SUMMERFIELD HOUSE

BOTHAM

BOTHAM
A BIOGRAPHY

•

Patrick Murphy

J. M. Dent and Sons Ltd
LONDON

First published 1988
© Patrick Murphy 1988

Printed in Frome by Butler & Tanner Ltd
for J. M. Dent & Sons Ltd

British Library Cataloguing in Publication Data

Murphy, Patrick, 1947–
Botham: a biography.
1. Cricket. Botham, Ian——Biographies
I. Title
796.35'8'0924

ISBN 0–460–04725–6

Contents

●

Colour Plates

●

Photographs 1, 3–6, 8–14, 17 and 23 are reproduced by courtesy of
    Patrick Eagar. No. 2 is kindly loaned by Ava McCombe and no. 6,
    of Ian and Kath, is kindly loaned by Gerry and Jan Waller. All
    other photographs, including the colour, have been reproduced by
    permission of Graham Morris.

Acknowledgements

●

This book is an attempt to place in perspective the jaundiced, apopleptic view of Ian Botham that has gained currency in recent years. Having known and liked Botham for a decade, I am convinced he does not deserve the blanket condemnation visited on his head from some quarters. Like all of us, he is a human being, with as many redeeming features as behavioural defects: Botham's are writ large because of the nature of the man's profession and the consequent media coverage. In that sense, Botham's life is a parable of our times, in which the trivial takes precedence over the relevant, the cheque-book triumphs over the altruistic and newspaper editors separate the wheat from the chaff – and then print the chaff.

Mark Twain once entreated a friend: 'Live so that when you come to die, even the undertaker will be sorry.' No one can accuse Ian Botham of ignoring Twain's dictum. He has in turns enriched, enraged, delighted and baffled us over the years and, along with countless others, I am glad to have known hin.

My research on this book has taken two years. The statistics have been compiled with characteristic thoroughness by Robert Brooke. Any other errors of fact or interpretation can be fairly laid at my door. My sincere thanks for advice, anecdotal help and effecting of introductions go to the following ... David Acfield; Jim Alldis; Paul Allott; Dennis Amiss; Keith Andrew; John Arlott; Jack Bannister; Richie Benaud; Dickie Bird; Len Bond; Allan Border; Kath Botham, Ian's wife; Marie and Les Botham, Ian's parents; Brian Brain; Mike Brearley; Chris Broad; David Brown; Tony Brown; Robert Burston; Tom Byron; David Capel;

ACKNOWLEDGEMENTS

Tom Cartwright; Ian Chappell; Eric Clapton; Brian Close; David Constant; Geoff Cook; Nick Cook; Sam Cook; Jim Cumbes; Basil D'Oliveira; Kapil Dev; Graham Dilley; Paul Downton; Alan and Ray Dyer; Phil Edmonds; John Emburey; Matthew Engel; David English; John Farrar; Duncan Fearnley; Keith Fletcher; David Foot; Roger Forrester; Graeme Fowler; Phillip De Freitas; Trevor Gard; Mike Gatting; Sunil Gavaskar; Norman Gifford; Graham Gooch; David Gower; David Graveney; Tony Greig; Richard Hadlee; John Hampshire; Roger Harper; Reg Hayter; Eddie Hemmings; Mike Hendrick; Graeme Hick; Michael Holding; Imran Khan; Robin Jackman; Bill Jones; Sally Jones; Frank Keating; Allan Lamb; Chris Lander; Brian Langford; Jim Laws; Geoff Lawson; John Lever; Tony Lewis; Richard Lines; Andy Lloyd; Clive Lloyd; Jeremy Lloyds; Vic Marks; Rod Marsh; Malcolm Marshall; Barry Meyer; Geoff Miller; Graham Morris; Mushtaq Mohammed; Phil Neale; Dr Ken Oakshott; Chris Old; Andy Peebles; Pat Pocock; Nigel Popplewell; Paul Pridgeon; Derek Pringle; Clive Rice; Viv Richards; Greg Ritchie; Steve Rhodes; Peter Roebuck; Paul Romaines; Harry Sharp; David Shepherd; Jack Simmons; Gladstone Small; A. C. Smith; Peter Smith; Micky Stewart; Andy Stovold; Chris Tavare; Bob Taylor; Bernard Thomas; Jeff Thomson; Derek Underwood; Mike Vockins; Jan and Gerry Waller, Ian's in-laws; Peter Willey; Bob Willis; David Willis; John Woodcock; and John Wright.

Patrick Murphy
April 1988

Introduction

•

September 1987 in the committee room at the Worcestershire county ground. As usual Ian Botham is the attraction. He faces the familiar dilemma: acquaintances thinking they are intimate friends and strangers striving to become acquaintances. All except one elderly man in the corner. He is dying of cancer. He knows this is the last time he will be able to stare out at the Cathedral, at the vista beloved of cricket photographers throughout the world. He turns to Duncan Fearnley, Worcestershire's chairman, and utters the words that have preyed on his mind for some time. 'You know, Duncan, before I go I'd love to meet Ian Botham – just this once.' Fearnley detaches Botham from the crowd, makes the appropriate introductions and Botham gestures towards a quiet corner. He spends half-an-hour with the dying man, making him feel the most important person in that room. The 1988 season started without one loyal Worcestershire member, but Ian Botham made that man's final day on the ground a memorable one.

That same weekend Botham made another grizzled veteran ecstatically happy. Minutes after Worcestershire had clinched the 1987 Sunday Refuge Assurance trophy, the rituals were under way – players and officials vied with each other to waste decent champagne by impersonating Grand Prix drivers, while the crowd roared for Botham, the man who had done so much that day on the field, the man who had told his colleagues all week that they would win. Botham paused for a moment to seek out Jack Turner, who has been the Worcestershire dressing-room attendant for fifteen years. While Jack wondered how many hangovers he would be supervising the following morning,

Botham thrust a small box into his hand with the words, 'That's for you – for all you've done for me this summer.' Jack mumbled his thanks and, when Botham returned to the fray, looked down at his right palm. There was Botham's medal, plus a few fivers. Two days later, Jack Turner was still wandering around the ground, showing off his proudest possession, posing for photographs with his hero.

These two examples are hardly the Ian Botham of tabloid demonology, but the Torquemadas of the press do not want too many of those insights. For them, Botham takes his place alongside their other one-dimensional caricatures like John McEnroe, Alex Higgins, and George Best – preconception rather than reflection their stock-in-trade. It is true that Botham does not help himself in this respect. Too often the aggression that is the very lifeblood of his game spills over into his private life. There have been occasions in his career when he has seemed obsessed with emulating Icarus – and not just because he has a contract with the *Sun* newspaper.

Botham is a paradox, worthy of prolonged study by his former England captain, Mike Brearley – now forging a career as a psychotherapist. Botham the right-wing Tory and ardent monarchist – yet a social iconoclast, fitting easily into the louche world of his rock star friends. The apostle of self-help, of Thatcherite endeavour, yet with a deep commitment to charitable causes. Paranoid about the media, he offers his exclusive thoughts to a newspaper house which makes up interviews with war widows. Anarchic on the cricket field, he is regarded by umpires and players as a sportsman of Corinthian mould. The supreme individualist, yet touchingly supportive of team-mates with a fraction of his talent. He appears incandescent with self-belief, yet he is insecure and increasingly reclusive. He is gregarious yet also a passionate devotee of angling, one of the loneliest of sports. A self-confessed male chauvinist pig who nevertheless admits he would be lost without his wife and children, who dotes on his youngest child, Beccy, and buys his wife a dozen red roses every Valentine's Day.

Truly a study of Ian Botham recalls the words of Winston Churchill as he strove to discover the secrets of Russia: 'A riddle wrapped in a mystery inside an enigma.' After years of hacking away at the coal-face of bitter experience, Botham is now less gullible, more reflective. The wild, unkempt burly lad whose post-match evenings in Taunton used to consist of umpteen cans of lager and stentorian songs by Rod Stewart on the pub juke-box is now more inclined to mull over the bouquet of a red wine from Australia. His dress sense used to resemble that of an unmade bed in those early Taunton days – but now he takes time to prepare for public appearances. Neanderthal Man does reappear now and again, but not as often. In the common parlance, Botham is streetwise.

Botham now has a greater perspective on life than most of his fellow-cricketers. His marathon walks for Leukaemia Research have rammed home to him his own good fortune, namely that a god-given talent and a loving family are assets denied to many others. I have never seen him more generally relaxed than in his first summer playing for Worcestershire. The painful divorce with Somerset was over, the weary grind of England touring no longer beckoned, the challenge of playing for Queensland lay ahead, his new manager Tom Byron was busy closing several lucrative deals and his family life was settled and content. He was even nervous before several matches for his new county, a sure sign that he was again taking his cricket seriously. After the first day's play in his début game against Kent, Botham threw a party in his cottage. Like a child enthusing over his Christmas morning bounty, he pointed out where he would be fishing, and conducted guided tours of his new home. He supervised drinks and barbecued steak with his customary generosity, but then – not long after midnight – he disappeared upstairs to bed, anxious to be fresh for his first innings on the morrow. When, next day, Derek Underwood had him caught on the long-off boundary for 46, his main regret was that he had been too tentative, too desperate to succeed.

Geoff Miller, one of Ian's closest friends from his England days, noticed the change that summer. Miller, a warm, convivial companion who admits he has never done himself justice as a cricketer, was going through a bad time in his first season with his new county Essex: 'I read in the paper about a little lad who had lost both his mum and dad in the Zeebrugge Ferry disaster and I cut out the boy's photo and stuck it inside my cricket bag. Every time I opened that bag, I would see that lad's face and remind myself that this was only a game, not the real world. When we were playing against Worcestershire Ian noticed the picture and said, "Is that Jamie?" (my son, he's always been good at kids' names). I told him who it was and he said, "Quite right, mate, there's more to life than cricket." I could tell he meant it and I was glad that he seemed to be maturing.'

Will that maturing process be reflected in Botham's cricket over the next few years? So many imponderables are involved and they will be discussed later. For the moment let us simply consider if Ian Botham has been a great cricketer. Does a man with a Test batting average of around 35 and a bowling average of about 27 deserve the epithet 'great'? I believe he does. Botham has been the most influential English cricketer since W. G. Grace, on and off the field. Throughout my research, whenever the subject of Botham's place in the cricketing lexicon arose, I was told by his contemporaries, 'You just have to look at his record.' You can juggle around with statistics to prove many a point (and recent batches indicate a sad decline in Botham's relevance), but overall the facts support the towering reputation of an all-rounder who has never seemed to care a fig for his statistical reputation. Botham has played the game of cricket his way and he would not have lasted so long if guided by the overwhelming desire to check the national averages every morning. I cannot imagine Boycott, for instance, contributing to the dismissal enshrined in *Wisden* on Tuesday, 13 May, 1974: There it is – I. T. Botham c. Northcote-Green b. Stallibrass 2. The catch was taken at long-off, it was the last ball of the match and Botham had opted to try to end it in the grand manner. Somerset, on a run chase against Oxford University, had failed in a quest for 69 off eight overs and with no less than 19 needed off the final ball, Botham went for the big hit. It was the brash young man's first full season in first-class cricket, but he had given notice that he was not going to approach his career in the conventional manner. He would never be like the other rational, pragmatic English cricketers, never possess the courage of their lack of convictions. Who dares, wins for Botham.

Hardened commentators put down their racecards or snap out of their post-prandial slumber whenever Botham walks to the crease, arms whirling, flexing that railway sleeper of a bat. Richie Benaud, that unerring judge of a cricketer, says that he is one of the few people he'd pay money at the gate to watch, while Tony Lewis considers him the greatest entertainer on the field he has seen. Yet has he been a *great* cricketer? John Arlott, who has seen all the major players of the past sixty years and researched many others before that, considers that Ian Botham is the greatest matchwinner in Test history. 'There is no point in reducing his performances to bare statistics, you have to look at how many games he has won. That is why he is ahead of even Bradman, because Botham bowled many sides to defeat as well as scoring fast hundreds and performing brilliantly in the field.' David Gower puts it succinctly: 'He picks up a game by the scruff of the neck and throws it out of the window.' This has nothing to do with the towering list of records that Ian has established over the years – his greatness has been the way he has imposed himself on a game, shaped it to his desire. Botham once told me: 'If I'd been in the war, I'd have won the VC – but it would've been posthumous.' He has gloried in the fight, relished the responsibility of being a matchwinner. Allan Border reckons he'd be a good man to be near in the trenches: 'You'd feel better hearing him shout, "Come on, let's get the bastards" as he went over the top.'

Botham's importance to cricket is only loosely concerned with his achievements. He was simply in the right place at the right time to capitalise on the broadening appeal of the game. After the World Cup victory in 1966, soccer failed to consolidate on its popular appeal in Great Britain, for a number of reasons, ranging from hooliganism to sterile, negative play. Cricket meanwhile broadened its appeal through a proliferation of one-day competitions, the recruitment of star overseas players and the gradual realisation that it was no longer an esoteric pursuit, there for the benefit of just the players. In 1977 Kerry Packer threatened to split cricket asunder with his instant, high-profile version of the game. Whatever the traditionalists may now assert, Packer was a genuine threat to the established order: new heroes were needed to maintain the appeal of Test cricket. Ian Botham did exactly that. He made his England début in the summer of 1977, when Packer's captures were preparing their farewells to the Test arena. Within a few months, Botham had replaced Tony Greig as the popular hero with the flair for the unusual and the spectacular. Cometh the hour, cometh the man. The sophisticated marketing techniques beloved of Kerry Packer were taken on board when peace finally broke out between the warring factions in 1979 and thereafter cricket has been hyped up aggressively, not always to its advantage. Ian Botham's stirring exploits have been manna from heaven to the media as the game has increasingly touched the public. The BBC video of Botham's amazing Ashes series in 1981 still sells handsomely and the rapacious instincts of the electronic media do not countenance a more detached attitude to cricket. It is even more apparent with the printed word. Sports editors know that tabloid readers do not desire a learned treatise on the merits of the outswinger; they expect meatier stuff than that, preferably something along the lines of 'Botham in Sex Romp on Test Eve Shock!' So the 'quotes' man comes along to the big games, with the brief to come up with something only loosely connected with the action out on the field.

So many occupants of the press box are obsessed with Botham when he is playing in the game – and at times, even when he is not playing.

During an Old Trafford Test I happened to be passing the time of day with Chris Lander, Botham's 'ghost' with the *Sun*, the poor chap charged with the responsibility of gleaning the great man's thoughts, then writing them up. Chris was jolted from his musings by a message that Mr Botham was calling from the England dressing-room; would he come to the phone? Lander, relishing every moment, walked slowly to the phone, then assumed an air of *gravitas* for several minutes, occasionally punctuated by 'Really?' or 'You're not going to stand for that are you', plus an artful 'I'll get onto him right away'. The worthy denizens of the press box were busy performing the difficult art of watching the game, making the odd note, talking among themselves – all the while trying to sniff out a story from a one-way telephone conversation. When Lander replaced the phone and returned to his seat, that peculiar masonic code of the press box was scrupulously observed – no one asked him what was up. But every call Lander made thereafter was ear-wigged and his regular departures from the press box were monitored. Another 'Soaraway *Sun* Scoop' was feared, yet the truth was more prosaic: Botham had rung Lander to put some money on a horse in the next race!

Outside the members of the Royal Family, Ian Botham must have the best-known face in Great Britain. In the last decade, no male politician or public entertainer has been in the public eye so consistently. Bob Geldof may be a contender, but only since the closing months of 1984 when he tapped the conscience of the world. Why is Botham such a massive drawcard? Graeme Fowler, Lancashire's opening batsman and a close friend, has this theory: 'He's just a bricklayer who's good at something else. He's a man of the people.' Certainly Botham was the first captain of his country to come out of secondary modern school, and he wears his eleven-plus failure like a badge of courage. Before he came along, cricketers at English county level were generally drawn from middle-class roots, apart from the four northern counties of Lancashire, Yorkshire, Derbyshire and Nottinghamshire. They were still fairly middle-aged as well: the year before Botham's début more than half the England side were in their mid-thirties. One cannot now imagine the sight of Brian Close and John Edrich (sharing eighty-four years) opening the batting for England against the dangerous, intimidatory West Indian fast bowlers.

Other great cricketers (Jack Hobbs and Don Bradman, to name just a couple) came from out of the sticks but it has been Botham of Yeovil who has done more than anyone to popularise the game, based, it is true, on the influence of the modern electronic age. It just so happened that he fitted the role of popular hero, in the process generating massive publicity for the game. The corollary, however, has been a goldfish bowl existence for Botham and he has not relished that. At times he must have pondered the wisdom of Harry Truman's observation about a certain hot kitchen as he lurched from lurid headline to shock-horror exposé, some of them of his own doing. The tin-cans of scandal tied to his tail have clattered at regular intervals in the last few years and there have been times when Ian's friends thought he was trapped in a professional and personal death-wish.

Botham may be restless, occasionally boorish, with a sad record of social own goals, but he is also a loyal friend, ridiculously generous, with a deep well of charitable impulses, both to causes and to individuals. When he smashed a hundred for Worcestershire against Devon in the Nat-West Trophy in 1987, he took a rest from the carnage for one over. He deliberately blocked a maiden over from Doug Yeabsley, Devon's left-arm seamer. It was a tribute to a man who had played twenty-nine years in a row for Devon and of whom Botham is a great admirer. Even though Worcestershire hit a one-day record total of 404 for 3, Yeabsley (12-1-50-0) was the only bowler not to exceed 80 and he had Botham dropped three times. It would have pleased Botham if Yeabsley had got his wicket.

Botham does not forget his friends, irrespective of their status in life or in cricket. When Botham left Somerset, he was greatly missed by Trevor Gard, who ended up reserve wicket-keeper at Taunton in 1987 after the signing of Neil Burns from Essex. Botham kept ringing up Gard to cheer him up, to yarn over old times. One day he chartered a helicopter and flew down to Taunton to pay a surprise visit. He walked into the pavilion as Gard was just about to order the first round. Botham took him out for the evening and paid for everything. It was a gesture that greatly touched Gard.

In 1980, Botham promised his pal, Mike Hendrick, that he would play for him at an important golf day during Hendrick's benefit season. Hendrick knew that the three amateur golfers who drew Botham's name out of the hat would be the envy of everyone else that day – his main worry was when Botham would turn up. He was well aware of Botham's hectic social life and the demands made on him, but as he stood on the first tee with the excited trio of businessmen, he wondered how he could break the news to them that the star attraction was nowhere to be seen. At 9.58, two minutes before Botham was due to tee off, there was a screech of brakes, a crunching sound on the gravel and Botham stepped out of his Saab Turbo in his golf gear. He looked as if he would need match-sticks for his eyes and he hurriedly explained to Hendrick why he was so late. He had played golf with Nick Faldo the day before and after a pretty vigorous party, he had woken up at 8.30 – in Hemel Hempstead, more than a hundred miles away. He left Faldo's at 8.50 and drove at 120 mph all the way. Now he addressed himself to his first drive, after the preliminary introductions had been performed by a relieved Hendrick. Botham took out his driver, made one practice swing and landed the ball straight as a die, down the fairway to the brow of a hill 250 yards away. Only one other golfer reached the same distance that day off that first tee, and several professional players were involved. Botham seemed satisfied at the shot, winked at Hendrick and walked off with the awestruck trio. Hendrick was neither surprised at such a shot from a man who had just driven so far at such speed, nor that Botham had made the trip. He had promised months ago that he would be there and he had no intention of letting Hendrick down.

But the colossus has feet of clay. He is colour blind. He suffers from asthma, needing a spray before he goes onto the field of play. His left ankle has troubled him since, as a teenager, he turned it over playing football – on countless occasions he has bowled for England with it strapped up. A stomach ulcer has dogged him since the tour to Pakistan in 1977 and he takes pills for it: close friends have seen him walk away, doubled up with pain, and return a minute later as if there was nothing untoward. For most of his England career he has suffered from haemorrhoids. Creams at £27 a bottle are often used to assuage the pain and an operation – a particularly painful one – is always being postponed, partly because Botham is terrified of needles. His back – that media obsession from his England captaincy days – continues to worry him. He has a chronic kink in his vertebrae, a structural problem. The results of an X-ray on England's last tour of Australia did not exactly force him to crack open a bottle of Dom Perignon. Throw in wear-and-tear injuries (like the left knee from all those pounding deliveries and the big toe on his left foot which often seems to get hit by a full toss or his own bat), and it is clear that Botham has given more than enough of himself to the game without shirking. Botham never talks about these ailments and, if asked about a specific injury, merely replies 'I'll be okay.'

Above all, Botham is an entertainer. The mulish side to his nature sometimes surfaces after he has got himself out, but it is hard to fault him for giving such pleasure. He has made big hitting respectable and inspired a generation at least to contemplate playing with dash and bravado. When Botham hit McDermott for two straight sixes off his first three deliveries in a Test in 1985, it made the crowd's day. It mattered little that Botham had been told to crash on, with a declaration imminent, or that both deliveries were right in the slot for that marvellously uninhibited swing of his bat; to the spectators Botham had chanced his arm and it had come off again. A violent innings of 18 that did not even last long enough to be called a cameo had them babbling as they filed out at close of play – even though David Gower had just made a beautiful 215, Tim Robinson another impressive hundred and Mike Gatting had clubbed a century in just 125 balls.

Botham acts out schoolboy fantasies whether in hitting sixes, walking the length of the country, flying with the Red Arrows, learning how to pilot a helicopter, partying with Elton John, grappling with authority or giving the motorway police a run for their money up the M1. He is box office. Fifteen years after he saved the reputation of his mates on the MCC Ground Staff by downing a yard of ale in record time, he was offered $10,000 just to stand in the Bollinger Tent on Melbourne Cup day. Influential magnates who would have edged away from the brash extrovert in that London pub now fall over themselves to get their picture taken alongside him. Captains of industry, used to chairing meetings on a transatlantic link-up, babble nonsense at him when they have successfully engineered an introduction. Botham is amused when they haltingly proffer a scrap of paper, with the inevitable caveat: 'It's not for me, by the way.' Botham is happy to play along, he has seen it all before.

His present manager, Tom Byron, says that he is well on the way to realising his promise to make Ian a million pounds in their first full year together. Botham deserves that for what he has given cricket. The receipts from home Test Matches make up one-third of an English county cricketer's salary; without that subsidy, the county game would be on the breadline and the playing staff would be skeletal. In fact there would probably be nothing like the structure that we now recognise. Without Ian Botham's contribution over the past decade, Test cricket would not have attracted so much intelligent sponsorship nor such healthy gate receipts. When Botham's large army of detractors start fulminating again, they might like to ponder how much he has done for ordinary professional cricketers lucky to have a job. Knowing Botham's sincere respect for his fellow-professionals on the English circuit, I am sure that this one achievement gives him as much pleasure as the more tangible ones accomplished on the field of play with such flair and daring.

I

A persistent boy

●

It is part of the Botham mythology that he just breezed through all sporting obstacles till the England captaincy brought him his first setback at the age of twenty-four. Far from it. Botham had to batter down many an obstacle before he was respected for his massive ability. Indeed the pitfalls, the setbacks and the disappointments are all clues to his intensely combative character, as is the desire to be taken seriously. Today nothing irks Botham more than to be written off as a lucky cricketer who has outrun his effectiveness. Despite the natural talent, the young Botham also had to work very hard to conquer both personal and social prejudice.

He was born at Heswall in Cheshire on 24 November 1955. A Sagittarian: the males of that star sign are supposed to be enthusiastic, wilful, optimistic, gregarious and extravagant. It sounds an accurate piece of type-casting. This particular Sagittarian male saw the first light in Cheshire because his father, Les, was stationed at the Fleet Air Arm near Londonderry and the family home was just a hop across the Irish Sea. When Ian was three, Les retired from the Navy and moved the family to Yeovil in order to take an engineering post with Westland Helicopters. Ian's parents were both from Yorkshire and they shared a fondness for sport. Marie played cricket, badminton and hockey, while Les was a keen cricketer, ran for East Yorkshire, had a soccer trial for Hull City Boys and played for the Combined Services.

When he was just two, Ian showed he had inherited his father's competitive instict – taking part in a twenty-yard race, Ian led right away and bumped any rivals out of the way to ensure he would finish first. At the age of four, he astonished his mother by walking into the kitchen one day and asking, 'Do you know how to bowl the daisy-cutter?', then proceeding to deliver a prolonged dissertation on the subject before returning to the garden to put in some more practice. Around the same time, he took his younger sister, Dale, to ballet classes. The thought of Botham rubbing shoulders with the tu-tu brigade would amuse many a drinking companion in later years, but Marie remembers that Ian was always very protective of Dale, especially in the school playground. 'He would look after her at the ballet classes as well, and join in. Anyway Les always maintained that you can't play ball sports unless you have good footwork. Ian's footwork isn't bad, is it?'

Soon Ian was getting used to playing cricket with his elders and this stood him in good stead: 'It meant I had to hit the ball hard against them. Nobody was going to bowl underarm at me, so I had to try to get up to their standard. That just made me try harder.' Ian was lucky that his games master at Milford Junior School had spotted his raw natural talent. Mr Richard Hibbitt remembers the quiet dedication in the boy, the steely resolution to succeed. The kindly games master used to place a pile of pennies on a length down the line of the middle stump to encourage his young bowlers to develop accuracy – Master Botham scooped the pool regularly.

When Ian was six, he calmly announced to his parents that he was going to be a professional sportsman. He was not yet sure which sport would gain his attentions, but when his mother discovered him practising his signature, she was told that it was necessary because he would eventually have to sign a lot of autographs. His school reports were sadly less impressive than his budding sporting talent – 'Could do better if he concentrated less on sport' was the regular verdict – but it did not seem to bother him. His destiny lay on the playing fields, not the Groves of Academe. Les recalls his son's determination:

There was a simplicity in Ian that was touching and it's still there. He wasn't treated any differently from our other three children, but despite the discipline he experienced at home, he went his own way. He would always take his punishment – and at school he would often take the blame when others were the ringleaders. He always had an independent streak. I laugh now when I hear the experts debating the merits of Ian standing at second slip, with his hands on his knees: when he was ten he argued it out with me! He said he had more chance of getting the snicks from that position, and he stuck to it.

Ian's always had fantastic eyesight and amazing reactions. He can easily spot us in a crowd when he's out in the middle. A few years ago when we went to a football match I saw his speed of reaction at close hand. We were behind one of the goals, watching Leeds United, when some of the hooligans started their nonsense. It was getting rather nasty when suddenly Ian jerked back his head. A dart whizzed past him. Without his swift reactions, that dart would've landed on Ian's face.

Marie is proud that the ideals of sportsmanship they drummed into Ian have not been tarnished. 'Les and I can't abide cheats at any price and Ian knew where he stood early on. There was never any malice in him, he was just a rascal, full of bounce and good nature. He's the only child I've known who used to walk down the street, looking in at all the prams, talking to the babies. He had a simple, unaffected fondness for babies and dogs and that's never left him. Basically he still wants to be Peter Pan, to stay young all his life.'

When Ian was eight, his parents took him to his first county cricket match, at Bradford, Marie's home town. It was there that he had his first encounter with Fred Trueman, later to become Ian's principal *bête noire* in the commentary box. At the time, Fred was the game's biggest 'character', a magnificent fast bowler who occasionally found himself on the front pages due to alleged misdemeanours on and off the pitch. Marie was not impressed:

Ian was determined to get the great man's autograph, and at lunch and at tea he went to see if he could get it. Each time he came back disappointed but vowed to manage it at close of play. When the game ended I went looking for Ian and I saw the great Trueman abusing the young autograph-hunters, telling them to get away from his brand-new car and refusing to sign their books, in language that I would not repeat. I told Ian to come away from him and I have never forgotten that. When Ian was first asked for his autograph he was in Somerset's Second Eleven; he looked at me, I nodded and he signed. Since then I think he has been very good about autographs, when he has the time and he's not walking off the field after a long day.

Marie is right about that. I have seen Ian oblige with the leaky pens and the grubby pieces of paper on innumerable occasions. He was particularly helpful on a July day in 1987 when he visited Londonderry for a game: after play had ended, he called for a chair, sat down and signed around 250 autographs in an hour. Anyone who accompanied him on his walks for Leukaemia Research will confirm the same freedom with his time – except when he was walking and he feared losing his rhythm. Botham also showed the appealing side to his nature one filthy night in the early 1980s at Ashton Gate, Bristol, when he was involved in a series of floodlit cricket games. It was such a dreadful evening that the football club officials staging the event confirmed that their first-team players would not have ventured out onto the pitch. Viv Richards refused to go out while Joel Garner had the presence of mind to stay in Manchester. None of the other West Indian stars would entrust their highly prized limbs to the English weather, despite the entreaties of the sponsors. Botham had no such qualms: there were hordes of families in the stand, waiting to see their heroes, and he felt that they should not be cheated because of the weather. He believed he owed both sponsors and fans an appearance and he cheerfully accepted a soaking.

While Ian surreptitiously polished up his signature in the certain knowledge that he was going to be a star sportsman one day, he continued to find his progress frustrating. He was obviously talented – Mr Hibbitt remembers a straight drive that landed in a far-flung playground that was worth a six at Taunton or Lord's, a powerful blow from a ten-year-old. He was strong for his age – at twelve, he returned from a sports competition at Motspur Park, London, with a trophy for throwing a cricket ball more than seventy yards. Yet Ian's restless self-confidence was not satisfied by good performances in schools cricket; that was kid's stuff. Even when he was nine he would turn up at Milford Recreation Ground, in Yeovil, asking each team captain if he was short of a player. Occasionally he would get a game while Les played for the Westland Helicopters side on the sports complex: 'I'd take him along to watch us play but after a time he'd wander off on his own looking at the other matches, hoping to play. If he did wangle a game he'd never get a bowl – he was too young – and hardly ever a bat, so I had no real idea how good he was. But one day, after Ian had played for us, one of my team-mates said, "Did you notice how he stopped that ball on the boundary and threw it in? He threw it further than I could." But I never forced Ian along, he knew what he was doing even at that age.'

After a couple of years, Ian started to play for the Boys' Brigade, but even then he did not walk into the side. One day, Marie noticed in the paper that A. N. Other was down to play for the Boys' Brigade the following weekend and she contacted the club secretary: her son had paid his annual subscription, so why was he not being considered? 'I was told he'd get a chance, but I must realise he wouldn't get in the first team every week. But he did – and stayed there!' Next stop, Yeovil Town's second eleven when Ian was around twelve. Again no one really took him very seriously. Les played a few games with him in the Seconds: 'Now and then he'd get a bowl but no one thought that much of him. His batting looked very mature for his age, but nobody seemed to rate him. Many clubs are full of tight little cliques where the adults prosper at the expense of the youngsters and this was the case here. They kept telling Ian that he'd have to wait another seaon before he could be considered for the first team and he got frustrated. Nothing came easy for him.'

By now, Ian was attending Buckler's Mead Secondary School in Yeovil. The hoary old tale is that he deliberately failed his eleven-plus because he wanted to play soccer at the secondary school rather than rugby at the grammar school, but Ian never really had a choice in the matter. He was bright enough, certainly, but lazy; scholastic matters had no appeal at all for him and if the secondary school played soccer, well that was just his good fortune. At Buckler's Mead he captained the under-sixteen side at the age of thirteen and inevitably his prowess was recognised by Somerset Schools. The thirteen-year-old Botham made his début for the county's under-fifteen team and in the process relieved his father of some cash: 'Rashly I said I'd give him sixpence a run. That night he came running down the garden path and I shouted "How did you get on?" "You owe me a lot of money!" he cried. "How many did you score?" "80!" The following game I was watching him walk out to bat for Somerset against Wiltshire and I overheard someone say, "Watch this lad bat." It began to dawn on me that he was rather special. Even then he was developing a reputation for hitting the ball hard and far.'

That 80 in his first game for Somerset Schools was in typical vein. He came in with two men out for just one, proceeded to club a few through the covers and hit a six over mid-wicket into an adjoining garden. Although he impressed with the bat, his captain, Phil Slocombe, did not rate him as a bowler. In his time with that under-fifteen side, the young Botham was never trusted against anyone other than tail-enders. Slocombe decided that the burly boy from Yeovil was a specialist batsman. To this day it rankles with Botham that he was not then deemed to have an all-rounder's potential and he never lost a chance to remind Slocombe of that when they subsequently shared the same dressing-room at the county ground in Taunton.

By the age of fifteen, Ian was built like a man, almost six feet tall. Marie recalls the time he seemed to shoot up in height, a story that also underlines the legendary Botham competitiveness: 'When he was fourteen he went off on a fortnight's cruise in the Mediterranean with the school. After just two weeks away, he looked as if he'd been stretched, he'd shot up. He and Dale used to measure each other up against the kitchen door and it would annoy Ian that she was taller. After the cruise he said, "Measure me, measure me" and when he knew that he'd grown so much, he went running into the garden shouting, "Dale! Dale! Come here, I want to measure you!" He'd finally passed her in height and he was delighted. All of a sudden it was important to him to be that tall.'

As he filled out, Ian's all-round sporting abilities increased. He was Somerset's under-sixteen badminton doubles champion, captain of the school soccer team and as keen on soccer as he was on cricket. Marie had to go out and buy royal blue wallpaper to match Chelsea Football Club's colours, and then he festooned his bedroom with Chelsea rosettes, scarves and pictures. It was typical of Ian that he would support Chelsea rather than the more efficient Leeds or Liverpool: at that time, Chelsea was the glamour club, with the likes of Peter Osgood, Charlie Cooke and Alan Hudson dazzling the King's Road. They were also the kind of characters who enjoyed a night out, a few drinks, then some more drinks, and an occasional fraças at a night club. It is interesting that Botham found an empathy with these flawed heroes, rather than with the stereotyped functionaries under the charge of such managers as Don Revie and Bill Shankly.

If Chelsea had approached Botham with the offer of a playing contract, he might easily have been tempted. But it was another First Division club from South London that was interested in Botham. Bert Head, the manager of Crystal Palace, was convinced he could make it: he had natural physical co-ordination and the added bonus of an enormous determination to win. But after a family conference Ian decided to stay with cricket. Somerset had already registered him and he was well aware that the next year or so would determine if he would ever be a professional cricketer. For once, Botham did not opt for the glamour: training and rubbing shoulders with so many famous footballers in a fashionable part of London came second to the burning conviction that he would eventually prove a better cricketer than footballer. Already he was beginning to understand the underlying complexities of cricket, the tactical nuances, the individual challenges. 'I was never coached by Dad at home, I just knew instinctively what to do. In my life I think I've only had about six hours' coaching and the only ones I've listened to have been Tom Cartwright, Kenny Barrington and Viv Richards.'

Before the fifteen-year-old committed himself to a career in cricket, he faced another setback. It was all the more galling because it seemed so unjust. It was not a case of having to kick his heels because he was too young (as in those days on Milford Rec. or with Yeovil Seconds), it was simply a matter of being passed over, having done exceptionally well in a trial. It was the summer of 1969 and Ian had been summoned to Liverpool to take part in some trial games to decide who would play for England Schools against the Public Schools at Lord's. Les Botham is still bitter about the experience:

> I sat near the selectors to see if I could glean anything from their conversations. At last Ian came on to bowl – not a common occurrence in those days. I could tell by the precise way he set his field that he had a tactical plan. The first wicket he got came after he did the batsman in the air and had him lunging a catch to mid-wicket. I overheard one of the selectors say, 'Ignore that, it was a fluke.' I couldn't believe my ears, Ian had worked for that wicket. Anyway he took six wickets in the innings by bowling to his field, exploring the weak points and outwitting the batsmen. Yet Ian wasn't picked for England Schools. He had been categorised as a batsman, not as a bowler, and his all-round capabilities were not appreciated. I often wonder if those same selectors blush at their decision when they see Ian winning a Test as an all-rounder!

Ian was not the only future England cricketer to be disappointed at Liverpool. Graham Stevenson – later to be captained by Botham in the West Indies – left the ground in tears after the team was announced. Paul Romaines, now a Gloucestershire batsman, was equally disppointed. All three players, born within a month of each other, struck up a lasting friendship with each other that week. Romaines recalls the favour that Botham did him: 'Ian was a great lad in those days and he hasn't changed a bit. He never forgets his old mates and he helped me to resurrect my county career. I had had a couple of years with Northants, didn't make the grade and went back to league cricket in Durham. Ian had a word with David Graveney when Gloucestershire were looking for batters and they took me on. I owe him a lot, it was typical of his thoughtful good nature.'

Botham needed all his reserves of good nature to shrug off the disappointment of not playing at Lord's. To make matters worse, Vic Marks and Peter Roebuck had been selected for the Public Schools and it would have given Ian great pleasure to square up to his two colleagues from Somerset's under-fifteen side. It would be wrong to say that that reverse gave Ian a chip on his shoulder or coloured his judgement about selectors: he always thought he was destined to be a great cricketer, that it was just a matter of time before everyone else saw the light. It was not a case of feeling socially inferior to public schoolboys like Marks, Roebuck and Slocombe – after all he came from a comfortable, loving, close family, a fact he readily acknowledges: 'I couldn't have asked for more from my parents. They had great faith in me and always encouraged me. Les gave me so much time and patience and was always there to run me to matches even as far away as Wiltshire.'

If you are born on the wrong side of the tracks, a Mediterranean cruise is hardly on a fourteen-year-old's agenda. Perhaps the geographical location was more important than anything to do with class, privilege or excellent public school wickets. Len Bond played cricket and soccer with Ian before playing for Bristol City in the First Division at the age of eighteen. Like Ian he grew up in Yeovil, that sleepy engineering town on the Somerset/Dorset border and he thinks he understands the roots of Botham's fierce determination: 'Where we come from, you have to be something pretty special to make it in sport. He's a punter made good from the sticks. That's still in his mind when he goes out on the field.'

Botham's immense drive and competitiveness, however, were now about to be tested in the arena that had been denied to him by those myopic England Schools selectors. Lord's cricket ground finally beckoned. Somerset County Cricket Club was impressed by the tyro – but he was too young to be taken onto the staff, even if he was thought to be good enough. There was no justification yet for thinking he would make the professional grade; many another big fish in a small pool had shrivelled when the competition got tougher. Young Botham was talented, but untutored. A spell on the Lord's Ground Staff would stiffen his backbone, knock the cockiness out of him, teach him to play himself in before trying to hit sixes – and disabuse him of the fanciful notion that he could actually bowl. Les and Marie knew that they had to give up the unequal struggle to improve his academic record; Ian would not pay any attention to anything other than a sporting career. But they were concerned at the job prospects awaiting Ian if he failed after his two years at Lord's. There was talk of a place at Millfield, that centre of sporting excellence – if he had gone there, one feels that for once Peter Roebuck, four months his junior, would have outshone him, at least in the exam room! – but Ian would not be swayed. He wanted to go to Lord's, to test his mettle against the other young players and broaden his horizons. His parents learned that if he failed to be taken on by a county, the experience at Lord's would at least qualify him for a coaching position at a school. 'Lord's Ground Staff Boy' carries a certain professional cachet; yet the very idea of Botham attempting to coach cricket to a group of pampered, untalented schoolboys is surreal – on a par with the Rev. Ian Paisley checking the Pope's Latin diction during a rendition of the Ave Maria! The unimaginable horror of a lifetime of coaching was a real incentive for Botham to succeed as he packed his bags for London.

2

'A fellow of infinite jest'

•

The works of J. B. Priestley have never been on the required reading list of I. T. Botham, but he would approve of the famous Yorkshireman's opinion of the members of the Marylebone Cricket Club at Lord's. Priestley referred to the owners of the famous egg-and-bacon tie as 'complacent, overweight males in the terminal stages of alcoholic poisoning', adding that 'it is always difficult to know where the Church of England ends and the MCC begins.' It was inevitable that Botham's direct, convivial attitude to his teenage years would conflict with the feeling of some MCC members that ground staff boys should treat them with, if not awe, then at least grovelling sycophancy. His memories of his time at Lord's are jaundiced by all those hours spent bowling at MCC members, and even now he stiffens at the sight of that famous tie. Extolling the virtues of the MCC in his company ranks in tactlessness with a British Airways steward asking Joan Collins if club class will do.

Apart from that inevitable conflict between oil and water, Botham had an uproarious time at Lord's. He still hates London, as you would imagine from a country boy with outdoor hobbies, but he was not averse to making the best of his stay there – sampling the capital's beer and exploring its low life with characteristic verve. A wage of £12 a week left him ill-equipped for his preferred social activities, but his mother's prudence ensured that he would be subsidised whenever he returned to headquarters.

Botham's exploits are ingrained on the memories of his friends on the ground staff. At sixteen he seemed amazingly mature, confident and strong for his age. No one else in his family had had such a rugged physique and although he regularly tucked into plates of spinach, not even Popeye would claim that such fondness for the green stuff leads to the kind of structure possessed by young Botham. Soon after taking up his place in the junior staff dressing-room, Botham was called upon to demonstrate that he was no shrinking violet. Those of a delicate constitution may wish to skip the next few lines, but they revolve around a bucket of whitewash, some bored young cricketers and the private parts of a robust youth from Yeovil. Jim Alldis, head boy at the time, remembers Botham's rearguard action with awe: 'After shrugging off a handful of the lads, it took another half-dozen to pin him down and apply the whitewash. He got the highest marks in history for resisting. He was just sixteen and some of the blokes he'd seen off were in their early 'twenties. A week later, it was raining again and we were all sitting around, bored. There was a knock on the door of the senior dressing-room and in walked Botham – that was taboo for a start. He asked if anyone fancied whitewashing him again!'

Soon Botham struck up a close friendship with Rodney Ontong, now Glamorgan's all-rounder. Rodney was at that time a shy lad of Botham's age, but there the similarity ended. He was on his first trip out of Johannesburg and Botham took him under his wing. He introduced Ontong to the delights of drinking, by saving up their daily luncheon vouchers and cashing them at a nearby pub at the end of the month – Botham always contrived to find someone to buy him double gins! One night Botham was carried out of a club in Pinner minus his trousers: nobody dared ask the circumstances. At one stage Botham and Ontong shared a flat, just around the corner from Lord's, but after various misdemeanours – like breaking windows, failing to pay the rent, waking up the neighbourhood at dawn – the landlady lost patience and threw them out. Undaunted they dossed down for a couple of weeks in a dressing-room at the Nursery End of Lord's itself. Had they been discovered, it might have been the end of two promising careers.

Yet it seemed that Botham was set for no more than a useful county career, for nobody rated him very highly. The ground-staff coaches were Harry Sharp, the former Middlesex batsman, and Len Muncer, who used to bowl spinners for Glamorgan. Muncer and Botham did not really get on: Muncer thought Botham spent too much time slogging the ball out of sight. Harry Sharp, on the other hand, would deal with him differently, standing behind the nets, ribbing Botham about the position of his feet, but encouraging him to play the same way if it worked. Sharp and Botham got on well together, not least of all because the coach did not drone on about the old days and his social philosophy was simple: 'Do what you want tonight, lads, but you'd better be fit for play tomorrow.' The hedonistic streak in Botham needed no second bidding. Today Harry Sharp chuckles at that brash youngster from Yeovil: 'He had a wonderful belief in himself. He never thought anyone could play the game apart from I. T. Botham. Yet Ian Gould, who later played for Middlesex and Sussex, was by far the most talented of that crop of youngsters. I liked Botham immensely, he was a big strong lad who saw the funny side of everything – but no one can tell me that he had the makings of a great cricketer when he was at Lord's.'

Amen to that from Bill Jones, who succeeded Jim Alldis as head boy. Botham had a healthy respect for Jones, partly because he was the captain but mainly because he was fifteen stone and perfectly willing to take his young charge on at any form of physical derring-do. Bill Jones went on to University College School, Hampstead, where he became a games master, but the two friends still keep in touch. Even after Botham got in the England side, he would talk about the intricacies of bowling with his imposing drinking partner. At seventeen, Botham outlined his career to his head boy and Jones says his forecast was amazingly accurate: 'He was convinced he would soon be playing for England, taking a stack of wickets. But we had a very strong bowling team and he rarely got on – when he did, he'd spray the ball all over the place. Big away swingers, it's true, but no control. And a lot of bouncers. One thing about him impressed me – he was as good a fielder as I've ever seen at that age. In the outfield, he was very fast to the ball for a big lad and wonderfully brave at short-leg. He caught some blinders there off my bowling. I used to gee him up when I captained him. Whenever he got out to a rash shot, I'd say "Number ten, next week" in front of everybody and he'd go away and brood about that. He so much wanted to be respected for his ability, and my taunts made him think more about his batting.'

It may surprise those who think Botham's attitude to the disciplines of the game has been far too cavalier, but initially he was very keen on net practice when he was at Lord's. Not in the Boycott class – who is? – but he was always first to the nets and last to go. With Rodney Ontong for company, he would stay on in the nets for an extra half-hour, trying to harness the rudiments of swing bowling. It was infinitely preferable to the sundry other duties of a ground-staff boy – like cleaning the pavilion windows, pushing the roller on matchdays, selling scorecards, pressing electronic buttons on the scoreboards and rushing bowling analyses to the dressing-room.

Amid all the pranks, the drinking contests and the simmering resentment against the more reactionary figures and customs at Lord's, Botham kept his eye on the ball. He would make the sceptics pay one day. In one game against a weak team from the City of London School, he managed to reach 50. The convention was to get out at 50 against poor teams to give other players a chance but Botham ignored Len Muncer's entreaties that eventually became commands. 'It's dog-eat-dog on the ground staff,' Ian said, 'you only get one chance.' He had scored few runs in recent games against far stronger sides and he had no intention of passing up this chance. Not until he passed 100 did he hit one up in the air and stride back to the inevitable rollicking.

Ian just could not see why those in influence did not share his high opinion of his all-round abilities. He was hurt that the summons to Somerset Seconds kept coming to Keith Jennings and Nick Evans, hardly ever to Ian Botham. Len Muncer confessed to Ian's parents that he too was amazed that the call hardly ever came from Somerset, but in those days the strong amateur sides in the county were gathered in the Weston, Bath and Taunton areas, not a sleepy town almost in Dorset. Talent scouts on behalf of the county would rarely venture as south as Yeovil, despite Ian's obvious raw ability.

He had to stay behind in London when he wanted to return home at weekends, like a conquering hero, to dominate second eleven cricket with his new-found technical sophistication. In truth there was very little finesse to display. In his last year at Lord's he was still hammering the ball like a shell out of the nets, while all around shook their heads and said, 'He won't do that in county cricket, why doesn't he learn to defend? And where does he get the idea that he's a swing bowler?' Clearly Ian's experience at Lord's shaped his attitude to cricket and to anyone who doubted his talents. Years later, he is still angry about the lack of faith shown in his bowling:

> I had to bowl for bloody hours in the nets because nobody would give me a go out in the middle. I wanted to prove a point to all those who wrote me off. The times I had to bowl at those MCC members! Almost every night – this after training all day. They'd shout 'Bowler! Come and bowl at me!' Sometimes they'd vary the command and call you 'boy!' Never your surname. Often we'd try to hit the change in a member's pocket as he stood at the crease, so

that he would feel he should give us a few bob. All that time in the nets at Lord's finally put me off them for life. I hate them now, I feel I'm hemmed in as if I'm in a shooting gallery, like the duck bobbing up and down in the water, waiting to be picked off. I feel claustrophobic and can't concentrate, because the ball is being hit around in adjoining nets. All I want to do is get out in the middle and play properly.

Tom Cartwright was the first major cricketing influence on Ian Botham. It is fair to say that without his guidance and insight, Botham would not have become that most dangerous of bowlers, one who swings the ball away from the bat at speed. Cartwright, a fine all-rounder with Warwickshire, Somerset and England, was nearing the end of his career when he first saw Botham in the winter nets at Millfield School, where he was coaching. Botham was fifteen at the time, and Cartwright noticed how the big lad moved his feet so nimbly, and was impressed by his overall physical co-ordination. To Cartwright he was the most talented of all the boys present and he was pleased to hear that Somerset had an option on his services and that he had been sent to Lord's to refine that raw talent. He was sorry to hear that the cricket cognoscenti at headquarters did not share his excitement:

> I got the impression from Ian that they thought of him as just another cricketer. Yet the use of his arms was magnificent, so natural. By the age of seventeen he had the physical maturity of a twenty-five-year-old and he was desperately keen to be an all-rounder if someone would only take him seriously. I said to him, 'Do you want to be a swing bowler?' and he was very enthusiastic about it. Soon Ian proved to me that he had a very intelligent cricket brain. He picked up the elements of swing bowling astonishingly quickly. An awful lot of swing bowling is a mystery – some swing it one day and can't the next – but Ian caught on right away. I used to despair when he tried to bounce people out – he's always been the same – but he was an ideal, willing pupil. Ian worked very hard indeed at the nets. He didn't show the dedication of a Boycott, but it was there, he just didn't make a fuss about it.

Thanks to Cartwright's perseverance and advocacy in influential quarters, Botham was blooded in two Sunday League games for Somerset at the end of the 1973 season. He did nothing special with the ball – his only wicket, a full toss, trapped Geoff Howarth of Surrey lbw – but he took a catch that demonstrated his athleticism. It was at Hove in his first match. Tony Greig mistimed a pull shot and Botham, running in full-pelt from deep backward square leg, dived forward and caught the ball just as he hit the ground. It was the catch of a natural cricketer. Somerset's officials were sufficiently impressed by the boisterous youth to offer him a one-year contract. Other novitiates would be that trio from the public schools, Marks, Slocombe and Roebuck. They would also be joined by one Vivian Richards, who had completed his qualification period at Bath. Richards had already played with Botham in Somerset's second eleven and they quickly discovered they were kindred spirits. Soon Vivian knew every watering hole around South Somerset, courtesy of his bluff new friend.

So Botham left Lord's, although many of the friends he made during those two years are still in contact today – among county cricketers, Ian Gould, John Hopkins and Rodney Ontong, plus Jim Alldis and Bill Jones who have turned to coaching at schools. Jim Alldis remembers how, during the Test against Sri Lanka in 1984, he had arranged for a quiet drink with Ian, but events conspired against them: 'I had two friends over from New Zealand and when they heard I was going to see Ian, they kept on at me for an introduction. I thought that was a bit much but finally, with some trepidation, I knocked on his hotel room door. He grabbed me round the throat in his usual playful manner, saying "Where the bloody hell have you been?" and when I explained my problem, he said, "Let's go and see them, then." For the next two hours he stood at the bar with a man and a woman he would never see again and made them feel important. He didn't need to do that; all the other England lads were going out and he could've joined them. That was typical of him, he really hasn't changed with his old friends.'

Bill Jones would agree. That same year – 1984 – Botham made a humanitarian gesture he will never forget: 'My father was dying of cancer in the Royal Free Hospital at Hampstead. It was a lingering, horrible death that took five months. Ian and I were due for one of our regular drinking sessions we have whenever he's in London and I rang him to call it off, explaining about my father. "Where is he?" he asked. We got a cab to the hospital and he sat there with Dad for half-an-hour, holding his hand and chatting about this and that. Then he drove to Taunton to play cricket. Dad died six weeks later. Believe me, he wasn't worried anymore about death. Ian had made him happy.'

In 1974, as Botham took his first confident steps into professional cricket, a number of people who would influence him significantly put down roots in his affections. Tom Cartwright we have already met: he would play alongside Ian for the next two seasons, relishing the heartiness that he brought to a jaded, defeatist dressing-room full of old sweats hanging on for their benefit or collecting a few 'not outs' to boost their averages. Recalls Cartwright: 'One or two of the senior players wanted to knock him down, but I would have none of it. He was a breath of fresh air. Sometimes I'd take him into the back room and give him an almighty bollocking for something daft he'd done on the field and he'd look sheepish and take it like a man. Then one of us would burst out laughing. Nothing will ever alter my affection for Ian, even though I always want to kick his backside for something every time I see him!'

For Cartwright the most gratifying moment that season came when his young charge took a remarkable catch at Bath in the match against the Pakistanis. Asif Iqbal stepped out to Dennis Breakwell and drove him high to long-off. Botham sprinted from long-on, dived forward and held the ball six inches from the ground. Cartwright still speaks of that catch with wonder: 'It was one of the greatest I've ever seen. The ball was going away from him, it was on the curve, the crowd was right by the boundary edge and he had to ignore the sightscreen as he sprinted. It was wonderfully brave, wonderfully athletic.'

A few weeks later, Botham played the kind of innings that suggested the boy had the mark of heroism on him. His match-winning 45 not out to win the Benson and Hedges quarter-final tie against Hampshire is now the stuff of legend. The photograph of Botham being mobbed as he stalked from the sunlit field still hangs in the pavilion bar, a reminder of the many good times that Botham shared with the home crowd before the sad divorce in 1986. Yet it was touch-and-go whether Botham would play or not. He only made the team because the pace bowler Allan Jones suffered a leg strain, so he was picked primarily for his bowling. In those days, Derek Taylor stood up to the stumps for Botham's bowling and when he bowled the great Barry Richards, the master batsman stood his ground for a second or two, convinced that the ball had rebounded from the keeper's pads, astonished that this young new bowler had beaten him all ends up.

Botham took another wicket and fielded with his customary brilliance, but then he found himself with an even greater challenge than bowling to Barry Richards. He came in at number nine at 113 for seven, with 70 needed to win off the next 15 overs. Immediately his mentor Tom Cartwright was caught at mid-on, and as the infuriated elder statesman stalked out of the ground to walk off his frustrations, his young protégé took charge. Hallam Moseley, a negligible bat who could at least hit the ball hard, kept him company until Botham was hit in the mouth by a lifter from Andy Roberts. That summer Roberts was decimating English county batting, giving notice of his later development as one of the most intelligent and hostile fast bowlers in the coming decade. It was easily the fastest delivery Botham had encountered in his short career; he managed to get his hand up to his mouth at the same time as the ball crashed into his face. Botham spat out blood and a couple of back teeth, swallowed some water, shook his head and carried on, clipping the next ball through the legside for three. Yet these were pre-helmet days, Roberts was the nastiest of propositions and surely Somerset were going to lose anyway? Why was this foolhardy young man staying out there? To win the game was the simple answer. He nursed Bob Clapp, the last man, through the closing overs and made the winning hit with seven balls to spare.

That night as Botham sat in the Stragglers' Bar, fingering his medal, anxiously flexing his jaw, he was told by a couple of old players, Bill Alley and Ken Palmer: 'Today you're everybody's hero, tomorrow they'll have forgotten you.' It was doubtless a well-intentioned attempt to keep the young man's feet on the ground, but he surely deserved his place in the sun. The following day, as well-wishers thronged the family home, Ian's mother was asked, 'Didn't he do marvellously?' only for the hero of the day to interrupt: 'There's no use saying that to mother, she never gives me any praise.' Ian's parents have always felt that he gets enough praise from other quarters and they have tried to keep his feats in perspective. Yet they were terribly proud of him, and justifiably so. The way he organised the situation was so impressive, even more so than his physical bravery. Hallam Moseley and Bob Clapp were a good deal older and more experienced than their inspirational partner, but he shepherded them, shielded them from Roberts and took on the responsibility willingly. It was a remarkably mature piece of cricket.

Was Botham physically afraid after that blow from Roberts? 'Not really, it seemed to settle me down for some daft reason. I knew he'd bowl me the yorker next one and I was ready for it. I was just pumped up after that. I've only ever been afraid on the cricket field once – funnily enough, in the same season in 1974. Mike Procter knocked out Derek Taylor and as I walked out to bat, they carried him off right past me. I played the first ball from somewhere near the square leg umpire!'

Botham's *tour de force* against Hampshire was watched with growls of approval by his captain, Brian Close, another man destined to play an important part in shaping Ian's career. They have many similarities – impulsive, warm-hearted men with fearsome tempers, fanatical, combative sportsmen, fast drivers (Botham technically far superior), hardened drinkers, and mulishly stubborn. Each man lost the captaincy of both county and country, each knows what it is like to flee the sanctuary of their own homes to escape harassment by the media. Close captained Botham for four years and they had some hilarious disagreements on and off the field, which were usually resolved amid much back-slapping and purchases of large whiskies in the bar afterwards. Close admired Botham's natural talent immensely; perhaps he saw something in him of the young D. B. Close who played for England and did the 'double' when he was just eighteen. He tried to counsel Ian against rashness saying, 'You're such a good player, lad, no one should get you out. What did you play a bloody awful shot like that for?' Close would upbraid him for bowling too many bouncers, but the young tearaway would go his own sweet way on the morrow. Even now, they still argue fiercely about cricket whenever they meet, or on the Easter holiday in the Lake District that they invariably share every year. Close's biggest influence on Botham was not a technical one, it was one of attitude. He encouraged him to take chances in the field, to back his judgement with a bowling change. Close's legendary attitude to pain found a suitable response in Botham, whose reaction to pain has always been that you feel what you want to feel. So when Botham shook his head clear, and whipped Roberts away through mid-wicket on that sunny day in 1974, it was no more than his captain expected.

For his part Botham thinks the world of his first county captain: 'He made me realise that a game is never finished till the last ball, that you can alter its course if you have the willpower and the self-belief. He was a breath of fresh air at Somerset and all the players who were destined to make the grade were better professionals after Closey had worked on us. We never really had many rucks, you know – I reckon about two in four years, and each time we ended up laughing about them. I used to travel everywhere with him, listening to his tales, and I'll always have a lot of time for him. I think he was second to Mike Brearley among my captains – I loved his attitude that you were better off losing a good game than boring everyone to death with a dull draw.'

Another Somerset player watched that mighty innings with great admiration. Since 1973 Vivian Richards and Ian have been as close as any cricketers can be; indeed before their respective marriages they seemed to be joined at the hip. Both young players had excited each other with their positive approach to the game that season and, as far as Botham was concerned, his performance against Roberts was no more than Richards had done a few weeks earlier in a Benson and Hedges game. At that time, Mike Procter vied with Roberts as the most dangerous fast bowler in county cricket and Richards destroyed Procter in one dazzling over. It was a muggy, thundery day with the hint of thunder and lightning in the air as the young Antiguan climbed into Procter. He smashed two balls in a row through the covers and when the inevitable bouncer came next ball, Richards hit him in front of square, to the boundary. It was an electrifying display and it left a deep impression on Botham. They both were aware that the game had to be played with flair and a positive approach. Richards agrees:

> When I first saw Ian, I thought he was marvellous. He was the only Englishman who played in the uninhibited way of a West Indian. In those days, the typical county pro played in a conformist manner, as if expecting to fail. They were taught how to play up and down the line with the left elbow pointing to the sky. They were full of technical jargon, yet nobody wanted to watch them bat. Botham was different from all the others. He'd heard all the mumbo-jumbo and pleased himself what he wanted to do about it. He'd race round the boundary, pick up the ball with one hand, and send it whistling into the keeper's gloves – while his captain would moan about him not getting two hands to the ball! Ian had so much self-confidence that it was exhilarating to be on the same side as him. I knew he'd be a great player, even though his performances in those days were erratic.

Over the years Viv has been a steadying influence on Ian. During Ian's wild, bacchanalian moments, Viv would lead him quietly away. He would never get into trouble while Viv was around. There is no question that both men love each other, but it is interesting to speculate which is the stronger man in the relationship. When Viv telephones Ian, it is the Englishman who slips into the sing-song Caribbean dialogue that is indecipherable to all but the initiated. Viv does not try to speak like an Englishman. It was Viv who turned Ian on to the music of Bob Marley, to the extent that Ian once visited Marley's grave in Jamaica to pay his respects. Viv takes Ian down to the ghettoes at St John's in Antigua, where an Englishman is a rarity. Viv was always the snappy dresser when they lived together (his flat-mate used to joke that he took longer to get ready than his mother!) but now, much to Viv's amusement, Ian takes a fair amount of time to dress. Ian says of the West Indians, 'these are my people', and his closeness to the West Indies side confirms his sincerity about multi-racialism.

One always gets the feeling that Viv has been one jump ahead of Ian in a rivalry that is undoubtedly friendly. They never had many batting partnerships together, partly because they would always try to out-do one another (leaving Richards invariably at the crease with Botham getting himself out). Viv now has the West Indies captaincy, while Ian has lost his chance of getting back the England job. Richards invariably came off best in their international jousts together, to a certain extent because West Indies had the superior bowlers, but also because Richards was mentally tighter. When they first opposed each other in a one-day international in 1976, Botham moved across to congratulate his pal on his century, only to be cut short chillingly: 'We're not playing for Somerset now, I'm playing for the West Indies.' It is difficult to imagine Botham adopting such a blinkered policy to a close friend, least of all Richards. He has always been one for the heartening word of congratulation on the field of play.

The next influential figure came into Botham's life in 1974 – although Kathryn Waller's independence of mind is less obvious compared with a Botham or a Richards. Nevertheless, without a chance meeting at Grace Road, Leicester, in June of that year, Botham's promising county career might have been interrupted by a spell of 'porridge' at Her Majesty's pleasure. Ian freely admits that the best day's work he ever did was to marry Kath, and nobody who knows them would demur at that. He was a wild lad in his early days on the Somerset staff – in the opinion of Vic Marks, 'a hooligan in the nicest sense of the word' – and although no one ever doubted his fundamental good nature, the roaring boy was a considerable handful. When the day's play at Taunton was over, Ian would head for the Gardeners' Arms, a favourite watering hole less than a mile from the ground and he would plan his social campaign for that evening. Jim Laws, a betting shop manager, used to accompany him on some of his escapades and he still shudders at the narrow escapes:

He used to order large gins and someone else would pay. Then he'd start a competition to see how many cans of lager we could consume. Whoever finished last had to buy the next round. You can safely say that Botham didn't have to buy any! I have never seen anyone hold his drink so well. You just couldn't keep up with him. At nine o'clock in the evening his day was just starting, so he'd drag me off to the 88400 club in Taunton. We'd get in there, I'd be hoping for a quiet drink and then I'd hear someone say 'I see Big Head's in.' Ian would ignore it but after a while he'd go and sort them out. I must say he never looked for trouble, but once it started he wouldn't back down. If he hadn't got married when he did, I reckon he'd have been inside.

Ian's saviour was a reserved Yorkshire lass who has more than made up for her apparently docile image with admirable strength of character. Kath and Ian decided to get engaged within six weeks of their first meeting. Kath's mother, Jan, thought him 'a nice polite young man, not at all like the rowdy youngsters of today'. Clearly Jan had not darkened the doors of the 88400 club! Yet Ian has always had a good relationship with Jan and Gerry Waller. They were impressed that Ian went through the formalities of tracking Gerry down on a business trip for permission to marry his daughter and they liked his openness of nature. In the winter of 1974/5, Ian came up to Thorne, near Doncaster, and lived with the family. Gerry gave him a rep's job in his business that made drums and drumsticks, and the boss thought he did a very good job out on the road, despite picking up an occasional scratch and dent on the firm's car. Kath and Ian became engaged at Christmas 1974, much to the wrath of Brian Close, an intimate friend of the Waller family. He told Kath that she would ruin a highly promising cricket career by such a distraction and, as for his young all-rounder, he simply was not good enough for such a smashing lass. But the happy couple battened down the hatches, waited for the storm to subside (Ian would witness similar eruptions every day of the cricket season), and made their plans. They bought a cottage in Mowbray Street, Epworth, eight miles from Kath's parents, and Ian set to work on it with the help of his flat-mate in Taunton, Dennis Breakwell. Jan and Gerry gave them the deposit for the cottage as a wedding present. Ian was hardly flush at the time – he used to borrow off Gerry so that he could buy his daughter flowers – and it was clear that he needed to be 'capped' by Somerset to improve his long-term prospects. That did not materialise in 1975, when he had a mundane season. In Close's opinion, Botham was too impatient, not realising that a promising young player invariably suffers a reaction in the second season. Yet that reverse did not dilute the famous Botham self-confidence. One day, Jan was clearing out Kath's bedroom and she came across one of Brian Close's England caps that he had given to his god-daughter. 'Would you like to try this on, Ian?' she asked, only to be told, 'No thanks, Jan – I'll wait for my own.' He was not joking, it was said with quiet conviction.

From the age of about twenty to his middle twenties, Botham was very wrapped up in cricket. He knows he was lucky because he had more ability than many others, but he worked as hard as anyone at his game.

> I really wanted desperately to succeed and I was so lucky to have Kath's support. We had nothing when we got married and if we spent twenty quid, we'd be worried about extravagance. Now I'm very irresponsible about money, I just live for today, but I've had to fight for everything I've got. I soon realised that you've got to be very single-minded and thick-skinned to get to the top in professional sport and you've got to be able to ignore the rubbish that's thrown at you. A happy home life allowed me to do that.

As the weeks ticked by to his wedding, Ian busied himself on the road, selling Gerry's handiwork, and back in Thorne he played football or enjoyed quiet nights by the fire with his fiancée – light years away from his last summer as a bachelor, when he used to win countless bets that he could drink three pints of beer in a minute, then round off the evening with an Indian takeaway! Before his wedding, however, he had one of the most serious setbacks of his life. He had taken the family dogs out to Robin Hood's Bay, near Whitby and blew away the cobwebs for an exhilarating half-hour, running up and down the rocks. A few minutes after he stopped running, Ian was overcome by a tightening of the chest. He found it very difficult to breathe for a time and was very distressed. Jan remembers the evening vividly: 'He came home, looking terribly upset and threw himself on the settee, saying "I can't even get through training without feeling breathless. I felt awful coming back in the car just now." He was devastated, he thought there was something seriously wrong with him, perhaps heart trouble. Well we packed him off to the family doctor, but unfortunately he wasn't there that night. His stand-in took a brief look at him and said "You may as well give up all sport if you want to feel well again." You can imagine how Ian felt.'

Jan had the presence of mind to contact the family doctor for a second opinion and Dr Len Oakshott sent him to a specialist at Doncaster Royal Infirmary, who moderated the initial diagnosis. He was told that he had exercise asthma. That distressing feeling that someone is keeping a hand over the mouth was affecting Ian *after* he had finished running, not *during* the exercise. Ian still suffers from exercise asthma, but a spray usually clears up any discomfort. If Jan had not persisted in getting a second opinion, her future son-in-law might still be selling drumsticks, but it had given her an interesting insight into his character: 'When he first heard the news he despaired, but soon he was full of resolution. There was something within him that wouldn't take "no" for an answer.'

In January 1976, Kath and Ian married and they embarked on another momentous year. It was important for Ian to get his cap that summer and it arrived within the first month, handed over by the man who had warned him against marrying his god-daughter. That doubled Botham's salary, no mean consideration in the days when he used to try supplementing his cashflow by ringing up Jim Laws and asking 'What's Closey backed today? Whatever he's gone for, I'll have the same – a twenty pence Yankee on the same four.'

The summer of 1976 was an important one for the Bothams. Ian felt he had to break through onto the international scene and, with his usual brashness, he badgered Close to promote him up the batting order. After moving him up from number eight to six in the order, Close's faith was justified when Botham scored his maiden first-class century against Nottinghamshire in early August. At Trent Bridge, Somerset had been set 301 in just under four hours, and at 51 for 3 they were struggling. Yet they ran out winners by six wickets, with Botham 167 not out. It must be admitted that it was a benign Trent Bridge pitch and Clive Rice was unable to bowl, but for all that it was a mightily impressive maiden century. He opened his account with a pull for six and a further twenty-one boundaries embellished the score. It was the manner of his batting that impressed everyone there that day. He was not yet twenty-one but, just as he had proved against Andy Roberts two years earlier, he could play with calm certainty if allowed responsibility. Clive Rice, for one, had no doubt that he had seen a new star after that innings: 'I told everyone that day that he should play for England that summer. It was a phenomenal innings from someone so young. Okay, we were short of bowling, but he looked so secure, his strokeplay was so crisp. What was he doing earlier, down at number eight, for God's sake?'

A good question. Botham felt the same way when he savaged 97 off a Sussex side led by the England captain, Tony Greig. Yet Botham's name went into Greig's file and, later in the season, after England's mature batsmen had been seen off by the West Indian fast bowlers, Botham was picked for the one-day international series. He played in two of the games but did little of any note. Significantly though, Greig liked his style. He told Botham that he would vote for him when the touring party for India and Australia was to be selected. Botham thought that was no more than his just desserts, yet when the squad was announced he was not in it. If he was disappointed he did not show it – his belief in himself was so strong that he probably saw it as England's loss, not his. He would reflect on a satisfying season, a doubling of his salary, a new, supportive wife, his first taste of international cricket and Christmas in the matrimonial home.

Just before Christmas, however, the phone rang in the Botham cottage. It was Donald Carr, the Test and County Cricket Board secretary. Ian had been chosen for a trip to Australia from early January for the next three months. He would play grade cricket to gain experience and the expenses would be met by Whitbread, the brewery company. By the following Christmas, his life was beginning to change dramatically.

3

The halcyon years

●

Over the next five years, Test cricket must have seemed comparatively simple to Ian Botham. Certainly some of the opposition was sub-standard, due to many of the best players signing for Kerry Packer, but you can only steamroller what is on offer and Botham did that in spectacular style. Records tumbled to the husky all-rounder and the English crowds loved him, not least of all because he communicated his pleasure in being alive, gloried in his juggernaut of feats. With Tony Greig accepting Packer's vision of cricket, Botham filled his position so effectively that the charismatic South African was never missed. The gods may have been saving up retribution for Botham in later years, but this uncomplicated young man would have no truck with such imponderables: each Test Match day that dawned was a fresh challenge to him and invariably he would batter down the gate of resistance. Cricket, like life, was the most enormous fun.

Yet the year 1977 did not begin in the most auspicious manner for Botham. He was pleased to get the offer of a Whitbread scholarship for Australia, arrived in Melbourne in early January and, with Yorkshire's Graham Stevenson, settled down to teaching these cocky Australians a thing or two about cricket. It was not a success. For a start it rained a lot. Melbourne's reputation of providing four seasons in a day did not impress Botham, especially when the elements ruined so many of the games he was due to play in. When he did get on the field, he was indifferent against fairly weak opposition and the Australians lost no time in suggesting that England caps must be coming fairly cheaply these days. The combative nature in Botham's character would flare up, and he threatened all sorts of dire deeds against the Australians when they toured England later that year. When it comes to shouting down opposition viewpoints in a noisy crowded bar, Ian is in a class of his own: the compulsion of his presence is usually enough for the most cerebral of debaters. For once, though, he met his match. Ian Chappell had been a brilliantly successful captain of Australia, an excellent batsman and he might have been sent from Central Casting as the archetypal tough Aussie. Chappell had faced grittier social opposition than this loud-mouthed Pom and he would not take too much from him. Between them it looked as if Chappell and Botham would do for Anglo-Australian relations the kind of service Genghis Khan afforded Central Asia. It was not a demure encounter.

Legend has it that Botham knocked Chappell off his bar stool after the Australian had made derogatory remarks about the state of English cricket, and that Chappell threw another caustic remark at the Englishman as he left the bar, whereupon Botham chased him out into the street, vaulted a car and failed gallantly in his efforts to catch up with the slippery, cowardly Aussie. Good, knockabout stuff. The image of Australian cricket had been tarnished in recent years under Chappell's cynical leadership, with 'sledging' a vital part of their on-field tactics – and it was good to hear that a patriotic young Pom had put the ringleader in his place. He had it coming, that Chappell bloke. For his part, Chappell is fed up of seeing this hoary old canard bobbing along in the sea of gossip. Now that he is working as a commentator with Channel Nine he is a good deal more accessible to the Poms than in his snarling, boorish days as captain of Australia – and he says that the young Englishman started all the verbal provocation. Chappell agrees he was knocked off his stool by Botham, and that he declined to get involved in any fisticuffs. After a vigorous exchange of views, Botham was led away, according to Chappell. 'I then remember seeing him in the Centenary Test in London in 1980 and I gave him a serve about more rubbish he'd put in the press about me. He blew me a kiss and suggested I came over to sort it out. I pointed to my throat and head, suggesting that he was dead from the neck upwards. Then on the 1986/7 tour to Australia, he behaved very badly during the dinner in honour of Bill O'Reilly. As far as I'm concerned I give him nought out of ten as a human being and not much more as a cricketer.'

Botham thinks highly of Chappell, too. All he would say about the 1977 skirmish is that 'he's an animal'. A feud that has been an open secret in cricket for a decade at least threw up one humorous incident on Botham's last tour of Australia. Chappell had to interview Botham for Channel Nine and it was amusing to see both men prior to the recording; as the technicians busied themselves with the usual paraphernalia, they each acted as if the other was not there, rather like a husband and wife who are not speaking, yet have to share the same meal.

Botham's stay in Melbourne in 1977 did nothing to douse the flame of his international ambition; indeed, with the Australians due shortly in England, it was certainly fanned. When the England team came to Melbourne in March for the Centenary Test, Stevenson and Botham were deputed to help their preparation. Stevenson threw himself gladly into the round of net bowling and dressing-room dogsbody, whereas Botham publicly viewed it as a necessary interlude before he took his rightful place in the England eleven. In that squad there were experienced, respected cricketers like Greig, Underwood, Knott, Brearley, Amiss, Willis and Fletcher, yet Botham immediately saw himself as one of the lads. Every time a player was on the treatment table, he would walk in and tickle their toes playfully; if someone started to read a paper, he would try to set fire to it. Ice cubes in the socks and hot teaspoons on bare arms came later, but Botham seemed totally unaware that he was the junior, the skivvy of the dressing-room. John Lever recalls how he attached himself to the post-match social gatherings as if he were an England regular: 'His self-confidence was amazing. There he was, telling all the old players what he'd do when he played for England. It was a case of "when", not "if". He tried to doss down in my room as well, but I soon slung him out!' Lever was not to know it at the time but, within eight months, he would be the first room-mate on tour of Botham's England career and he would be bringing the young tourist a handful of pills to help with his dysentery.

Botham returned to England in the spring of 1977 to find a pregnant wife and the press indulging in the usual speculation about the formation of the England side for the forthcoming Ashes series. Against the Australians for Somerset, he enjoyed a fine all-round game, inspiring them to a thumping victory over the tourists for the first time in the county's history. He had no doubts that he would figure prominently in the selectors' thoughts, even after a bad game for the MCC against the Australians in the first month of the season. Botham's aggressive nature had got the better of him in that match as he tried to bounce out Rod Marsh. He was hooked several times as he lost line and temper and his captain, Mike Brearley, took him out of the firing line, suggesting that

macho efforts like that were just a waste of energy. It was the first time –
but far from the last – that Brearley would know when to cry 'enough'.

Yet Ian's immediate international prospects were not unduly harmed;
he was picked for the one-day series and even though he did not make
the side, he was able to sample the unique dressing-room atmosphere
of international cricket. Not that Botham was particularly overawed by
it all – he spent a good deal of time during the Old Trafford game trying
to sell his new colleagues some cheap watches that were allegedly the
bargains of all time!

Then it was back to county cricket, to create some impressive figures
to justify a call-up to the Test arena. After two Tests it came, courtesy
of that fairly common occurrence, a Chris Old injury. Botham was
picked in his place but it was another Yorkshireman, Geoffrey Boycott,
who grabbed the main headlines, returning to Test cricket for the first
time in three years. Botham was happy to let Boycott hog all the media
attention at Trent Bridge; he was sure he would get enough of it before
his own England career was done.

On that first morning, Brearley warned his young charge that he must
not overdo the bouncer in the manner of that recent MCC game – it
was to be bowled occasionally, for a specific purpose rather than just
to intimidate. That MCC game had been filed away in the sagacious
Brearley cranium. While Botham was digesting this advice, his family
were struggling to get over Trent Bridge to witness every minute of his
first day in Test cricket. Both sets of parents and a heavily pregnant
Kath piled into one car and Les Botham's inability to distinguish red
from green traffic lights is still remembered with amusement. Somehow
the family battered through the traffic and installed themselves before
Ian bowled his first spell for England. It was unimpressive, apart from
his second delivery, edged by Rick McCosker into the vacant third slip
area. Botham cursed himself because although he wanted four slips he
lacked the courage to ask Brearley for something so aggressive in his
first over in Test cricket. In future he would not make the mistake of
being retrograde in expressing his opinions.

That first spell was typical of many Botham has put in over the years –
too little on the spot, too many wide deliveries picked off to the
boundary – but his first wicket was equally characteristic. In their earlier
encounters Greg Chappell and his men had not been over-enamoured
by Botham's talents and his initial wayward spell confirmed their dis-
respectful opinion. When he returned for another go just after tea,
Chappell licked his lips in anticipation. He had reckoned without the

legendary Botham luck. The first ball of Botham's new spell was a long-hop, slowish in pace, wide of the off-stump, the kind of delivery the Australian captain would punish almost as an afterthought. Instead he dragged it on to his wicket as he tried to hammer it through the covers. Botham raised a right arm in salute and, as his colleagues raced towards him in congratulation, he charged down the pitch like an angry rhino. That charge, that swelling of the chest, the arms above his head – they would soon be a familiar sight on Test grounds all over the world. Down in Taunton, Jim Laws, Ian's betting shop friend, was preparing to pay out to him with a genuine smile, having promised sponsorship of £5 a wicket and £1 a run for England.

It was significant that his first wicket should be courtesy of a bad ball and a misjudgement by a master batsman, but Botham has never been bothered by such niceties. He admits it was a poor delivery, but reasonably points out that every bowler is often unlucky with a terrific ball that the batsman is not good enough to touch. Nevertheless, the legend of 'Golden Arm Botham' was born on his first day as an England player and it persists.

After Chappell was out, Botham settled down and did himself justice. The outswinger started to work and he ran in with purpose, gaining an extra yard in pace. He trapped Rod Marsh with an inswinger to the left-hander, a particularly pleasing dismissal – ignoring Brearley's strictures about bouncers, he first softened him up with one that whizzed just past his nose. Then with Marsh expecting another bouncer, Botham foxed him with a well-pitched up delivery and he was late on the shot. It was a good piece of bowling, the forerunner of many similar dismissals over the years.

The debutant finished with 5 for 75 and just to round off a perfect day, he was introduced to the Queen, a lady whose virtues always bring out a near-primeval loyalty in Botham. During the inevitable round of interviews he remarked: 'My wife was eight months' pregnant this morning, I hope she still is!'

That first day was to prove Botham's most influential part in the match. He made a sketchy 25, being dropped first ball (at slip by Greg Chappell), then playing and missing at the next two deliveries. He did not take a wicket in the second innings and did not bat again as England won easily by seven wickets. Chappell and his side were hurriedly revising their assessment of the uncomplicated young man from Yeovil, although they felt he had used up his allotted ration of luck with the ball at Trent Bridge.

In his next encounter with them – the Leeds Test – Botham did not shine initially. After sitting in the dressing-room for a day and a half as Boycott compiled his hundredth century, he lasted three balls and fell, slogging at Ray Bright's left-arm spin. He made amends with the ball, however: 5 for 21 as the ball swung in the cloudy Headingley atmosphere. That, to all intents and purposes, was the end of Botham's season, on August the fourteenth. He had felt a few twinges in his left foot the previous week, but had neglected to tell the England selectors about it. On the fourth day of the Leeds Test, he stepped on the ball in trying to stop a quick single and turned his ankle. When Derek Randall caught Rod Marsh to bring the Ashes back to England, Botham was flinching on the physio's table, as a hypodermic needle administered a pain-killer.

It turned out that he had fractured a bone in his foot but, although the injury robbed him of another England cap and the chance of the 'double' (88 wickets and 738 runs was his final tally), he was at least able to attend the birth of his first child. Liam brought his parents great joy and it is to their credit that he has turned out to be such a well-mannered, unspoilt young lad. Many a child would have been put off appearing in public after the sort of press harassment and playground leg-pulling he has had to endure, but he clearly inherited a good portion of his father's durability and his mother's common sense. It was a happy autumn for the Bothams, that one in 1977, with cricket honours keeping pace with domestic contentment.

Around that time, Botham took two more significant decisions. One day he popped into Musgrove Hospital in Taunton for treatment on his injured foot. By mistake he wandered into the wrong ward and came across a group of children; many of them were bald, they all looked terribly weak and Botham was too upset to stay in their company. He asked what was wrong with them and he heard the dreaded word – leukaemia. As a proud father of a matter of weeks, he was shattered to think that someone like Liam could be struck down with such a deadly disease. Botham arranged for a regular sum of money to be set aside for Christmas parties for the children in that ward and for travelling expenses for any relatives. He insisted on anonymity. Eight years later he was at last able to do something major for leukaemia sufferers by walking the length and breadth of the country.

Botham also started to attend to business matters. On the advice of Basil D'Oliveira, he took on the services of Reg Hayter as his agent. Reg, a highly respected journalist, has run a sports agency for more years than he cares to remember and it is no exaggeration to say that if every journalist covering Test matches had the integrity and values of Reg Hayter there would never be the sort of rift between players and media that exists today. Reg liked the young Botham straight away: 'Unlike most sportsmen I know, Ian was a generous man. He was always trying to pick up the tab after a meal, always first to the bar to get the drinks. I was never a father figure to him, simply his agent, but it was a happy relationship. He was the easiest of clients to deal with when it came to money because he trusted me. In the early days he never even looked at the details of his cheques because he knew I had his best interests at heart and would never try to put one over on him.' Over the next eight years, before Ian lost his heart to the egregious blandishments of Tim Hudson, Reg Hayter provided shafts of common sense and unselfish support in Ian's increasingly turbulent life. He also introduced his lawyer, Alan Herd, to Ian, a relationship that has proved mutually satisfactory.

By 1977 another business relationship that has provided both parties with great satisfaction was taking shape. This was the first summer in which Botham used Duncan Fearnley's bats. He had shaken hands on a contract that saw Botham using Fearnley bats for the princely sum of £150 a year. By the time that four-year contract was up, Botham was England captain and his dashing batting had popularised the distinctive Fearnley symbol all over the world. The next contract was for a slightly higher sum! Today, Fearnley manufactures around 50,000 bats a year, the biggest amount in the world, and he freely admits his debt to Botham: 'He's done more for me than any other cricketer, the kids love him and want to use bats with his name on them. Early on, money didn't mean all that much to him, he just wanted the right product. I was there in the England dressing-room when he told Tony Greig where to get off, because he was going to use my bats rather than Greigy's firm. He had complete trust in me and I appreciated that. I suppose we've gone up the ladder together, but Beefy's remained the same with me. His word is his bond and when he shakes you by the hand, that is enough for me.'

Botham gets through a couple of Fearnley bats a season on average. They weigh just under three pounds, not as heavy as many believe. He likes a light pick-up and there is a good deal of wood in the lower part of the blade, in the drive area. 'I take it as a compliment that people say Beefy mishits for six,' says Fearnley, 'that means I've done my job right.'

Soon Ian's Fearnley bat was doing him proud in New Zealand and he returned home a hot property, en route to being the world's best all-rounder. Tony Greig's departure to World Series Cricket left a gap for the all-rounder berth and Botham filled it handsomely – although not before he had to battle to earn his place. As usual in his career, success did not come immediately and the first part of the tour, to Pakistan, was a nightmare for him. For a large part of the trip he was ill with severe dysentery and, when he was fit, he had to convince Mike Brearley that he was a better all-rounder than Chris Old. It seems amazing now to conceive the possibility that the guru might have misjudged the respective merits of Old and Botham, yet Brearley does admit he was spectacularly wrong. In the previous English summer, Old had taken 30 first-class wickets and scored 341 runs, 107 of these coming in just 37 minutes at Edgbaston, when Warwickshire fed him with the fearsome bowling of John Whitehouse and Rohan Kanhai in search of a declaration. Yet Brearley felt he could develop as a batsman; when he failed twice at number seven in the First Test at Lahore, Bob Taylor was moved up to that position for the rest of the series, and Old's career as a prospective England all-rounder was over.

Even before Botham fell ill with dysentery, he had done himself no favours in the eyes of Brearley. In the first serious net practice at Rawalpindi, he tried to slog the local leg-spinners as far as the eye could see, with predictable consequences. Brearley wondered if he and the tour selectors had erred in taking this over-confident slogger on a senior England tour. It would be a few weeks before Brearley changed his opinion and that would only come when he rejoined the tour in New Zealand as a journalist, after breaking his arm.

A decade after this England tour, many tried to drum up a retrospective feud between Botham and another young hopeful on his first tour, Mike Gatting. When Gatting took over the England captaincy in 1986, the press speculated on how he would handle the mercurial Botham: it was alleged that he would get his own back for being treated dismissively over the years by Botham and some other senior players. The feature-writers delved back into the faded press cuttings and came out with the theory that the pair had been deadly rivals on that first tour, and that they had never really got on. Yet it was not a case of Gatting vying with Botham for a single place in the Test team: in Pakistan, Old and Botham were rivals for the all-rounder berth (it could hardly be Gatting on the strength of 14 first-class wickets the previous summer!). Gatting made his Test debut at Karachi, but there is no suggestion that he forced out Botham, who was still recovering from his illness. In fact Gatting took the place of his captain, whose arm had been broken three days earlier. When the tour moved on to New Zealand, Botham was fit and raring to vent his pent-up frustrations on green wickets that favoured his bowling. Gatting would never have supplanted him at number six, the pivotal position for the all-rounder, which the Middlesex player patently was not. In any event, Gatting also played in the Third Test at Auckland: the weakest England batting side in living memory had vacancies for anyone showing the remotest suggestion of class.

Gatting points out that it took some time for he and Botham to get to know each other, because Botham soon had his own circle of friends in the England side, while Gatting was never sure of a regular place until 1985. The England management soon worked out the kind of colleagues who would share rooms on tour with Botham – men of similar social inclinations like John Lever, Geoff Miller, Mike Hendrick or Geoff Cook – while differing characters like Derek Randall or Phil Edmonds were kept away from him. After the 1977/8 tour Gatting did not make an England trip until 1981, under Botham's captaincy in the West Indies, so it is hard to conceive a bitter rivalry between the two men that simmered over the years. Gatting is not immune from hearty japes at the hands of Botham (no one is whom he likes), but anyone who saw them together in Ireland on the 1987 Leukaemia Research Walk is well aware that under the bluff banter there is a healthy respect for the England captain. Botham has a typical response to the rumours of an early rift: 'The usual bollocks you get in the press.'

He had weightier matters on his mind during that Pakistan leg of his first England tour. At one stage he thought he was going to die, the conventional response of the tough character who shrugs off physical pain but cannot come to terms with more subtle challenges to his health. Anyone who has suffered from amoebic dysentery will understand how ill Botham and his room-mate Mike Hendrick felt for several weeks: thoughts of getting back into the England team were on the back burner, apart from one unintentionally hilarious afternoon when both tried to convince the selection committee that they were fit for the forthcoming Test. In front of a sceptical group of selectors, they tried to run around the ground – both managed fifty yards before their legs gave out on them and the dreaded stomach cramps returned. Bernard Thomas, the team physiotherapist, packed them off to their hotel and that was the last they saw of a cricket ground for some time. Hendrick takes up the grisly story:

We were rooming together and we were a sorry sight, taking it in turns to use the toilet, convinced we were going to croak. After we'd collapsed at the ground, a Pakistani doctor came in to examine us. He told us triumphantly it was amoebic dysentery and that we each needed an injection. He pulled out a phial containing what looked like syrup and then rummaged around for a needle. He found one in his top pocket and it had clearly seen better days. Thank God Bernard Thomas was there and he offered one of his. Then it took this doctor about three minutes to find my vein and the stuff in the phial felt like porridge going into me. I was moaning and groaning and Both said, 'There's no way that bloody stuff's going in me.' We stayed in that room for two days, drinking nothing but Perrier, staggering to the toilet, white as sheets. We convinced ourselves that we were gonners unless we got some decent English food in us, so we cabled our respective wives: 'Send food, a matter of life and death.' It took a month before it turned up, at Karachi.

That tour of Pakistan was the last of the old-style England tours, with long periods where teeth had to be gritted and hardships endured. By the time England returned there in 1984, they found themselves in luxurious hotels, with their hosts doing their best to accommodate their wishes. It was different in 1977, as Geoff Miller recalls:

I'll never forget the Sanjee's Hotel in Hyderabad. It wasn't a tourist trap! At close of play we'd all come back and take turns in trying to clean up under a thin trickle of water coming out of a wall at knee height – there were no showers on the ground. During the day, our food came from this huge cauldron, straight out of Macbeth, except that a little Pakistani stood in for the three witches. He kept throwing things into this cauldron and bubbling it up. By this time Beefy was convinced they were trying to poison him and he was clinging on to the desperate hope that his food parcel from Kath would turn up before he breathed his last. He got so annoyed with the mosquitos in our room that he bought a bull whip. The hotel was situated near a swamp and at night you could see a cloud of mosquitos rising up, just looking for flesh to bite. We had no nets, of course, so we'd lie in bed with batting gloves on and cricket socks and flannels. One night we kept the light on and Beefy enjoyed himself flicking the mossies off the ceiling. He got over-ambitious with one massive flick of the wrist and brought part of the ceiling down on top of me. He was pleased with that, he'd got rid of most of the mosquitos in one go!

Those England players agree that a terrific team spirit was needed to get through that Pakistan leg of the tour and Botham forged friendships with the likes of Miller, Hendrick, Old, Lever and Willis that are still warm and intimate. When the Air New Zealand flight left Karachi Airport, it was Botham who led the cheering. As Botham and Hendrick tucked into fried chicken legs and cans of beer, the spirits of the players lifted. Over the next six weeks, Botham was to be involved in more productive action than cracking a bull-whip.

The wickets in New Zealand were ideal for him. They were green and the shine stayed on the ball a good deal longer than on the mud-baked surfaces of Pakistan. By the time Botham started harvesting wickets in New Zealand, he had taken steps to refine his technique. In the week after his Test début at Trent Bridge he had experimented with outswingers bowled from the wide of the crease. He reasoned that the line of attack would confuse a batsman, who would be expecting inswingers from the extremity of the crease. The three wickets he took in that county match (against Northants at Weston-super-Mare) were all catches to the wicket-keeper from such a delivery. When he got to Pakistan, he was no-balled regularly early on in an up-country game at Peshawar. He was sufficiently concerned to enlist the services of his county captain, Brian Rose, and of Chris Old and Mike Hendrick. At close of play the quartet went out to the middle and spent an hour finding out the area of transgression. They discovered that his front foot was not grounded behind the popping crease at the moment of delivery. Botham practised hard at coming down well behind the crease, so that by the time dysentery struck him down he was cured of any no-ball problems. Since then, a no-ball from Botham is very rare, a point he expressed forcibly to umpire Alan Whitehead during their infamous difference of opinion in the Trent Bridge Test of 1985.

The significant point is that in late 1977 Botham worked really hard at his bowling. He knew that at Test level the basics had to function automatically, that he also had to master the surprise delivery to get class batsmen out. On his first tour, he spent a lot of time talking technique with the more experienced seamers, Old, Willis, Hendrick and Lever, and he also took a conscious decision to bowl faster. Before then, he had been erratic in speed, sometimes military-medium, sometimes sharp, as he was in his first Test. In Pakistan, on the rare occasions that he was fit to bowl, he saw that the line-and-length stuff was cannon fodder on those flat, lifeless pitches, so he decided to bend his back and try to beat them through the air at speed. Botham believes that, for a couple of years after that, he was the quickest English fast bowler after Bob Willis; certainly his attributes of speed and late swing made a deadly combination.

So Botham was ready for the New Zealanders, both as bowler and batsman. Soon he blasted an unbeaten hundred against Canterbury (missing a 'pair' by a whisker), and he harvested wickets and runs over the following weeks. His first Test hundred came in the Second Test at Christchurch, where he played with great maturity, allowing Richard Hadlee to exhaust himself with too many bouncers. Botham ducked them all and, when Hadlee tired, picked him off with calm assurance. Botham also endeared himself to the rest of the team by running out Boycott as our Geoffrey painstakingly tried to up the tempo. Most other players would have bowed to the status of England's best batsman (and the captain, in the absence of the injured Brearley), but not this 22-year-old. 'I can't seem to get the ball off the square,' lamented Boycott. 'Don't worry, Fiery,' answered Botham, 'I'll sort it out.' He did, running out Boycott by half the length of the pitch. The sacrifice of Boycott and Botham's 30 off 36 balls paved the way for a declaration and an eventual victory by 174 runs.

Botham took 17 wickets in the three-Test series, averaged 53 with the bat and took some superb catches. He had 'arrived', a fact that did not escape him. Paul Downton, another young man on his first tour, recalls being told by Botham that he planned to play for England until he was around thirty. Paul says: 'He simply said he was good enough. On my first tour as reserve wicket-keeper I was just happy to be on the trip, but Beefy had such enormous self-confidence.'

On that New Zealand tour, Botham came up against a player who would later rival him for the title of 'world's best all-rounder'. Richard Hadlee had some stirring jousts with him in the early months of 1978 and those duels have been written up as yet another 'feud' between Botham and an opponent. In the Canterbury game, Botham hooked him savagely, but then Hadlee had him caught at square leg in the First Test, won by New Zealand. In the following Test Hadlee again suffered at the hands of Botham, although this time Botham showed he had learned his lesson and refrained from hooking. In the same Test, Botham bounced Hadlee a few times, reasoning correctly that the New Zealander did not fancy the short-pitched delivery aimed at his face and tried him with a few more. Hadlee managed to flat-bat him over the slips, Botham lost his temper and went for five an over. That was the extent of their supposed 'feud'. Yet Botham behaved the same way towards Hadlee as he would to any batsman who he sensed did not fancy the bouncer, or to a bowler who thought Botham might get himself out to the hook shot. Botham's game then, as now, was all about challenge and any opponent would feel the draught of his competitiveness. Personalities were irrelevant, as Hadlee agrees: 'There was never any feud between us. At that stage I was just trying to sort out my bowling and to get my general game together. I didn't really start to promise much as a batsman till about 1983/4 so I was never till then a threat to Botham as an all-rounder. I was just another opponent in 1978 and we took each other on. I won a few jousts, he won the rest, end of story. We've never had all that much in common with each other off the field, but that doesn't mean we haven't got a healthy respect for each other.'

As the England party flew home, Brearley began revising his opinion of his dynamic young charge. 'He played in Tests as if it were a club game, but then he also showed great maturity when needed. In that hundred at Christchurch, he disciplined himself impressively. He also bowled long spells, showing hostility and variety. I had clearly under-estimated him.'

At that time Botham was still thought of as a front-line bowler who could bat well, if erratically, but in the next few months he established himself as the premier all-rounder in the side. And by the end of the 1978 summer, Botham was a star: two centuries and 37 wickets in the six Tests against Pakistan and New Zealand. In just over a year since his Test début, he had taken five wickets in an innings eight times – in only eleven Tests – as well as scoring three hundreds. His most memorable performance came in the Lord's game against Pakistan, when he became the first player to score a hundred and take eight wickets in the same Test. The story behind the hundred is interesting: it confirms Botham's zest for life and Brearley's tactful handling of his gifted matchwinner. Chris Old fills in the background:

On the first day, there was never any chance of play because of rain. It had rained the day before as well and, to me, there seemed little chance of play on the second day. Late in the afternoon I asked Mike Brearley if he thought we'd play tomorrow and he said, 'I think you'll be alright for a drink tonight.' Beefy overheard and said, 'Can I come too?' Well we had a fair old skinful, and didn't get to bed till about 2.30 in the morning. Friday turned out to be a beautiful sunny day and we started half-an-hour late! Brears came back after winning the toss and said, 'Looking at two of my main bowling strike force, I've decided to bat first.'

Late in the day, I joined Beefy at the crease when he was in the eighties. I told him he wasn't to do anything rash that evening and to play for tomorrow. I proceeded to hit the first ball to mid-wicket and as I passed him, Beefy was doubled up, laughing. He then hit three fours in double quick time and got his hundred in the last over of the day. I couldn't understand how he could see the ball so well the day after a big bender. I got used to that!

His bowling was even more spectacular on the Monday, a bright, fresh day, hardly conducive to swing bowling. But Botham took 8 for 34 in a magnificent exhibition of the art and the hapless Pakistanis were brushed aside. Botham was as amazed as anyone that the ball swung so much and Bob Taylor, England's wicket-keeper that day, told me that he has never kept to a more devastating display. 'It was perfect. His line was right and the ball swung late, at speed. Ian got everything right – he was hungry for success.' The ball that clean-bowled Haroon Rashid astonished bowler, close fielders, wicket-keeper and umpire David Constant. It started out in the area of middle and leg, swung late and knocked out the off-stump. As Constant recalls, 'No one could've played that one. The batsman was turned round, committed to the stroke on legside and he didn't have a chance'. Botham still thinks it was one of the best two deliveries that ever got him a Test wicket. (The other came in his second Test, at Leeds in 1977 and Jeff Thomson was the unlucky recipient of the unplayable ball. 'It was wasted on Thommo. It started leg-stump, it held its own for a time so that any batsman would've been into his shot, and then it went late and picked out the off-stump. I honestly think it would've beaten any batsman in the world, and Thommo missed it by the width of three bats.') As for the Haroon Rashid dismissal, Phil Edmonds, who was fielding at leg-slip, remembers the ball vividly: 'Haroon played the exact copybook stroke to the appropriate ball, except he was nowhere near it when it hit his stumps. It was an amazing delivery.'

Botham's performance that day was no fluke. Later in the season he took eleven wickets in the Lord's Test against the New Zealanders and one of them was a prodigious inswinger to bowl John Wright, their fine opening batsman. Mike Hendrick still talks about it: 'I was fielding at

The Benson and Hedges Cup Final of 1973 has ended with a win for Kent over Worcestershire and as Kent's Alan Ealham seeks the sanctuary of the dressing-room, a young member of the Lord's Ground Staff (right) attends to the duties of supporting the police in their crowd control. No doubt the brawny young man from Yeovil would have preferred to have been playing somewhere, rather than supporting the forces of law and order. Perhaps he told himself he would soon be back at a Lord's cup final, this time as a player. Even in 1973 Ian Botham was certain he was heading for great things.

The Somerset playing staff of 1974 that saw the start of some famous careers. In the front row, Ian Botham kneels on the left, with Vic Marks second right and Peter Roebuck first right. Viv Richards is second right in the back row. Brian Close, one of the major influences on Botham's career, is third right in the middle row and on his right sits Tom Cartwright, the man who first took Botham's bowling seriously.

Midsummer, 1974 and Botham has won a big match for Somerset off his own bat for the first time, against Hampshire in the Benson and Hedges Cup. Soon he would be used to ecstatic receptions like this one.

Batting for Somerset in the Gillette Cup semi-final against Kent at Canterbury in 1974, Botham's first year on the Somerset staff.

The summer of 1976 and the young Botham reacts to his first England appearances (against the West Indies in the one-day series) in the uninhibited manner that has marked his career. The wicket-keeper is Derryck Murray.

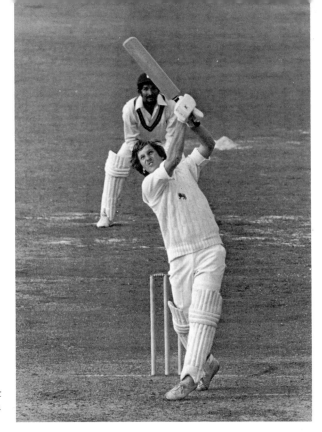

August, 1977 and the family boxers keep Ian and his wife Kathy company as they contemplate two eagerly-awaited events – the birth of their first child, Liam, and Ian's recovery from a broken bone in his foot.

Left: Australia, 1978 – and Botham's famous competitiveness is matched against John Lever, with Geoffrey Boycott labouring behind them.

Above: In the Lord's Test of 1978 Botham gave an inspirational display of high-class swing bowling in taking 8 for 34. Here Pakistan's Haroon Rashid is bowled by a ball that would have defeated any batsman after swinging late. Wicket-keeper Bob Taylor, first slip Mike Brearley and second slip Graham Roope hail a great delivery.

Below: Lord's, 1979 and India's Sunil Gavaskar becomes Botham's hundredth Test wicket, making him the youngest player to reach the target. Fittingly the man making the catch is Mike Brearley, the captain who did most of all for Botham's career with England.

The scalp Botham has always prized above all others – that of his great friend Viv Richards, during the Old Trafford Test of 1980.

With the England tour manager, A. C. Smith, in the lobby of the Pegasus Hotel, Georgetown as the 1981 tour of the West Indies comes to grief against political complications in Guyana.

The Lord's Test of 1981 against Australia and the moment when Ian Botham's career took a shattering nosedive. He has just been dismissed for his second nought of the match and MCC members greet his return to the pavilion with a deafening silence. A few hours later, Botham was no longer England's captain.

The right place at the right time.... Mike Brearley and Ian Botham were good for each other.

Botham during his historic 149 not out in the Leeds Test of 1981. Note the wide-eyed sense of enjoyment he exudes, one of his most endearing characteristics on the field of play.

second slip and in my peripheral vision I saw the ball and I honestly thought it was coming straight to me. It bent in like the proverbial banana, Wright was too late on it and his stumps were scattered. Don't forget that at that stage Beefy was quicker than me, about the pace of Imran Khan – so a delivery like that was unplayable.' John Wright sportingly gives best to the bowler: 'I knew he was trying to york me. He'd tried it a couple of times but they turned out to be a full toss and a half-volley and I got them away for fours. I thought I was organised, but that inswinging yorker was too good for me.'

It was a heady summer for Botham. His batting was considered a bonus because of his phenomenal success with the ball, and yet he was turning in the figures of a class all-rounder. He approached batting then in the same vein as in his famous innings at Leeds three years later. At Lord's he came in to face Iqbal Qasim's left-arm spin with four men around the bat. His second ball was crashed into the Mound Stand and by the end of the over, only one fielder was close to Botham's bludgeoning bat. His hundred that day came off 104 balls. Such was his confidence in his own ability that he even gave his captain a batting tip. He told Brearley, then having a bad trot as an opener, that he was gripping the bat too hard with his right hand, instead of just using the tips of the middle finger and thumb!

Botham could not wait for the trip to Australia later that year. He had been laughed out of Melbourne grade cricket eighteen months earlier and he would repay the jibes with interest. Before then, however, he and his family were to experience their first bout of prurient sensationalism from the popular press. It was an encounter that soured their concept of what constitutes fair reporting and it still rankles.

Just a couple of days before departing to Australia, Ian looked in at a farewell party for him at his local pub in Epworth, the Queen's Head. After half-an-hour, he was walking into the pool room when someone shouted out to him. He turned round, left his hand in mid-air and the door sprang back, with his hand shattering the glass. Ian tried to pull his hand back and in that instinctive reaction he severed two tendons. Blood pumped out everywhere and Gerry Waller, Ian's father-in-law, rushed him back home to get the car out for the inevitable hospital visit. Ian and Gerry told their wives there was nothing to worry about, even though they themselves were very worried indeed. Ian was kept in overnight and, after an operation, he was told that there had been no damage to the nerve and that it would take about three weeks to heal. The Test and County Cricket Board and the tour physiotherapist

Bernard Thomas were kept fully informed and it seemed that England's prized cricketing possession would after all be fit for the Australian challenge, even though he would have to wear a sling for a time and exercise the tendons.

But the Botham family reckoned without the desire of a hospital porter to make a few quid on the side. He tipped off a national newspaper and at ten o'clock on the Sunday evening – almost twenty-four hours after the accident – a reporter announced himself to Kath. Could she confirm that her husband had been badly injured in a pub brawl and that he was not going on tour? He persisted in his line of questioning and, after getting nowhere, announced that he would stand up the story by talking to people in the pub. He failed in that respect and, as he was phoning his copy over to his office, Kath's irate father arrived, hot-foot from Thorne: 'I pulled him out of the phone box, told him to come and apologise to my daughter and after that I watched him dial his office and tell them instead to kill the Botham story about a pub brawl. But the next day, they still printed the story, with the innuendos thrown in. They'd taken no notice of the background information we had given that reporter, which he hadn't really deserved, considering how rude he had been.' For Kath, at the time, it was an instructive introduction to the darker side of being married to a sports star.

Unsurprisingly Botham shrugged off his injury in Australia, impressing Bernard Thomas with his dedication to exercise and obedience towards his instructions. On that tour, Botham's ability to withstand pain was immediately noticeable but it was also the only time Bernard Thomas saw him really concerned for his own welfare. 'It was at Brisbane, just before the First Test. Beefy had eaten a bad oyster and he was throwing up all over his room. He looked absolutely terrible. He was in a worse state than when he had dysentery because then he at least had Mike Hendrick to share it with. This time he was on his own and bewildered. It wasn't a physical challenge like jumping out of a plane, hooking fast bowlers or wind-surfing.'

The tour management kept quiet about Botham's discomfiture in the hope that he would shrug off the debilitating effects. He played in the Brisbane Test, although not fully fit, and made his usual important contribution to a seven-wicket win. In Thomas's opinion, no other player would have got on the field, but Botham was cast in sterner mould than the rest. In the Sydney Test, he carried the bowling in enervating heat on the second day. It was 103 degrees when Willis tottered off, suffering from heat exhaustion. Hendrick also had to go off after seeing three sets of stumps; he sat under a cold shower for half-an-hour, trying to rid himself of dehydration. Botham rose to the challenge, taking two brilliant catches and bowling with great heart. After the rest day, with Willis still wobbly, and Hendrick drained, he still bowled on and on – sending down 28 overs (eight balls per over in those days). When it was Botham's turn to bat, he kept quiet about the virus that gave him a splitting headache and high temperature. Australia led by 142 on the first innings on a turning wicket. Keeping Derek Randall company in a crucial stand, he made just six singles in 90 minutes, telling the excitable Randall that he simply had to stay out there, to occupy the crease and wait for the pitch to break up. Botham had never lingered that long at the crease without hitting a boundary but, when he was out, the lead was 125. On the final day, with Australia needing 205 for victory, Botham was hit sickeningly on the helmet at short leg as Darling smashed an Emburey long-hop at him. Botham is convinced that he would have been killed without the helmet. A few minutes later, he ran out Wood from extra cover. Botham had been sent there to recover from the blow to the head: typically he would not leave the field. His example of personal courage, indomitable will and his unselfish encouragement of Randall were all crucial factors in England winning a Test by 93 runs that they really ought to have lost.

Botham's attitude to injuries over the years has been heroic, there is no other word for it. It was not as if he could cruise through a part of the game, hoping the injury could clear up – strike bowlers who bat at number six and field at second slip do not get much chance to rest. Bernard Thomas, who looked after Botham on seven England tours, says that if Botham was around 50 per cent fit he would expect to play. 'He was always very good at discussing with me what he needed to do to get on the field and he would always follow my instructions. But the will has to be there first. He was always positive about playing, he just wouldn't acknowledge the pain.' Praise also comes from an unlikely quarter, from a cricketer who would have been an even better player with a different psychological attitude to the pain barrier. Chris Old would never scoop the Brian Close Award for Indestructibility and perhaps that is why this highly talented performer is so rich in his praise for his old drinking companion: 'Half the time you didn't know Beefy was injured because he didn't show any pain or talk about it. He'd go and see Bernard Thomas when no one else was around. Beefy simply didn't believe in going on about injuries, he made himself go through the pain by force of will.'

With England winning that Australian series 5/1 there were hopes that they might win the World Cup in 1979. It was not to be. Yet Botham enjoyed another remarkable summer, an Indian summer in fact. In four Tests against the Indians, he set yet more records – the quickest to a hundred wickets (two years and nine days), the fastest to the 'double' (21 Tests), and the most sixes in a Test in England, when blitzing the Indians for 137 at Leeds. During that hundred, Phil Edmonds came in just after 1 pm, told Botham that the instructions were to play for lunch and do nothing silly. Botham proceeded to smash another 38 in that time, including 23 off six balls as he roared past his century – all this while grinning up at Brearley on the balcony, whose mock entreaties to play with decorum were met with a cheerful two-fingered salute.

At Lord's the captain had provided Botham with his hundredth Test wicket with a brilliant slip catch to get Sunil Gavaskar. That night Botham was the cynosure as the media and the other assorted back-slappers crowded in on him. After he had attended to the necessary public relations duties, he slipped an arm around his mate, Mike Hendrick, and suggested a celebration. As Hendrick toasted Botham's hundred wickets in a quiet Maida Vale pub, Botham said that he reckoned thirty of them were Hendrick's. The Derbyshire seam bowler was touched by Botham's generosity. They were totally different bowlers – Hendrick the nagging dentist's drill of a bowler, operating in a tight area that rendered the batsman unsure whether to play back or forward, Botham the expansive, occasionally expensive performer who had brought back the away swinger and the pitched-up delivery to an age where the stock ball seemed to be the one aimed at the batsman's helmeted head. Apart from the bravery to indulge in flights of fancy, to deliver the ball in wicket-taking areas, Botham undeniably had the invaluable assistance of high-class, accurate bowlers at the other end. From 1977 to 1979, England had a fine pace attack: Willis provided the pace and bounce, Botham the swing bowling at a clinking pace, while Lever, Old and Hendrick strangled the batsmen at the other end with their remorseless accuracy and craft. None of these bowlers begrudged Botham his success, even if they invariably joshed him about his luck with bad deliveries. Botham was always the first to praise the support he received and he particularly enjoyed bowling in tandem with Hendrick. Sometimes, though he would exasperate Hendrick:

> I used to get really annoyed at beating the bat time after time and
> then watching Ian bowl a joke ball that got a wicket. At Melbourne

in '78 I bowled four maidens in a row at Kim Hughes but then I had to go off to replace a broken lace in my boot. As I sorted it out in the dressing-room I heard this almighty roar and I thought, 'I bet that bugger Botham's come on and got Hughes out.' He had, first ball, his loosener, and Hughes hit a wide half-volley to extra cover.

How many times has he bowled crap, come off at 0 for 60 and ended up with 6 for 90? Perhaps it's because Beefy wouldn't tense up, he'd relax, enjoy himself, banter with the fielders or give a lucky batsman a mouthful. That ability to let the juices flow helped make him a great cricketer. Yet I never complained because he always appreciated what we were doing at the other end.

John Lever says that it was soon evident that Botham was to be the 'Golden Arm' of his era, but he deserved his luck because he bowled with optimism. 'Yes, he did bowl a lot of half-volleys, but they always swung and a wide half-volley that swings gets batsmen out if they go for the drive and don't get over the ball.' At Melbourne in 1978, Botham bowled Graeme Wood behind his legs with an outrageous slower ball, slower even than John Emburey's stock off-break delivery. Yet although Wood looked disgusted with himself, Botham deserved the wicket because he had tried something imaginative. He reasoned that if he bowled from around the wicket, Wood would not know where his off-stump was and would be forced to play at the ball, even though it was wide of the mark. In the end, the ball was so slow that the batsman essayed a sweep and was bowled leg-stump!

Apart from his natural ability, his luck and his self-confidence, Botham could actually make things happen on the field, mould the game into the shape he wanted. Take the Oval Test in 1979, that summer of Botham records. On the final day, Botham arrived at the ground nursing the uneasy premonition that Sunil Gavaskar was going to score a double hundred. He did – 221 to be precise, and India would have reached the unlikely target of 438 to win had it not been for Botham's refusal to bend the knee. When the last twenty overs began, India needed only 110 with nine wickets in hand, Gavaskar was untroubled and the bowlers were in disarray. Willis was spent, Hendrick off for good with shoulder trouble, and the spinners were being played with ease. When Botham, of all people, dropped Vengsarkar on the boundary at 365 for 1, it seemed that a famous victory was inevitable. Then Botham raised himself for one last surge and the Indians panicked. With eight overs left, 39 needed and seven wickets in hand, Botham was brought back for a final desperate effort. In his four overs he took 3 for 17 (including Gavaskar) and ran out Venkat after making a scintillating stop to rob the Indian captain of four runs. The match was left drawn with India nine runs from victory and two wickets standing. The way that he had imposed himself on the game in those final overs by his athletic fielding and inspirational bowling summed up the mettle of the man.

A few months later, Botham was testing his mettle against sterner foes. The Australians had been strengthened by the return of their Packer players and, in a professional manner, they won a shortened series 3/0. Botham took another 19 wickets in the series, but his batting gave cause for concern. He confided in Ken Barrington, the assistant manager – one of the few former players Botham ever talked to about technique – who told him he was toppling over when playing the shot, rather than standing still. After changing his guard from middle and leg to leg stump, he felt more comfortable. In the Melbourne Test, he made his fifth hundred for England, a mature effort on a pitch of low bounce that brooked no dramatic strokeplay. Botham's calm, four-hour innings was a masterpiece of its kind against one of the great bowling performances of recent Test cricket. Dennis Lillee took one look at the slow, low Melbourne wicket and cut his pace down. Lillee, the master craftsman, took eleven wickets with artful leg-cutters, in the process so impressing Botham that he tried to bowl the same way in Australia's second innings (a reasonable effort it was, too – 1 for 18 off twelve overs). Botham still talks about that masterly display of bowling by Lillee and it remains the main reason why he insists Lillee will always be the greatest bowler of his time. The virtuoso effort of Lillee only served to embellish the lustre of Botham's hundred. In the circumstances (the state of the pitch, the need to protect the tail, the quality of Lillee's bowling, Botham's 119 not out was his most laudable Test innings) up to that time. Perhaps the pitchers of gin and lime he was drinking at Rajah Sahib's Indian Restaurant the night before helped to compose his mind! The kindly proprietor often laughs about this unusual preparation for a big innings, and they yarn over old times whenever Botham is in Melbourne.

There was one more stunning example of Botham's all-round ability as both cricketer and socialiser before he returned to England in the spring of 1980. The team stopped off to play the Jubilee Test at Bombay, to mark the fiftieth birthday of the Indian Board of Control. Botham chose the occasion to turn in an amazing performance with bat and ball, becoming the first man to score a century and take thirteen wickets in the same Test. Perhaps the game did not deserve the status of a Test – there was a carnival atmosphere about the celebrations and certainly the Indian players seemed in skittish mood. Why else would Sunil Gavaskar hit John Lever back over his head in his first over? In humid atmosphere and on a soft pitch, Botham ran through the Indians twice. He also added a record 171 with Bob Taylor for the sixth wicket, playing himself in responsibly (57 for 4 when he came in) then unfurling some glorious strokes. On the third day, Botham bowled from lunch till close of play, then wrapped up the game on the fourth morning. The great all-rounder was fêted by all and sundry and hyperbolic statements came from the most surprising quarters. Ken Barrington said it was by far the most intelligent and hostile bowling performance seen from an England bowler since the days of Trueman and Statham.

I doubt if those two worthies ever prepared for a Test like Botham did in Bombay. At the end of a hard tour, he had decided that some fun was as desirable as winning the forthcoming game. This time Derek Underwood had drawn the short straw and roomed with Botham. Now Derek, a dedicated smoker, and an ardent sceptic of the new-fangled obsession with gymnastic exercises to get fit for cricket, was as keen on a drink or two as any self-respecting cricketer but he blanched at the prospect of being billeted with the apostle of self-indulgence. 'We had a period of time to kill before the Test and on the rest day, which came on the second day because of an eclipse, Beefy was not to be denied. I escaped from him after midnight and he wasn't too pleased the next morning.' A third party to the bacchanalian exercise was Chris Lander, later to be Botham's 'ghost' on the *Sun* and, at the time, writing a book on the tour with Underwood. 'Every night was party night during that Test', recalls Lander. 'One evening we had a huge amount of tandoori chicken in my room and we ended up throwing them around, trying to catch them. Beefy was on brandy and we helped him demolish a very expensive bottle of the stuff, this after a series of cocktails, containing tequila, gin, other lethal stuff, plus orange juice to make it look respectable as we sat in the hotel bar. On the fourth morning of the match, I was lying in bed around eleven o'clock, totally incapable of moving. I vaguely noticed that the television was upside down and when I eventually turned it on, it smelt of curry and started steaming. Some of those chicken legs must have got in the works. Anyway, through the steam I could just about make out the figure of Botham running in to bowl. With his first delivery, he got a wicket and he looked as fresh as a daisy. I couldn't believe it.' That first ball accounted for Yadav, Botham's thirteenth wicket of the match. Underwood walked over from mid-off, hurled his hat at him and chuckled, 'How the hell can you bowl like that after what you put away last night?'

When the Test was over, Botham displayed another appealing side to his character. As he sat down beside Bob Taylor he tossed the match ball to the wicket-keeper, saying, 'There you are – there's a world record ball for you.' Taylor had set up a new record of nine catches in a Test and Botham knew that such a landmark meant a great deal to the wicket-keeper. Today that ball, suitably mounted, occupies pride of place in Bob Taylor's lounge in the Potteries, proof that, despite all the bluster, Botham was never averse to the quiet, thoughtful gesture.

After the Jubilee Test, Botham had played twenty-five times for England with spectacular success. Before we examine just how statistically successful he was, it is worth appreciating this comment from Geoff Miller: 'Many times he would slump down on his bed and say, "I can't do it all, Dusty, we need everyone pitching in." Boycott would've said something like "That's another fifty today, so I need another 35 for my 8,000 Test runs and an average of 50." Beefy never cared about records, he was the most genuine team man I ever knew.' That only serves to make his early Test record even more remarkable. In his first 25 Tests ending with the one in Bombay, Botham accounted for 178 of the 393 wickets that fell to England while he was in the field, a total of 45.29 per cent – made up of 139 wickets, 36 catches and three run-outs. Nobody in Test history can rival such a high percentage of opposition wickets. Truly he never seemed to be out of the game in those early days.

The quality of opposition has to be taken into account when assessing Botham's remarkable start in Test cricket. His detractors have always maintained that Kerry Packer's interference robbed the established game of many world-class players between 1977 and 1979, thereby diluting the standard of Test performances. That is true, but only up to a point. Of the eight series that Botham played in before June 1980, only three of them were affected by absenteeism through Packer's influence. The Pakistanis missed Imran Khan, Zaheer Abbas, Mushtaq Mohammed, Majid Khan and Asif Iqbal when they toured England in 1978, but all bar Imran and Zaheer were on the wane by then. Doubtless these players would have stiffened the Pakistani batting, but none of them ever had outstanding records in Tests in England because of the way the ball seams around. They would probably have made a lot of runs in the 1977/8 series in Pakistan, although they did not seem short of batting in that series. Mohsin Khan and Mudassar Nazar, two batsmen who might not have played if the Packer men were included, did not exactly fail in Test cricket over the next few years. The effect of Packer on the Australian side was more marked. In the 1978/9 series, the Chappell brothers, Lillee, Marsh and Thomson would undoubtedly have posed a greater challenge, as they proved a year later. Yet Rodney Hogg and Alan Hurst took 66 wickets between them, while batsmen like Kim Hughes and Allan Border developed. The crucial difference between the two sides in that 1978/9 series was in the quality of captaincy, with Mike Brearley stealing most of the tricks from Graham Yallop. That tactical superiority manifested itself in England's excellent team spirit. The following year, Botham's all-round performances in the three-Test series were even more outstanding than in 1978/9, once he had sorted out his batting difficulties, culminating in that excellent century at Melbourne. In any event, when Botham took five wickets in an innings twice at the start of his England career, the only Australians of stature missing from the line-up were Lillee and (arguably) Ian Chappell. Nobody suggested Botham got cheap wickets then.

Of course, Botham did not come up against the West Indians during that period, so his position as the world's best all-rounder was not put to the ultimate test. In the light of subsequent events, that has to be a relevant consideration. Yet in any era of cricket you can only do what you can against the best available opposition, and in most of the series that involved England from 1977 to 1980, Packer was irrelevant. Botham was highly relevant in all of them, apart from the one in Pakistan.

Certainly Botham did not expect the golden run to continue. Sterner battles lay ahead – two series against the West Indies and one against Australia in the next eighteen months – and Botham simply enjoyed his place in the sun with his usual fervour. I remember one worrying note, though, in that spring of 1980 and it was struck by Ian's great friend, Bob Willis. After returning from the tour to Australia and India, he told me that Botham had been over-bowled by Brearley. In the Perth Test, he bowled 80 overs as Willis (his run-up and rhythm awry) was relegated to third seamer, and the novice Graham Dilley was too exhausted to do justice to the new ball. Botham willingly shouldered the extra burden and took eleven wickets. He bowled another 40 overs at Sydney and 51 at Melbourne, as well as cheerfully accepting the responsibilities of middle-order batting and fielding close to the bat. Willis feared that Botham's desire to be always in the game and Brearley's understandable preference for his inspirational efforts when a wicket was needed, would rebound on Botham in years ahead. We were not to know, as we chatted about the recent tour, that Botham's much-publicised back injury lay just a few weeks ahead, nor that he was about to endure the worst year of his Test career. Willis's fears were justified. Whatever the reasons, Ian Botham was never the same bowler after he tossed the match ball into the hands of Bob Taylor in that Bombay dressing-room, and told him to put it on his mantelpiece.

4

The captaincy ordeal

●

Hindsight can be a deluding instrument in the shaping of opinions. Many people assessing Ian Botham's career suggest that his elevation to the England captaincy was the most ludicrous appointment since Caligula spotted senatorial qualities in his horse. Yet was it such a foolhardy decision? Those critics who lambast the England selectors for their pusillanimity and conservatism might like to reflect that it was at least a bold response to the dilemma of finding someone to succeed Mike Brearley. It failed and Botham declined as a cricketer, with the team suffering as a consequence. But many imponderables jostle with incontestable facts over the nightmarish year of Botham's captaincy. He proved deficient at the job but at least he retained his dignity at the end of the sorry saga. Others in a less public position did not. Perhaps the words of the Chinese proverb are relevant – 'When the wagon of fortune goes well, spite and envy hang onto the wheels.'

The received wisdom is that Mike Brearley forced the selectors' hands and made them turn to Botham in May 1980. Brearley had told them that he would be unable to tour again due to his desire to qualify as a psychotherapist. Yet he played three more years in county cricket, and appeared in four more Tests in 1981, and was still available for England in the summer. Lest that sound too heretical, it must be remembered that England captains of the past have declined to tour, for reasons varying from standing for Parliament to a desire to establish a career in the City of London, or even an antipathy to the Indian sub-continent. Today Brearley still maintains that Botham should not have been pitched straight into the job without the vital grounding. 'It was callous of them to throw him at the West Indies for his first two series. They could have kept me on for part of that first series, or even all of it, helping Ian to absorb what was needed for the job. Then he could have taken the side away in the winter with the media pressures less intense on him. I made it quite clear to the selectors that I was willing to carry on the job in 1980.' Botham would have been more than happy with such an arrangement: 'I would've learned a lot from him. Brears would've taken a lot of pressure off my shoulders, especially from those at Lord's who clearly didn't like me.'

Brearley admits that Botham was strongly recommended by him for the captaincy. On the last tour of Australia, Botham had been co-opted onto the selection committee and the captain had admired the self-assured way he had tackled his duties. 'He was particularly good with Boycott. He gave him good technical advice about transferring his weight onto the front foot but, more interestingly, he handled him very well on a personal level. Boycott could have been prickly – he must have thought his seniority and prestige entitled him to Botham's place on the selection committee or even the vice-captaincy – but Botham handled him with good humour and tact.' In retrospect Brearley admits he was wrong; he had not bargained for Ian's loss of form, nor his over-sensitivity to criticism, both of which drained him. He notes with sadness that Ian's tenure as Somerset captain was also a failure.

Brearley's initial advocacy of Botham was not shared by one good judge, a man who knew Ian better than most. Brian Close was dead against the idea. He admired Ian's vibrant style immensely and was well aware how valuable he was to the team; that was why he wanted him to turn down the job. When Botham captained the MCC against the champion county at Lord's in April 1980, Close spent half-an-hour trying to talk sense into the brilliant young player he had led from the ranks of the erratic to those of heroic stature. Close was an England selector at the time and he kept telling his co-selectors that Ian was not ready for the task at the age of 24 years and six months. 'At that age, he was just an instinctive cricketer, whereas a brilliant one was desperately needed if we were to have any chance against the West Indies over the next year. Nobody in his right mind should've taken on a year like that and I told Ian that Brearley was leaving him a poor side, that he hadn't improved the performances of the others apart from him. The job needed an experienced, thinking bloke who had stopped working out his own game and now had time to look after the others in the side.'

Botham must have realised that there was little that Brian Close did not know about the art of captaincy. A talented all-rounder himself, Close was in his thirties before he was appointed Yorkshire captain and 35 before the call came from England. His sincere, caring advice came not only from the heart, but from first-hand experience. Yet Ian agreed to take the job. He has always justified his decision on simplistic lines – 'You just can't turn down the captaincy of England, can you?' – and such a view must be respected. We have seen how Ian had to fight for recognition at every level of his cricket, right from the age of eight; he had been written off as a village-green slogger many times, and Somerset only picked him for his 1973 debut because they were desperately short of players. The Australians underestimated him in 1977, and so did Mike Brearley on that first England tour. Ian would not be human if he occasionally harboured grudges against those who had undervalued him and the England captaincy was without doubt an irresistible prize to a lad who had had to make his own way through the game's upper echelons, with just his natural talent as his shield. He may have nurtured seditious thoughts about some of those who work at and visit Lord's, but Botham has always been enough of a traditionalist to respect the office of the England captain. He saw the honour as something he deserved and his unquenchable optimism would force Close's misgivings to the back of his mind.

In any case, who could be a logical contender? If the selectors ruled out Brearley, where else could they turn? The name of Roger Knight was bandied about: a fine fellow, likely to turn in an excellent performance at press conferences, but not a good enough player to justify an England place. Keith Fletcher? Shrewd, successful and still a useful batsman – perhaps a worthy stopgap till Botham matured. In the England side, Boycott would be anathema after his performances as stand-in captain in New Zealand two years earlier, while Willis was uncertain of a regular place in the side. The sensible alternatives were thin on the ground and there was much crossing of fingers and toes as the roulette wheel stopped at Botham.

Now here is one to ponder among the great might-have-beens in cricket: how would Ian Botham's captaincy career have turned out if he had refused to bowl against Oxford University on a cold April day in 1980? Botham, cocooned in sweaters like a Michelin man, was reluctant to turn his arm over to any great extent against the novices from the dreaming spires but his captain, Brian Rose, insisted. Even in his pomp, Botham was never a paragon when it came to loosening up before a bowling spell (hence the usual lollipop delivery at the start), and he hurt his back that day. He bowled 25 overs and, on the final day, with the back still sore, contented himself with off-breaks. He was still bothered by his back when the First Test started at Nottingham more than a month later; his bowling clearly suffered and, with it, the balance of the England side. Ian had put on weight after returning from Bombay. Giving up smoking in the spring did not help, nor did the steroids used to combat his asthma. He also kept from the press the fact that he wore a corset in the Trent Bridge Test, which only served to make him look bulkier. Bernard Thomas, the England physiotherapist at the time, says Ian was caught in a Catch-22 situation: 'His increased weight irritated his back problems. The steroids were helping him to exercise but he had to keep taking them to ward off his asthma, so the exercise was not helping him lose weight. His back injury is still with him, it's a kink in the vertebrae. An operation would only put extra strain on the adjoining areas.'

Predictably Ian makes light of such gloomy prognostications, but he admits his back did not feel right until after the West Indies tour in April 1981. In the intervening months his back became an obsession with the media while Botham, typically, refused to use it as an excuse for his below-par performances. Yet with the bat at least he started the 1980 season triumphantly. He hammered Gloucestershire for 228, the highest score of his career – a majestic, imperious innings containing ten sixes, made in just 48 overs. His dominance cowed the bowlers and it was a subdued trio of players that made its way up the motorway that night to Old Trafford, where Gloucestershire was to play a Sunday League game the following day. Not a word was exchanged for the first forty miles between Brian Brain (the driver), David Partridge, Alan Wilkins and the scorer, Bert Avery. After yet another cigarette was wearily stubbed out, Brain broke the silence: 'Bloody hell, there's 350 runs in this car!' He was right. All three bowlers had passed their century, a fact dolefully confirmed by Bert Avery. Botham's butchery was so savage that Sunil Gavaskar, playing his only season of county cricket, hardly got a mention in the press for his beautiful 75 before lunch.

Back problems notwithstanding, Botham was in cheerful spirits as his first England squad assembled for the one-day internationals, the traditional pipe-opener before the Tests. England lost at Headingley but won by three wickets at Lord's, with Botham batting responsibly and thrilling the crowd when he smashed Joel Garner into the Mound Stand for six. It was difficult to read too much into a couple of one-day internationals when trying to assess a new captain's credentials (after all, limited-overs cricket is an exercise in negative tactics when fielding), but Botham seemed to have got most of the basics right, and he had shown his inspirational qualities with the bat at Lord's. One man went back to his county full of praise for the new captain – his team-mate Vic Marks: 'I was very impressed by his all-round performance as captain and player. I had known Ian for years, of course, but I was surprised by his maturity. He was relatively restrained in his judgements, compared with when he was just a member of the team, and he handled me very sympathetically when I bowled. He brought me on early, encouraged me by saying, "Come on, you're the best one-day spinner in England," and he showed more faith in me than I had in myself at that time. When we batted together at Lord's he was incredibly motivated. Usually there's always a jokey side to our batting partnerships, but not this time. He would bash me on the chest between overs, saying. "Come on, do it for England, do it for me, just *do* it!" '

So to the Test series, and another imponderable: if England had held their catches, would Botham have been labelled a failure a year later? At Trent Bridge, on a wicket that seamed about all the game, West Indies squeezed home by two wickets, after Mike Hendrick and Chris Tavare dropped two slip catches and David Gower had spilled one at cover off Andy Roberts, with only thirteen needed. Roberts chanced his arm and his audacity won the match, but it was a very close thing. If Botham had been fully fit to bowl, if Hendrick had not still been hampered by his injured shoulder, if, if, if. . . . That was to be the nearest Ian Botham ever got to a win as captain, in the first of his twelve Tests. As the damp summer proceeded, the gap in class between the two sides grew and Botham's public comments grew more and more repetitious. No, he was not down-hearted, yes the spirit in the side was very good, no he was not worried about his trough of poor form. It was not Botham's fault that he sounded like a familiar gramophone record, it was simply that the media was seemingly unconcerned about anyone else in the side. Botham was news, whatever his state of mind or form.

Some of the 'gentlemen' of the press stunned the Botham family by their insensitivity. It was bad enough to pick up a paper and see 'before' and 'after' pictures of Ian, it was pathetically trivial to see Taunton's lunchtime menu reproduced faithfully in the tabloids, but it was appalling to drag Ian's young son into it. Liam was occasionally stopped by reporters on the way to school and asked what his daddy had for breakfast. Botham's next-door neighbours were quizzed about Ian's appetite the last time he had come for dinner. One reporter spent three days outside the house, scavenging for evidence of potato peelings in the dustbin, then haranguing neighbours and shopkeepers about the Bothams' food bill. Gerry Waller, Ian's father-in-law, remembers it as an appalling time: 'The press cuttings of that period seemed to refer to nothing else but Ian's weight. People used to shout "Fatso" at him from the other side of the street and whenever he was in a restaurant someone always came up to him and said. "You shouldn't be eating that, you know, you'll put on more weight." They'd get half a story from the papers, then think they were entitled to invade his privacy or shout rude things at him.'

Kath began to dread shopping. Whenever she went out, someone would bring up the subject, conjecture that her husband was not doing very well and ask her if he was going on a diet. She was walking round the Taunton ground one day with Ian's mother when a particularly nasty specimen abused her, concluding with the verdict that her husband was a disgrace to the England team. The family received threatening letters and the police were informed. All because a sportsman had suddenly lost the Midas touch. A year earlier, Bernard Thomas had been nagging Ian to lose half a stone to improve his flexibility, but that did not interest the media because Ian was performing wonders on the field. If he had only maintained some semblance of his usual form the press might have relented, but they were determined to wring every last drop from the story.

Down in Yeovil, Ian's parents were not immune. Reporters would ring up, asking to speak to Ian, unaware that he was actually playing for England at Leeds or Old Trafford. As members of Somerset CCC, Les and Marie would sit in their regular seats, without publicising their identities, and they always enjoyed the cricket chat, never taking their son's side if he was being criticised as a cricketer. They have always agreed that Ian deserves to be taken to task for his deeds on the pitch but Les came to resent other forms of criticism: 'That year, 1980, Ian was playing golf in the Bob Hope Classic at Epsom. We were treated regally in a vast suite in a marvellous hotel. On the third day, after he had driven off the tee, I heard one chap say to a steward, "Oh that's Ian Botham – I'm told he was blind drunk in the bar last night." Now I'd been with Ian all the time and it was a complete lie. The bloke shot off when I put him right. On the same day, Ian shanked a shot at the sixteenth when partnering Ken Brown. It was the kind of shot that everyone plays at some stage. I heard a complete stranger say, "What a bloody awful player he is, and what a bloody awful man." How can these people say such things about someone they have never met?'

The Bothams have never bothered to go ex-directory or even change their telephone number, just because they have a famous son. With so many friends it would be too much of a burden to inform everyone of their new number. Besides, Marie has her own distinctive method of dealing with difficult callers – she simply blows a referee's whistle down the phone! One day, as Les was being treated in hospital for a disc problem, Marie had a call telling her that her son was in danger and that her husband would spend the rest of his life on his back once he came out of hospital. Marie gave a shrill blast of her whistle and phoned the police. Another time, Ian spotted a letter with a Bath postmark, addressed in red ink, and told Marie not to open it but to hand it over to the police. Obviously he had suffered at the hands of the writer in red ink, but he never mentioned it again. His parents are philosophical about the dangers of stardom: 'We put such nasty things against the pleasure he's given so many people, and the happy memories come out top.'

On the cricket field in 1980 Botham kept trying to turn the tide. His clarion call to the troops at dinner on the eve of each Test was different from Brearley's more analytical approach, but he was no less sincere. 'Let's stop telling ourselves how good they are,' he would say, 'and get out there and prove they're not world-beaters. You're all good players, we can do it.' Nor did he forget the human touches. At Old Trafford, Bob Willis was badly mauled by Viv Richards after the tabloids had whipped up yet another pathetic 'feud' story between batsman and bowler. That night, as Willis contemplated ruinous figures and the possible end of his Test career, Botham took him out and tried to console him. 'Beefy stood by me when I needed help,' says Willis. 'I could barely bowl a legitimate delivery because of no-ball problems, but he never stopped encouraging me. He was just as loyal to the other players.'

Yet it was not enough. The team badly missed Botham's ability to conjure wickets through either a hostile spell of bowling or the outrageous slices of luck he had hitherto enjoyed. In five Tests that summer (four against the West Indies and the rain-scarred Centenary Test against Australia), he scored just one half-century and took fourteen fairly expensive wickets. His many admirers hoped that it would prove to be the kind of one-off summer that has affected the greatest players at some stage and that the much-trumpeted back injury would be of blessed memory when he took England to the Caribbean early in 1981. The press, meanwhile, had a problem. Having largely plumped for Botham as Brearley's successor, they could hardly admit they were wrong so soon. Those 'Captain Marvel' and 'Captain Fantastic' headlines were itching to be dusted down and set in bold typeface.

Before that could happen, Botham had to face up to headlines announcing 'England Captain on Assault Charge.' For the first nine months of 1981, the charge hung over Botham, another test of his enviable *sangfroid*. Just before Christmas 1980 he had joined his fellow Scunthorpe United players on their stag night out. Botham was training and playing the occasional game with the club to keep fit, and, as one might expect, he soon became a popular figure in the dressing-room. The lads recognised he had talent as a footballer, and, above all, relished the high spirits that he exuded. They loved the way he prepared for one particular game that season. The manager sent him off for a week with the advice to keep himself fit by daily training in readiness for Saturday's match. Botham went up to Scotland for a week's fishing and proved his fitness in distinctive fashion – getting to bed around dawn after telling endless stories in the pub once he had gone through the card of its marvellous selection of malt whiskies. On the Saturday morning, he got to bed at three, left Callander at 8 am, drove 270 miles to Epworth for a couple of hours' sleep, arrived at Scunthorpe's ground at 1.30, to be told he was the substitute. Perhaps the manager knew that Botham's fitness for ninety minutes might be in some doubt! He got on after half-time, but could not prevent a 3-1 defeat. By nine o'clock that evening, he was back in the pub at Callander, telling further tall stories! Such a free spirit was a godsend in the world of professional football, where grown men are told what to eat on the lunchtime of a game and their passports are taken away from them at the start of the season.

Ian was particularly close to the Scunthorpe goalkeeper, Joe Neenan, and it was that friendship which brought him damaging publicity. After receiving a few abusive words outside Tiffany's Night Club in Scunthorpe, Neenan had followed one Steven Isbister down an alley and gripped him warmly by the throat. Botham went to check on his mate and the upshot was that both were charged with assault. Botham elected to go for trial before jury, denying the charge – so that it was not heard until September of the following year. Neenan admitted he had hit Isbister and was fined £100 with a further £100 costs. The press loved the story; they had a new angle on Botham and, within the laws of contempt, they pushed it as hard as they could before Botham left for the West Indies. It was a worrying incident and one could understand that it constituted a genuine news story, rather than ludicrous 'jack-ups' about Botham's girth.

When Botham appeared at Grimsby Crown Court, he was cleared of occasioning actual bodily harm on Isbister. It emerged that Isbister, a 19-year-old naval rating, had two previous convictions, one for attacking a man of fifty, the other for causing criminal damage. Furthermore, two of the witnesses called on by the prosecution had previous convictions, for theft and criminal damage and for causing bodily harm. Botham had cleared his name, but the conflicting evidence at the three-day hearing hardly endeared him to the more reactionary elements in English cicket or society. To those who simply did not care for the chap it was a case of smoke and fire coalescing.

Before that trial, Botham endured the worst six months of his life. The forthcoming hearing at Grimsby Crown Court was a mere pin-prick compared with his feeling that he was on trial every time he stepped out onto a cricket field. His family all say they never knew a time when he was lower, as his tenure of captaincy drew to a close. Nothing seemed to have gone right for him, in stark contrast to his days of joyous invincibility. Would Botham ever see glad, confident morning again? To be fair to him, the problems he faced on that West Indies tour would have tested the resolution of a Jardine, the diplomacy of a Cowdrey and the equanimity of a Brearley, never mind a 25-year-old coming to terms with the job as well as with an alarming loss of form. On the field of play, the series was lost 2/0 to fast bowlers who seemed to improve every year. Off the field, the Robin Jackman Affair led to a hasty departure from Guyana and the inevitable muddying of diplomatic waters through the mixing of sport and politics. Worst of all, Ken Barrington died of a heart attack in his hotel room during the Barbados Test. England's assistant manager was much loved, not least of all by the young captain. He was probably the biggest influence of all on Ian's cricket because he never lectured him, never harked back to the old days. Barrington admitted it was a good deal harder to play in the 1980s than when he was England's rock in the middle of the order. Ian genuinely respected Barrington's enduring batting skills, of which he had given a tantalising glimpse two winters earlier, on a dampish net in Australia where the ball seamed about all over the place. Kenny was finally persuaded to put the pads on and, ten years after he had played his final first-class game, he showed his ability. It took Ian a long time to get over Kenny's death and when his widow asked him to read the lesson at the memorial service, he deemed it an honour.

It is tempting to speculate on what course Ian's career might have taken had Kenny Barrington lived. Some believe he would have kept him on the straight and narrow of regular net practice and temperate socialising. Bob Willis, close friend of both men, thinks that, though Botham and Barrington enjoyed a matey relationship, with no commands involved, Barrington would have made little difference to Botham's approach to the game. It must also be borne in mind that Barrington's position as assistant manager (in effect, cricket manager), was not wholly favoured in influential circles at the time. A year earlier, the Test and County Cricket Board had had to revise its original decision to tour Australia without an assistant manager, and Barrington was hurriedly drafted in. A cricket manager on tour has only become the vogue in recent years, as England kept losing series abroad.

Despite losing that series in the West Indies, the tour manager, A. C. Smith, felt Botham had acquitted himself well. 'The tour might've fallen apart but it didn't and the captain deserves some credit for keeping the blokes going. We were often confined in our hotels, with armed guards everywhere, but the party never lost its spirit.' The professionalism of men like Peter Willey, Geoffrey Boycott, John Emburey and Graham Gooch was also admirable, as the side batted with courage and tenacity to save the last two Tests. Now and then, though, Botham pressed the self-destruct button. On the rest day of the First Test in Trinidad, he announced to the scribes that the wicket was so good that if England lost, 'heads will roll'. Alan Smith, sitting alongside his young captain, winced inwardly, knowing that Botham had given a hostage to fortune and an inevitable follow-up story if they did lose: 'I thought, "Oh my God, you don't really mean that", but I could hardly lean over and get him to retract it. It showed his inexperience with the media at captain's press conferences.' Sure enough, England lost by an innings and the chief culprit was the captain. On the final day, England faced the not impossible task of batting out for a draw. There was rain about and every prospect of a curtailed day's play. Obviously Botham's was a prized wicket and the West Indies picked it up because he could not resist trying to hit his great friend, Viv Richards, out of the ground. Richards enjoyed the encounter: 'When Clive Lloyd brought me on, I just knew that Beefy would eventually have a go at me. I kept running up, tossing up the ball and he kept blocking me, smiling ruefully, knowing full well what I expected of him. Finally he could take no more – I pushed it a little wider, tossed it up a touch more and he holed out at deep extra cover to Michael Holding. I still pull his leg about it!'

Off the field, Ian still veered between the Scylla of good-natured, high spirits and the Charybdis of tactlessness. John Woodcock, *The Times* cricket correspondent and a Botham fan, was appalled at the sight of the captain and Graham Stevenson wearing two extravagant party hats at a function organised by the Jamaican High Commissioner. One night in Barbados, Ian called an impromptu team meeting in a bar and moved the resolution that Graham Gooch should be barred from going on any more early-morning runs. Gooch pointed out that he kept bumping into the captain coming home from a night's carousing as the Essex opener returned from his pre-breakfast run. At Bermuda Airport, en route for home, Botham grabbed Henry Blofeld by the throat after reading some unfavourable comments in a cutting sent to him, that he had stuffed into his England blazer some weeks earlier. Alan Smith agrees that that incident perturbed him and he made a point of getting both parties together as soon as he heard of it: 'I kept telling Ian not to read the papers and to stop being so paranoid about them, but he's fundamentally insecure and very sensitive about criticism.'

Viv Richards is not sure that the whole team was behind his soul-mate on that tour: 'I think there were a few people happy to see Ian go down. I used to watch them at functions attended by both teams and a lot of the players stood on the sidelines, not mixing with us or anybody. I used to tell Ian to watch out for the back-stabbers, but he just shrugged it off.' Clive Lloyd, Ian's opposite number, sympathises: 'He was the obvious choice for the job and he helped create a good atmosphere between the two sides, but in the end he was relying on pop guns against our heavy artillery. There was nothing he could do against the quality of our fast bowling.' Ian smiled when he read a letter from Mike Brearley: recognising the herculean task he faced, Brearley suggested that Ian should find a country other than the West Indies to face. Instead they had been the opposition in nine out of his first ten Tests as captain. Napoleon was not alone in wishing his generals to be lucky.

Yet underneath the bravado, the genuine sportsmanship in defeat, the occasional social gaffes, Botham was hurting. He missed Ken Barrington's warm companionship, he would have understood the various pressures. Had not Kenny worried himself into a heart attack and early retirement in 1968? When the party arrived in Antigua, Botham was cheered by the presence of his bosom pal from the Somerset dressing-room, Trevor Gard and his wife, Mandy. Gard recalls how low Ian seemed: 'I've never seen him like that, he was withdrawn and negative. It looked as if it was all getting on top of him, but he cheered up in our company for a few days at least.'

One member of the England party knows how low Botham felt at the end of the tour. Robin Jackman must be one of the few cricketers ever to see Ian Botham in tears. It happened on the last night of the tour in Jamaica, as everyone busied himself with packing. Jackman says: 'The phone rang in my room and it was Ian asking me along for a drink. He opened a bottle of whisky, and we just talked about the tour and general things. He was emotionally drained and I think he saw the writing on the wall about the England captaincy. I got the impression he wanted to talk to someone older than himself who was still a player. I wasn't sure what advice I could give him, but it was an emotional half-hour. Earlier in the tour he had genuinely felt sorry for me, with all that Guyana business, and this time it was my turn to offer a comforting shoulder.'

Botham is still hurt by the dismissive criticism of his England captaincy: 'My record against a terrific West Indian side isn't that bad, you know. Three defeats out of nine Tests and a shared one-day series is better than the subsequent hammerings we took. We should've won the Trent Bridge Test and, if the weather hadn't mucked us up, we might have sneaked the one at Old Trafford. I needed some luck at vital times and I just didn't get it.'

When the party returned to England for the Ashes contest, Botham felt even more on trial. He surprised his Somerset team-mates by his negative attitude to Michael Holding early in May when that great fast bowler was gliding in menacingly on an Old Trafford wicket freshened by rain: Botham announced he did not expect to last more than a few overs. It was uncharacteristic of Botham to admit he had had enough of West Indian fast bowling but it was also indicative of the way he had been worn down by it in the Caribbean.

A few weeks later, he was given the England captaincy for the First Test only. It was lost, by four wickets, when the result could easily have gone the other way. The crucial moment of the match came when Allan Border was dropped behind the wicket by Paul Downton off Mike Hendrick's bowling: it was a routine nick at regulation height, but poor Downton took his eye off the ball. Border went on to make the highest score of a low-scoring match on a 'result' wicket and that was that. Ian now clearly lacked confidence in his bowling, waiting until the fifty-fifth over before he put himself on when he should have revelled in the conditions. The relentless drip of criticism had dented even his massive self-confidence. At home he was remote, as Jan Waller, his mother-in-law recalls: 'He got very morose. Kathryn and I just couldn't get through to him.'

The sad dénouement to Ian Botham's career as England captain occurred at Lord's. Before it began he had decided to pack the job in at the end of the game, because he saw no point in being kept on, match by match. There was no continuity in the selections, no coherent strategy. Bob Taylor noticed this when he returned to the England team after an interval of fifteen months: 'There was none of the usual zip about Ian, he was listless. I stood beside him at slip and it was a sharp contrast to the days when he and Brearley used to be beside me, swapping all sorts of ideas. As captain, Ian didn't seem to be able to get the other lads going in that Lord's Test; we all just went through the motions in the warm-ups and the nets. It was a sad return for me.'

Ian Botham's 'pair' in that Test just about summed up his state of mind. Uncharacteristically, he had made up his mind to sweep Ray Bright's first ball, only to be bowled behind his legs. Ian has never been one for the premeditated shot unless in desperate circumstances, but he clearly decided that the exigencies of the game, with a declaration needed, demanded an immediate, positive response. As Ian walked back to the Lord's pavilion, the deafening silence which greeted him would have struck a chord in the breast of a tenth-rate comedian at the Glasgow Empire. Possibly embarrassment had something to do with the crowd's silence as they averted their eyes, like maiden aunts spotting a piano leg in Victorian times. Certainly some well-heeled troglodytes in that pavilion snapped shut their ironed copes of *The Times* and marched to the bar a-quiver with righteous satisfaction. That bounder Botham had got his comeuppance, he must be drummed out of the side now. Hands that contemplated a clap moved upwards and straightened out knots in egg-and-bacon ties as the England captain stalked from the sunshine. You could have heard a pinstripe drop.

Ian's parents watched that moment on television at home in Yeovil. Les, the most equable of men, says he will never forgive those MCC members for their rudeness. Gerry Waller puts it more forthrightly: 'All those pompous jack-asses in that pavilion, there by privilege rather than merit. What had they ever done for cricket? If Ian never played another game, he deserved at least a round of applause for what he had done for English cricket.' Kath did not see Ian's second nought of the match – she was sitting behind 'Q' stand talking to Reg Hayter and his wife,

Lucy. In any case she could no longer bear to watch the ordeal and when she heard the news of Ian's resignation she was relieved.

Since that day, Ian Botham has never raised his bat to the Lord's pavilion during the ritual obeisances for landmarks in an innings.

> Nor will I ever do so – I shan't forget that silence as long as I live. They didn't want me, simple as that, and I'd had enough. I was fed up with staggering from one Test to another, feeling on trial all the time, listening to the saga about my weight. How many games have I missed in fifteen years, for God's sake? I can't be that unfit. I refused to make excuses about my back bothering me for a year, so they droned on about my weight instead. I just wanted some peace of mind if I wasn't going to get support. It was so ironic because I was scoring lots of runs for Somerset that year, yet couldn't get them in the early Tests because of freakish dismissals. The players know that such things come in patches and that if you're good enough, you'll come through, but the press wouldn't see it that way. They had their story and they wanted blood.

By the time Ian had resigned, his mentor Brian Close was on his way back to Yorkshire. He had been down in London since the previous Wednesday and had kept on at his fellow-selectors to make a decision about the captaincy. Close had wanted Ian to be relieved of the job at the start of the series, but after being out-voted on that he agreed to offer it to him on a match by match basis. On that final day at Lord's John Edrich wanted Botham out, Charlie Elliott was undecided and the chairman Alec Bedser was also wavering. With the press darting back and forth, looking for the story, Close ran out of patience, never an uncommon event. He told Bedser that his vote was for another match for Botham but that the chairman had the casting vote and he would abide by that. When Botham found out that he was not going to have the job for the whole of the series, he resigned. He could have done without Bedser's public comment, 'Well we were going to sack him anyway,' but by that time Ian was well shot of it. He just wanted to get out of Lord's. He rang up his Somerset team-mate, Jeremy Lloyds, and asked him to keep their local pub in Taunton open till he got there.' I don't want to be on my own tonight,' he told Lloyds, and when Botham walked into the Four Alls he was among friends who proffered some consoling liquid. After an hour or so, Viv Richards was handed a bottle of gin and took him back to his flat to talk it all out.

Was Botham sold short over the England captaincy? His face takes on a Mount Rushmore appearance when the subject is aired, but he genuinely believes he was getting the hang of the job. Yet his stubborn refusal to accept detailed criticism is roughly reminiscent of the obscurantism of the pre-Reformation Papacy and it is necessary to turn to other qualified observers for a detached view. Richie Benaud, a man who knows a thing or two about captaincy, feels Botham was hard done by, that he might have settled down into the job, given time. Allan Border, his great friend on the Australian side, felt that Ian was playing too much like the expected image of an England captain, rather than like a great, swashbuckling cricketer who happens to be in charge. Perhaps Ian needed someone like Brearley to run up to him and say, 'Come on, Both, you're the best player.' Maybe there was nobody left who could inspire that sense of challenge or responsibility in him that Brearley had managed to do. Perhaps Ian's tactics on the field were too much in the mould of Marshal Foch – 'My flanks are turned, and my centre is surrounded. I shall attack.' This had proved particularly counter-productive in the Caribbean, where four slips and no mid-off or mid-on is risking a lot against openers like Greenidge and Haynes. At least Botham kept trying to win, even though he was unable to master the off-field responsibilities of captaincy, as Brian Close had feared.

There was also the problem of marrying up Ian's relaxed attitude to life with the perceived responsibilities of the England captain. Graham Gooch sums up the problem: 'My biggest criticism of Beefy was that he couldn't expect the younger players to knuckle down and then go out drinking till all hours. He didn't change at all, that was his downfall.' Mike Hendrick agrees: 'A lot of the lads were his mates. They didn't really get stuck in behind him about things like nets because they knew him as a terrific bloke and a great player who wasn't that hot on self-discipline. He was still a boy at heart, he lacked judgement in certain situations.' Whatever his defects, he had at least convinced many doubters that he had a keen enough cricket brain for the job, a fact acknowledged by everyone I interviewed. The feeling persists that he came out of it all rather better than some sections of the media who had made his private life a misery over the past year. This did not apply just to the fiction pedlars in the tabloids. The item on BBC TV's 'Newsnight' programme in the summer of 1981 ('The Trial of Ian Botham' with 'fors' and 'againsts') must rank as one of the tackiest, insubstantial offerings since Tiny Tim invited us to tip-toe through the tulips.

The whole saga took a lot out of Botham. He had become slit-eyed with suspicion whenever he met anyone he did not know and trust.

That made his public appearance at a testimonial dinner around that time even more admirable. Months earlier Ian had promised the great Welsh rugby player Phil Bennett that he would speak at a dinner for him in Swansea. It fell between the Trent Bridge defeat and his resignation at Lord's, at a time when he was being accorded media interest that was totally out of proportion for a sportsman. Vic Marks remembers how Ian surmounted the hurdle: 'A few of us went along to support him in this difficult time and I must say he stole the show. Gareth Edwards and Mike England also spoke but Ian outshone them. He was brilliant, taking the mickey out of himself about his weight, his poor form and his captaincy. I didn't think Ian had it in him at that time, because he was so down and dispirited but from somewhere within himself he dragged out a terrific performance. Many others in his position wouldn't have honoured that commitment but he showed immense strength of character and humanity.'

When Botham returned to the Somerset dressing-room the day after his resignation, he found a warm, welcoming cloak to wrap himself in, as he settled back into that masonic sanctum. He said cheerfully: 'Right lads, I'll be with you for the rest of the season now, so watch out!' Not for the first time, Botham's crystal ball was murky.

5

Phoenix from the ashes

●

One month of cricket half-way through Ian Botham's twenty-sixth year
served to establish him among the game's immortals. Any international
cricketer would have been proud of just one of the three performances
he put in between 20 July and 15 August 1981 but to accomplish them
in a row was ridiculous. The remarkable feats he engineered at Leeds
and at Edgbaston were worthy of Pearl White at her best in those silent
two-reelers of the 1920s. A British nation already *en fête* for the marriage
of the heir to the throne was captivated by the deeds of the England
side. Trading at the Stock Exchange was once temporarily halted,
factory productivity slumped at crucial phases of the three games and
lager sales around Earl's Court took a dent. Sports editors hitherto
obsessed with Ian Botham's allegedly porcine qualities now had to
concentrate on his inspirational ability on the field of play, while the
England captain Mike Brearley seemed worthy of membership of the
Magic Circle.

As ever in sport, luck played a vital part in the equation. Turning
points jostled with each other over the next month like shoppers at the
sales, but perhaps the most significant one was the rationale behind
Mike Brearley's reinstatement. In his resignation interviews, Botham
had plumped for the recall of Brearley as a stopgap, yet the issue was
far from cut and dried. The selectors were unhappy about turning to
the man who would no longer tour for England, and there was an
uneasy feeling that continuity was as important as stopping the rot.
Alternative candidates were not plentiful, apart from one man, Keith
Fletcher. Over the past decade, Fletcher had shown himself to be a very

shrewd, capable captain, leading Essex from genial obscurity to regular success, while at the same time managing to retain the side's humorous, relaxed attitude to the game and life in general. His batting record in Tests was immeasureably superior to that of Brearley, and at 37 he was the right, mature age. Fletcher could take over the side for the next four Tests, shape it in his fashion, then lead England that winter in India. He would certainly make more runs than Brearley, he would not be that far behind in tactical sagacity, and his popularity with players from all sides was a byword.

Yet there was one major fly in the ointment. The next Test was due to be staged at Leeds, a city that ranks in Keith Fletcher's scale of affections alongside W. C. Fields's opinion of Philadelphia. Since 1968 Fletcher had never been popular with the Headingley crowd, after being preferred for the Australian Test to Yorkshire's own Phil Sharpe. Fletcher had not only failed to score on his Test début but had put down a couple of slip catches that Sharpe, the greatest English slipper of his generation, would probably have swallowed. Hell hath no fury like a Yorkshire crowd frustrated and, ever since, Fletcher had been brusquely treated by cricket-watchers at Headingley. Brian Close, one of England's four selectors in 1981, remains convinced that Fletcher would have been chosen ahead of Brearley if the Test was due to be staged anywhere else.

So it came to pass that Brearley was reinstated. Thoughtfully he rang Ian before the selection committee met to pick the team for Leeds. He confirmed that Ian wanted to play, a desire repeated on the day before the Test started. The captain joked that the wheel of fortune would probably veer so greatly that Botham would get a century and twelve wickets in the match. It was a shrewd way of making Botham realise he was still vital to the team as the main all-rounder, an acknow-ledgement that he had been through a hard time and that a few runs and wickets would make all the difference. Yet after the first day, it looked as if luck would remain stubbornly on the side of Australia. On a cloudy day, ideal for bowling at Headingley, Australia finished on 210 for 3. It was another frustrating day for Botham. He had Trevor Chappell missed at third slip by David Gower, then Botham himself dropped an easy one off Bob Willis and, in the next over, put down a hard chance offered by John Dyson. On top of that Brearley took him off after just three overs of his second spell, telling him he did not want half-volleys bowled at medium pace. The next day, Brearley cleverly gave the new ball to Chris Old and Graham Dilley so that when Botham eventually came on he bowled with much of his old fire in conditions that favoured swing bowling. Figures of 6 for 95 were his best since the Jubilee Test in Bombay.

By Saturday evening, England supporters had just a few scraps of comfort. Botham's return to form (six wickets and 50 off 54 balls) was the main consolation. But England had been forced to follow-on and lost Graham Gooch before the close. The obsequies would be observed around mid-afternoon on Monday and Australia would go two-up in the series. Several England players gathered at Botham's house for a Saturday evening barbecue in philosophical mood, aware that Australia had bowled better, and made plans for a rare day off on the Tuesday.

It was in that relaxed, resigned mood that Botham walked to the wicket on Monday with England 105 for 5. Soon it was 135 for 7, still 92 short of making Australia bat again. Yet it was Graham Dilley who played the more attacking shots early in their stand. Botham had made 39 in 87 minutes to tea. Afterwards, he decided to join in the fun. After smashing one particularly outrageous boundary he wandered up to Dilley and uttered the famous words: 'You don't want to hang around here for the next two days, do you, Dill? Let's give it some humpty!' It was hardly the most technical advice ever given on a cricket field but it proved mightily significant. Botham, using Graham Gooch's bat, played textbook drives interspersed with authentic slogs, but carried on enjoying himself, as Dilley recalls: 'It never occurred to me to block it out, I'd have probably gone first ball if I had, and all I looked to do was whack it in the middle of the bat. It was just a bit of fun, neither of us thought we had any chance of getting out of the mire.'

By the time Dilley played on to Terry Alderman for 56, the stand was worth 117 in 80 exhilarating minutes. Since tea they had put on 76 in 44 minutes. Yet England were still, in effect, 25 for 8. That made the contribution of the next batsman doubly vital. Chris Old was a talented striker of the ball but he preferred the spinners, or enough room to swing his arms at the ball. Pace bowlers of the class of Lillee, Alderman and Lawson would be expected to follow Old's movements towards the square leg umpire or beat him for pace. Yet the three bowlers were tiring. Lawson's back was beginning to trouble him (it was to rule him out of the rest of the tour), and they were bowling the wrong line now at Botham. The England dressing-room had sensed that the initiative was swinging towards the home side; if only Old could stay with Botham, see him to his hundred then garner precious runs to the close. Mindful of the reception he would get if dismissed quickly, Old stiffened the sinews and played with great responsibility and no little flair. He remembers that hour in graphic detail:

> Beefy knew the situation had changed during his partnership with Dill. He said to me, 'We've got 'em going, let's get a good lead' and he went berserk as I kept up my end. They were demoralised, they all started bitching at each other – Marsh, Lillee and Chappell were ignoring Kim Hughes eventually – and the wheels gradually came off. The field started to spread in all directions, they were standing in places where they thought the ball would be edged, rather than hit, and Beefy just annihilated them. He hit everywhere, not just in one particular region. I was surprised Hughes didn't bowl Ray Bright until late on; Beefy would have tried to hit a spinner into Bradford in that mood and he might've got a top edge. I could feel the crowd willing us on, and when I got out, I was furious with myself. I thought I'd lost the game.'

Old did not need to chastise himself. He had played heroically to add 67 invaluable runs. As he clumped up the pavilion stairs, he went straight to the balcony to watch a highly significant last twenty minutes. In that time, Botham was truly magnificent – not only did he ensure that Willis, the last man, faced just five balls, but he helped plunder another 31 runs. At the close, England led by 124 with Botham 145 not out. Looking at it objectively, the odds still favoured Australia, but that would take no account of their state of mind, the frustration of having to come back to battle in a game that they ought to have won that day. Bob Taylor, popping into their dressing-room to get some benefit bats signed, was told to go forth and multiply in no uncertain terms. He was delighted to oblige, not least because he felt the Australians were sliding into a fear of defeat. He reported back to his team-mates that it looked like the end of the world in the opposition dressing-room. In their negative state of mind, something around 150 would be a tall order on a pitch of uneven bounce.

It was a remarkable, gung-ho effort from Botham. When he first came in, after a couple of speculative slogs to the boundary, Barry Meyer, one of the umpires, said to him: 'Both, what the hell's going on? Aren't you going to play yourself in?' Botham laughed and replied: 'I just have done, Bas.' Such *chutzpah* deserved to change the course of the series, and it did. That evening, as Botham tucked into fish and chips with his family, no one came up to him to suggest that he should watch his calories!

If Ian Botham established the platform for a victory surge it was Bob Willis who hammered home the advantage. After Botham thumped one more boundary on the final morning before Willis was out, Australia needed just 130 to win. Willis knew that his Test career was over unless he bowled like a man possessed. At this stage, his confidence was low. He had been drafted back into the squad for Leeds after originally being left out because of illness. Although he maintains that he had bowled well in the first innings, he had not taken a wicket and was plagued by no-ball trouble. To a cricketer of Willis's keen perceptions, the options were minimal: 'I simply ran in and bowled as fast as I could without worrying about no-balls. If I failed I'd never be playing for England again. What greater incentive could there be?'

After Botham made the initial breakthrough (confirming the luck was running his way again, as Graeme Wood got himself out to a wide half-volley), Willis took charge. He took 8 for 34 and the moment when he won the match by plucking out Ray Bright's middle stump has been replayed on countless video recorders around the world. In the space of 24 hours, two cricketers had recovered their golden touch and Australia had been swept aside. The press hailed a glorious recovery, even after Willis delivered a bitter attack on newspaper standards during a television interview on the player's balcony.

Within a fortnight, Botham had done it again and the circumstances were even more remarkable this time. On the fourth day of the Edgbaston Test, Australia, needing 151 to win on a flat wicket, were 87 for 3. Graham Yallop and Allan Border were well set after some early flutters and England's only hope seemed to be John Emburey, who was bowling his off-breaks teasingly and tightly. Botham managed to catch Yallop at silly mid-off off Emburey but as the score passed 100 with only four wickets down, an Australian victory seemed inevitable. The ball was not swinging, Willis was spent after a magnificent spell in the morning, the pitch was slow and blameless and the only hope for England was the off-spin of Emburey and Peter Willey. At 105 for 4, with 46 needed, umpire 'Dickie' Bird was party to an interesting conversation.

Brearley: 'What do you think, Dickie?'
Bird: 'I think you're struggling, Skip.'
Brearley: 'I think you're right.'
Bird: 'Best thing to do is put the spinners on and that'll get us off early.'
Botham: 'Yeh, he's right, Brears, put both spinners on.'

Two balls later, Emburey got Border with one that bounced sharply. Five down, 46 needed. But now Brearley decided to abort his plan to bring on Willey and gambled on Botham's sense of responsibility. 'Keep it tight for Embers,' he told him. In the next 28 balls Botham was hit for just one run – and he also took the last five wickets. To be frank, it was not the most impressive spell Botham ever bowled – but he overwhelmed the batsmen with his presence. Botham responded to the bull-ring atmosphere that day like a true public performer. The chest seemed to swell with each wicket, the bull-like charges down the pitch became more dramatic and he would not be denied. It was one of those occasions when the bowler, rather than the deliveries, triumphs. Any other bowler would have been played on his merits, but the Australians were like lemmings against him. Marsh hit across the line to be bowled, Kent did the same, and Lillee chased a near-wide to be caught behind. Bright was done for pace, to be lbw first ball, while a straight delivery was enough for Alderman, whose defence was never in the Maginot Line class. The last five wickets had fallen for just seven runs and England had done it again. At the fall of the final wicket, Botham grabbed a stump, and ran exultantly from the pitch, waving it high like Excalibur. The noise from the crowd was incredible; they had supported England vociferously all day, roaring on Willis through his unlucky spell, then galvanising Botham. It was all most un-English. The overwhelming brute force of Botham's character had disorientated the Australians and made them shrivel in the remarkable atmosphere. Among contemporaries, only Dennis Lillee in his pomp could have matched Botham's psychological hex over an opposition that day.

Two of that Australian team still shudder at the memory of Edgbaston, 1981. Rodney Marsh, whose rash stroke precipitated the slide, says: 'I could eventually accept the Leeds result – the glorious uncertainties of the game and all that stuff – but not Edgbaston. That destroyed us as a team for the rest of the summer.' Allan Border feels that the state of mind of the Australian side was crucial: 'We had got into a negative state on the last day of the Leeds Test and we played that way from there on in. The English guys just thought they could now win everything, whatever the state of the game. I've never felt worse about a result in my life. The only consolation for me was that no one else but Botham could've done it.' In the immediate aftermath of that game, the face of Kim Hughes, Australia's captain, was a study in shell-shocked consternation. He looked like one of those vapid junior Government Ministers Margaret Thatcher likes to savage with a curt couple of sentences and a glint of her gamma-ray eyes. Poor Hughes was bewildered at the sudden change of events. His standard of captaincy never improved after Edgbaston and it knocked the stuffing out of his team. In subsequent Ashes series, Botham has always seemed to the Australians to be a brooding, influential figure, even when he is simply standing at slip. To the Australian cricketers, the words, 'Botham 1981' have the same effect as 'Calais' must have had on Mary Tudor.

Exactly a fortnight later, the praise now heaped on Botham reached the proportions of mountain lava. His wonderful century in the Old Trafford Test led to *The Times* devoting a front-page article to the innings, with the headline 'Was Botham's Innings the Greatest Ever?' The sub-editor cannot possibly have been a cricket expert, because the accompanying text by the esteemed John Woodcock, the paper's cricket correspondent, outlined the opinion that it was probably the greatest innings *of its type*, something rather different. Once again, England's uncomfortable position in the match brought out the greatness in Botham. He came in, on a 'pair', with England 205 ahead, five wickets in hand, but on a pitch that looked full of runs. If he could be swept aside quickly, the Australians had a genuine chance of squaring the series. Botham seemed to be aware of that because he started circumspectly. Off his first 30 balls he made just three singles, a rate of progress to satisfy even those Roundheads, Brearley and Willis. When he had scored 28, the new ball was taken: he needed just another 33 balls to reach his hundred. He hit Lillee for three sixes in two overs and a couple of them epitomised both the appeal and the enigma of Botham. Two bouncers came at him, straight and at head-height, ideal deliveries of their type – Botham ducked at the last moment and swatted them over the two long-legs by about thirty yards. It was wonderful, heady stuff, but how many would have pilloried him if he had holed out on the boundary? Those who rail against Botham for irresponsibility cannot then laud him to the skies for sensational batting displays like this one.

He hardly played a false shot that day at Old Trafford. He gave two steepling, horrid chances to third man and mid-off and he reached his hundred with a top-edged sweep off Bright that cleared the fielder and went for six. Apart from that, it was a frothy cocktail of authentic, crashing drives off front and back foot. Botham was particularly pleased with the treatment handed out to Lillee, a bowler he has always revered, but in truth no one was safe from an awesome onslaught. Chris Tavare, who shared in a stand of 149 with Botham, describes it as the greatest experience of his career: 'It became almost dream-like, such was the perfection of Ian's batting. I couldn't believe what was going on and in that highly-charged, euphoric atmosphere I felt rather emotional, standing there at the other end. It was a privilege to be so near to that display. I didn't even have to worry about manipulating the strike – Ian managed that himself. I was so pleased for the crowd, because I had bored them to death in the morning!'

England won that game despite brave hundreds from Border and Yallop. It had been another tremendous all-round performance by Botham – a glittering hundred, five wickets, and four catches, two of them in the grand, prehensile manner. At the Oval, in the final Test of this historic series, he failed twice with the bat, but took 10 wickets and again showed his lion-hearted appetite for the fray. He bowled 89 overs in the match, far more than any other bowler, yet after the first day he could only operate at medium pace. He had trapped a nerve in his back and could barely get his socks on that first evening, yet he took three wickets on the second morning. The injury was kept from the press, the official line being that he had cut down his pace to allow the ball to swing more. Then Mike Hendrick pulled a rib muscle and Bob Willis strained a muscle in the stomach area, so Botham just had to keep bowling in the second innings. When the Test ended, Botham drove to Edgbaston for a county game and slept for most of the next two days in the dressing-room; I recall his bleary eyes after I had woken him up for a television interview! He had given almost everything to the England cause that summer. It had been just seven weeks since obscurity with Somerset beckoned after that painful day at Lord's.

Botham was the hero of the land, cogent proof of the value of sport in a society dogged at that time by the spectre of unemployment and rising tension in the inner cities. Just as Denis Compton delighted so many in the immediate years of post-war austerity, so it was with Botham in 1981. No other English cricketer has brought so much unalloyed joy to so many people, many of whom had the vaguest knowledge of cricket. It seems a shame that Compton and Botham have little else in common, with the generation gap and the tabloids' cash register combining to place them in opposing corners.

In retrospect it could so easily have gone wrong for Ian Botham at regular intervals. If Kim Hughes had captained Australia with just a modicum of finesse on that Monday at Leeds; if his bowlers had concentrated on line and length; if he had trusted the spin of Ray Bright earlier than at 309 for 8; if the Australian batsmen had treated Botham's bowling on its merits at Edgbaston; if one of those chancey hook shots had not soared into the Old Trafford crowd off Lillee's bowling. Yet Botham had been unlucky before the gods relented in his favour – remember the dropped catches at Trent Bridge?

The great imponderable is the influence of Mike Brearley and the lack of inhibition in Botham from Leeds onwards. To this day Botham attests that the captaincy was not relevant, that his luck simply changed. Yet he did play more in character after Lord's, he did attack the crease more in his bowling. On the second day at Leeds, Brearley told him to run in more positively; he goaded him, calling Botham 'The Sidestep Queen', a reference to the fact that his momentum was being reduced by stepping in towards the stumps at the last moment. He needed to run straighter and with more bounce. At Old Trafford on the last day, Botham was getting tired and tetchy and he bowled the first few balls of one over off his short run. Brearley called to him from slip, 'Run in and bowl, don't just put it there!' Botham pointed out with feeling that it was his thirtieth over of the innings and that it must be hard to stand at slip all day when you are Brearley's age – but the next ball was much quicker. After lunch on the fourth day at Edgbaston – with Australia 68 for 3, just 83 short of victory – Botham was not wearing his bowling spikes as the team prepared to take the field again. For a couple of minutes, the difference of opinion went back and forth between captain and all-rounder, with Botham insisting his rubbers were satisfactory. Brearley stuck to his guns, and made Botham change into bowling boots. They were to prove rather important within an hour. Brearley usually prevailed in the battle of wills: at Adelaide in 1979, he told Botham that he ought to be wearing spikes when batting, but Botham mulishly stood his ground. Yet he wore them after lunch without mentioning his change of heart to Brearley.

It would be wrong to read too much of the guru syndrome into their relationship, but Brearley seemed to be able to get the best out of his star player. At Perth in 1978, Botham was at his most infuriating, testing out a theory that Peter Toohey did not like the short-pitched delivery. He went for fourteen in one over. He was also annoyed at being told he could only bowl one short-pitched delivery per eight-ball over at Geoff Dymock, a tail-ender. The result was impetuosity triumphing over common cricketing sense. With the new ball due, Bob Willis shouted at Brearley, 'For God's sake, don't give it to Botham, he could go for twenty next over!' Brearley, inwardly annoyed at Botham, maintained his cool façade and opted for Hendrick, who bowled Dymock in his first over after replacing Botham. It was that sort of capability that was so important. Some of it must have stemmed from the age difference, a point acknowledged by David Gower: 'To captains like myself, Bob Willis and Mike Gatting, who have grown up with Beefy, it was sometimes a problem that we were of similar age. It was different with Brears, he was so much older and therefore found it easier to assert authority.' He usually seemed in control: a part of the side, yet apart from it when difficult decisions had to be made. In Botham's early days, when he was sweeping aside the opposition, it was simply a case of opening the cage at various times and letting the carnivorous Botham gorge himself on comparatively easy pickings. On the occasions when Botham did not brush the batsmen aside, Brearley could motivate him shrewdly. From his position at slip, he would make two-handed gestures akin to stirring a pot while Botham walked back. Willis at mid-off would take this as the cue to wind up Botham ('You're not going to let him hook you, are you? Call that quick? You're just slow-medium'). During the next over, Hendrick or Taylor among the close fielders would also attempt slyly to emasculate Botham to his face. Stung with pride, snorting with fury, he would invariably snatch the ball with fervour within a few minutes.

At Sydney in 1980, Botham slogged one up in the air to be caught off Greg Chappell for nought – this after Derek Underwood had laboured valiantly as nightwatchman for around three hours. Botham had thrown away the advantage won by Underwood's obduracy. Brearley was not pleased. He took a piece of paper, drew nine fielders around the boundary and handed it to Botham with the words, 'I think that's the kind of field I'd always have for you.' Botham was stung by the public rebuke. He received a more private dressing-down from Brearley in Tasmania on the 1978/9 tour. He was rooming with Mike Hendrick and they were taken aback when Brearley knocked on the door, and politely asked if they were enjoying themselves on the tour. On being assured that they were very happy, Brearley told them: 'Will you please stop saying "Only a couple of Tests to go before we can go home"? I know you don't mean it, but there are certain players in the party who aren't having as good as time as you two, and they will get even more homesick if they hear any more of that.' Hendrick accepts that was good man-management, 'and Both took it in the right way too. It would have been easy for someone of Beefy's background to see Brears as a Southern wimp, but he had a lot of respect for him.'

In Botham's opinion, Brearley's captaincy was in a class of its own. 'He was tactically superb, honest and a fine man – but his biggest asset was the way he seemed to understand every player and what motivated them. It was brilliant psychology when he asked me if I wanted to play at Leeds. "Course I bloody want to play", I said. Brears knew that I'd do everything to get back on top. He was a great influence on my career. You could talk things over with him. He got me wrong in Pakistan on my first England tour and I told him so – but he accepted it. It was a sign of his strength of character that he encouraged us to air our views, even if he eventually disagreed.'

Botham liked the way that Brearley would jokingly acknowledge his boisterous social life. Sometimes in the dressing-room he would inquire with a faint smile. 'Was it three or four in the morning?', for Botham to reply with bravado: 'Five o'clock, actually, Brears.' That would not be the case but the captain knew that, like fishermen, Botham liked to tell tall stories of alcoholic consumption. Brearley operated on a very long leash. His *laissez faire* attitude stemmed from the belief that men playing for their country know how to handle the various distractions. When Paul Allott played his first game for England in 1981 he was amazed at the air of relaxation in the England dressing-room: 'Beefy threw Boycott into the bath not long before he was due to go out to bat, with all his gear on. Everybody laughed. When we went to Mottram Hall the night before the Test started, we were upstairs for just a few minutes, then out to the pub down the road for vodka and tomato juices. One night we went to this wine bar in Alderley Edge, and Beefy polished off the best part of two bottles of wine while the rest of us drank vodkas or glasses of white wine. I learned it was the regular thing to do during an Old Trafford Test. I couldn't believe how cavalier they all were in the dressing-room. But Brearley never minded the high jinks or the drinking as long as they performed out on the field.'

Phil Edmonds, that thorn in Brearley's flesh when they shared the Middlesex and England dressing-rooms, feels that captain and all-rounder were close because they did not pose a threat to each other. 'Beefy needed to dominate a dressing-room physically whereas Brears wanted to shine intellectually. Brears relied heavily on Both's animal strength and they respected each other enormously. It was almost a paternalistic relationship.' Paul Downton, another Middlesex and England man, feels that Brearley was insecure as a player and admired Botham's boldness: 'I opened the batting with Brears and he wanted to be reassured even by a young player like me from the other end. He was acutely conscious about not doing it at Test level. In contrast Both would just take on anyone and Brears warmed to that attitude. Beefy also liked Brearley's non-conformity – the frayed collar, the casual dress, the support for his players, if necessary against the authorities – and, of course, he admired his perception and the fact that he could easily out-argue him.'

Brearley accepts some of this, although he does not go along with all the Svengali comparisons.

> I felt an empathy with Ian, I never got as angry or impatient with him as I did with others. I found I could be firm and strong with him as well as being friendly. To be in charge successfully you have to have elements in common with your players, and I felt that Ian and I shared a sense of humour. We always seemed to enjoy each other's company if we sat around at an airport and I could share in his boyish humour – I'd find myself giggling when he threatened to set fire to Kenny Barrington's hair as he slept on a plane, or I'd tip shampoo over Ian's head in the shower and share a harmless laugh about it.
>
> In the end I simply feel I was the right person at the right time. It helped that there was no sense of rivalry between us; I was a good deal older and already England captain when he first came into the side. Somehow I could say 'no' to him and stir him up when it was needed. He had good ideas and I encouraged him to be adventurous as a cricketer, rather than suppressing him.

Whatever the influence exerted by Brearley on Botham's career, there is no doubt that 1981 will always be the seminal summer. The kaleidoscope of emotions that Botham passed through and the spectacular shift in his fortunes are the stuff of pulp fiction. 'I wasn't oblivious to what it all meant to the nation', says Ian:

> It was Boys' Own stuff, but with a difference because it was Australia and we were one down against the oldest enemy. I've honestly got no idea why it all fell into place for those three Tests, other than the luck coming my way at last after earlier setbacks. In our profession you make the most of it when the wheel of fortune sticks in your slot because it doesn't happen all that often. I was lucky at Leeds and I've often felt that Bob Willis and Graham Dilley didn't get as much credit as they deserved. I just swatted it around at Leeds, but I played much better at Old Trafford – one of my best knocks from a technical point of view. At Edgbaston, they just caved in after losing a couple of early wickets through bad shots. I didn't bowl all that

brilliantly, but my competitive instinct was the crucial factor. I loved the support from the crowd that day, the Union Jacks flying around, all that 'up and at 'em' stuff. Right up my street, that kind of atmosphere. It's inevitable that 1981 crops up whenever someone talks about cricket to me and I'm proud of it. I honestly think I could still do it if the circumstances were right.

That summer marks both the apogee for Botham and his nemesis. No cricketer could expect to enjoy such a golden run again, to achieve so much by playing totally in character – yet Botham is still expected to step into the time machine and transport himself back to 1981. During the Edgbaston Test of 1987, Bruce French was booed as he walked out as nightwatchman on the Saturday night, ahead of Botham. After French went quickly, the crowd was transported with delight when Botham came out to join in thrilling battle with Imran Khan. On the Monday morning, everyone on the ground was waiting for vintage Botham but he mistimed a hook and was gone within the hour. It was the kind of dismissal that happens to every batsman. Yet such is the burden of expectation he carries that Botham is expected to work miracles time and again. The stunning displays of 1981 are now a millstone around his neck and he has since been judged from a totally different standpoint than other cricketers. He is, after all, a human being and it would be inhuman if he had managed to reproduce consistently the batting of Leeds and Old Trafford, the galvanic bowling of Edgbaston. We should simply be grateful that he has managed to dazzle so often in the intervening years, while those of us there in 1981 are glad to have special memories for our dotage.

6

England expects

•

Over the next couple of years, Ian Botham's press image was to veer from the near-canonisation of 1981 to an opprobrium stemming from a desire to cut him down to size. There was no discernible change in the general public's attitude to Botham, other than a heightened expectation that he could work miracles as a matter of course, and an understandable frustration whenever his style of play undermined his effectiveness. Yet the popular press had a problem; Botham was under exclusive contract to the *Sun* and although his regular columns were never masterpieces of insight the rival tabloids were having to work maniacally to come up with new Botham angles. Preferably derogatory angles – there had been enough Phoenix from the Ashes stuff, it was now time to spin another dice in the one-dimensional game. Soon the obsession with Botham's weight was to rear its ugly head again and, by 1983, the unthinkable was openly discussed – should Botham be dropped? For his part, Botham reacted in his usual Pavlovian manner – 'the press build you up to knock you down again.' For years Reg Hayter his agent had warned him that a public figure struggles to have a completely private life, and that the perks of stardom carry responsibilities. Yet Ian thought he could remain the same, with the media turning a Nelsonian eye to all but his performances on the field.

It did not help that England started to lose rather too many Tests series for comfort. Tours to India and Australia in successive years ended in defeat, while Pakistan and New Zealand gave England a fright at home. Elimination at the semi-final stage of the World Cup in 1983 did not make things any easier for Botham, especially as he performed moderately in all the matches. He was circumscribed by his great deeds of 1981; he was now expected to win matches as a matter of course. If Botham did not deliver the goods, there had to be reasons other than loss of form or superior play by the opposition.

On the first England tour after his incredible summer, Ian was his usual sociable self within the team unit, and he was still the best player. At the crease he was majestic, a fusion of discipline and aggression, giving a tantalising glimpse of Botham as specialist batsman. He enjoyed a very friendly relationship with the captain, Keith Fletcher, who had replaced Brearley as the Middlesex captain pursued his new career in psychotherapy. The team spirit rarely flagged, despite losing the series after batting badly in the First Test at Bombay. Botham maintains that his bowling at Bombay (9 for 133 in the match off 50 overs) was one of his best performances for England and the way he could still swing the ball in bright conditions was encouraging. Perhaps Fletcher then made an error in giving Botham the next ten days off before the Second Test. At Bangalore he took 2 for 137 when England needed a breakthrough to get back in the series. Mike Brearley, who was out there for a few weeks in a journalistic capacity, thinks Botham ought to have been in better shape for such an important game: 'He bowled like a rusty, creaking machine and wasted the new ball. It was our only chance but Ian wasn't tight enough.' Fletcher will have none of it. 'There's no point in telling gifted players like Botham or Gower how to do their job because you stifle all their flair in the process. I just got the other players to work in a unit and let Beefy operate around them in the game. He's such a great trier that there would never be any worries about him supporting us out in the middle.' Nor did Botham's famous resilience desert him. Just before the Madras Test he picked up a virus and a lesser man would never have got on the pitch. He had a temperature of 103 at one stage and Kath and Bernard Thomas had to change his sheets every hour. For two days, they worked to get his temperature down and he made it, bowling 39 overs in the match and scoring 52.

Botham was as popular as ever with the team on that tour. His occasional elephantine humour would often rebound on him, but he retained the ability to laugh at himself. He poked fun at Boycott for most of the time he was there and, at the traditional fancy dress party at Christmas, Botham came loosely disguised as Gandhi, with a placard on his front saying '8,000 Test runs' and one on his back saying, 'I love me.' Botham was not alone in his antipathy towards Boycott's obsession with topping Gary Sobers's tally of Test runs, and when Boycott

returned home early through mental exhaustion, few tears of regret
were shed. His departure gave a chance of England recognition to Geoff
Cook, the Northants captain, who had correctly reasoned that he was
there as stand-in for the senior batsmen in the event of emergency.
Cook roomed with Botham for most of the tour, making the correct
assumption that expendable players were paired off with a cricketer
whose pre-Test preparations had always been a shade unconventional.
Cook, an unpretentious, warmly humorous man from the North-East,
was the ideal companion to keep Botham happy. Geoff Cook is also
one of the game's best drinkers, but even he had to give best one night
in up-country Jammu: 'Ian put me to bed at three after we demolished
a fair amount of whisky. Around mid-day, I attempted in vain to stand
up long enough to play golf – Botham had been gone six hours at the
crack of dawn, shooting pheasant and duck to bring back for the lads
to roast.'

At Indore, he gave an even more remarkable demonstration of his
iron constitution. Along with the *Guardian*'s Frank Keating, he wiped
out a bottle of brandy after sampling other alcoholic delights and, by
six in the morning, Frank was en route for a couple of hours' precious
sleep. Botham did not go to bed because he did not want to wake up
Geoff Cook, who needed runs later that day to claim a Test place. So
Botham stayed up. A few hours later, Cook was cheated out as his drive
to mid-on was taken on the second bounce, only to be given out. Botham
told him, 'Don't worry, I'll get him for you,' and proceeded to score the
fastest hundred ever seen in India, off 48 balls. He then went straight to
the badminton court with Cook and beat him in three sets. Next day,
with his second ball, he broke the finger of the man who had claimed
the catch to dismiss Cook. An even happier sequel came during Botham's
innings, as a certain newspaperman had to eat humble pie. During Frank
Keating's drinking session with Botham, he had been told by a fellow
reporter: 'I've seen another former England captain ruined by his
friends – don't forget he's got to bat later on. He shouldn't be drinking
so late.' No names, but the jeremiah has never been a Botham fan and
labours under the impression that the England side would have been
unbeatable in recent years if the selectors had simply picked the entire
Middlesex team, apart of course from Wayne Daniel. As Keating
watched the abashed correspondent file his copy later that day, he
allowed himself a wry, knowing smile.

That tour launched a firm friendship between Botham and Cook. It
is instructive to observe them together. Cook is one of the few who

regularly punctures Botham's balloons of absurdity by a shaft of common sense or even ridicule. They have shared rugby trips to Dublin and many a carousing evening and there is no doubt that Ian has a great deal of time for 'Tosh' Cook, even if their political and social attitudes are at opposite ends of the spectrum. At Kanpur, on the eve of the final Test, Ian made a rare mention of his own performance on that tour, delivering the opinion that he had been pleased with his batting. 'You've got to be kidding, Beefy,' Cook told him. 'With your ability, on these flat wickets and against these bowlers, you should be scoring hundreds, not just fifties.' At that stage, Botham had made four half-centuries, but not a big score. At Kanpur, he scored a disciplined 142, which took him five and a half hours. It would have been interesting to see Geoff Cook captain Botham if he had been a good enough player to hold down a regular England place – at that stage he was highly thought of as a leader by the selectors. Cook's frankness with Botham has always stemmed from a great fondness for him: 'He's a man full of paradoxes. I was struck by his forcefulness, his occasional lack of patience and his quick temper, yet he often showed the caring side to his nature. He chided me along on that tour, knowing how frustrated I was at not getting in the Test team. He was fully appreciative of the kind of role that Chris Tavare and I would play in an innings, even though he would be bored to tears watching us. He surprised me with his insight into the game.'

By this stage, however, hardly an eve-of-Test meeting went by without Botham asserting that most of the opposing batsmen were vulnerable to the bouncer. In India, such repetitious assertions became farcical. On the night before the Madras Test, Botham joined the squad and told them he would be fit to play, despite the effects of his virus. They settled down to sift the respective merits of the opposition and how to dismiss them. The captain Keith Fletcher went through the roll-call:

Fletcher: 'Gavaskar?'
Botham: 'Good player but he can't hook.'
Fletcher: 'Vengsarkar?'
Botham: 'He doesn't like it up him.'
Fletcher: 'Viswanath?'
Botham: 'He's a dwarf – a bouncer will do him.'
Fletcher: 'Yashpal Sharma?'
Botham: 'No problem. Last time we played him, he hooked my bouncer, and he smiled at me. The bouncer will get him.'

Collapse of England players into paroxysms of laughter. Botham could not surely believe all this rubbish; it was possibly a time when he was feeling physically vulnerable and he wished to reassert his overtly masculine presence on the series. No one took his statements seriously as he worked his way through the entire Indian team, coming to the dogmatic conclusion that each one was vulnerable to the bouncer. Good old Beefy was just having one of his daft days again. Indeed Yashpal Sharma was soon to disprove Botham's theory, batting an entire day at Madras, with England failing to pick up one solitary wicket. Botham tried his heart out, even indulging in some gestures to Yashpal that owed everything to Tony Greig and nothing to the MCC coaching book. The press took him to task for such behaviour, yet neglected to mention that as Yashpal Sharma walked of the field at close of play, Botham waited for him to shake hands and offer congratulations.

Botham's popularity with the rest of the tour party survived his idiosyncratic interventions in team meetings and, more importantly, his decision to pull out of the proposed tour to South Africa by several of England's top players. This plan had been mulled over throughout most of 1981, and Botham was very keen on the idea for a long period. He took an active part in secret discussions about the trip while in India, along with Boycott, Lever, Underwood, Emburey, Gooch and Willis. By December, however, Botham had decided to withdraw. His solicitor, Alan Herd and his agent, Reg Hayter, flew out to Bangalore to advise him against going to South Africa, on commercial grounds. Both men are certain that by the time they had got to Bangalore Botham had already decided to stay with the official brand of international cricket, despite the lavish sum he had been promised by the sponsors. He would have been the major draw card of that South African tour but he pulled out fully three-and-a-half months before it was to materialise. The other England players involved accepted Botham's decision with no hard feelings at the time, apart from Boycott, who viewed it as an act of treachery of Greville Wynne proportions.

Four months after that meeting in Bangalore, Ian's knack of entwining foot with mouth again rebounded on him. Instead of keeping a low profile on the South Africa excursion (as refuseniks like David Gower, Mike Gatting and Bob Willis did), he allowed himself a moralistic homily in the *Sun* about the evils of apartheid. Ian's exclusive column contained the view that he wouldn't have been able to look Viv in the face again if he'd gone. Now there is no doubt that Viv Richards possesses strong views on the apartheid system, that Botham shares them to a degree – after all Viv is a godfather to his son, Liam – and that many of Ian's admirers were pleased that he had taken such a stand. Yet it was tactless to make such statements in public, thereby unconsciously damning his friends as racialists chasing blood-stained Krugerrands. If he had been so concerned about Viv's reaction, why had he allowed himself to get involved in the first place? The truth of the matter is that Ian did not bother to read the column written by his ghost-writer in the *Sun* before it was published. His trusting nature had again let him down, in the process hurting former colleagues with whom he had shared many laughs and many emotional moments on previous tours. Worse still, he somehow allowed his sentiments to be read out to an anti-apartheid rally in Hyde Park, making Gooch and company feel even more like pariahs. Why not just keep quiet or trot out that cliché beloved of most sportsmen about keeping politics out of sport or the one about the individual's freedom to choose? The *Sun* had to have its pound of flesh, that is why, and Ian failed to exercise strict control over his public statements on the matter. In later years Graham Gooch admitted that he could never trust Ian fully after that episode, and Mike Hendrick took him to task over his comments when Somerset came to Trent Bridge early in the 1982 season.

Once the South African Breweries' tourists were banned from Test cricket for three years, Botham's continued good form was of prime importance to an England team shorn of several of its best players. England's new captain, Bob Willis, relied on him greatly but, although he generally performed well in England during that time, the side's poor showing away from home was mirrored in Botham's indifferent form. Soon the knives would be out for both captain and star all-rounder – but not before some thrilling batting by Botham in the summer of 1982. In the Old Trafford Test against India, he savaged 128 off 169 balls, despite being hit painfully on the toe by a full toss when he had scored 67. He went one better at the Oval, scoring a double hundred off 220 balls – a marvellous display of dominant, punishing batting in the mould of Wally Hammond. He batted number five in this series, despite putting in a lot of overs, and he looked the genuine, finished product as an international middle-order batsman. His captain was annoyed at him for getting out, believing he would get a triple hundred.

Botham continued to bat with great panache as the season ended. Two county games that September convey both his all-round skills and his enormous zest for life. Matches against both Warwickshire and Worcestershire always bring out both Botham's ultra-competitive instincts and desire for a large social thrash – in both cases due to the enduring friendships he has with players and officials of both clubs. In the Warwickshire game, he limbered up in the first innings with 41 off 32 balls, then walked to the wicket with Somerset still needing 160 in 145 minutes for victory. Sixty-five minutes later they had cruised to victory with Botham 131 not out. He reached his hundred in 56 balls, the fastest of the season and hit ten sixes all told. Thirty runs came off one over from Paul Smith's fast-medium bowling. In the next game against Worcestershire, Botham plundered 98 off 51 balls on the first day. At lunch on the second day, Worcestershire had four wickets down and were making a fight of it. Botham had not bowled in the morning but, as he started his first spell of the innings, Jeremy Lloyds at slip whispered to Trevor Gard, the wicket-keeper, 'I bet he gets five bloody wickets.' The first second ball was a slow, swinging half-volley which Phil Neale nicked to Viv Richards at second slip. Botham took 5 for 50 off 7.4 overs (there *were* a few wide half-volleys!) and the game was wrapped up by mid-afternoon, with Somerset winning by an innings.

The background to that performance by Botham is also typical of him. Duncan Fearnley, later the man to secure Botham's services for Worcestershire, had come down to Taunton to watch a bit of cricket and socialise with the prized wielder of his bats. He describes how Botham prepared himself for that matchwinning piece of bowling:

That first night, after he'd got 98, he wasn't bothered at all about missing out on the hundred, even though it would've been an even faster one than the Warwickshire knock. He said, 'Right, Dunc, we're going to have a good night out,' and I feared the worst. We drove up to Weston-super-Mare where Beefy played a frame of snooker with Ray Reardon as part of Viv Richards's benefit, then we got back in the car and drove at the speed of light to reach Beefy's local by closing time. At the pub, the gin was downed in vast quantities, he started throwing ice cubes around, then the soda syphon got an outing. I finally beat the retreat around two o'clock, with Beefy still going strong. The next morning, Steve Perryman bowled out Somerset within half an hour and Beefy had to go out and field. He doesn't often have hangovers, but he did that day. He couldn't bowl before lunch because he felt so bad, but he polished us off quickly enough when he came on. At four o'clock he was on the outfield, playing football with the rest of the lads and shouted 'don't go yet, Dunc – the Red Arrows are going to fly past to salute me.' An hour later, there they were blowing red and white smoke over the ground, then whizzing over our heads. Typical Botham. The most amazing 24 hours of my life.

By 1982, Botham was having the time of his life, living out the fantasies that the rest of us could only ponder. He was famous, but not just as a cricketer – why else would an American ask him for his autograph at Caesar's Palace, Las Vegas at the time? – but because he brightened up a drab world. He symbolised the dream of any working-class kid from the sticks with enough talent to make a dent in life. His enthusiasms were touchingly childlike. After a practice run with the crack Red Arrows flying team, he announced to Reg Hayter that he planned to fly round the world. Now Reg was used to Ian's boyish wheezes, but he blanched at this one. He knew, even if Ian did not, that a flight around the world was not quite as simple as it sounded. Ian enlisted the help of Alan Dyer, a businessman who had completed the trip in 1974, flying 25,000 statute miles in eighteen days. Alan found the Botham optimism unquenchable:

He hadn't then got his fixed wings licence or had many flying lessons, but he was happy to trust me completely as his co-pilot, even though there would've been immense responsibility on me as the experienced partner. Ian wanted to raise money for Leukaemia Research and the National Children's Homes with the project, and it appealed to him because it sounded so adventurous. Ian fancied the proposed route – from London to Hong Kong, through the Pacific to Alaska then back to Scotland – but I had great difficulty trying to make him appreciate the pitfalls. I rolled out this map, pointing out the major problem – the Pacific, where you can only stop for fuel on small islands surrounded by 6,000 miles of water. If you miss one of those stops you're swimming, but Ian simply said, 'That's no problem, you'll sort that out.' Thank God there was no time to fit in this trip but he often says we'll do it one day. Since then I've flown with him in the King's Cup Air Race, the major race in this country, and down to the South of France. He takes the controls now and then and he adapts very well; you need a sharp mental aptitude to absorb heights and speeds on those dials and Ian has that, plus sheer determination to improve himself.

With so many exciting elements now in his life, it is hardly surprising that Botham was not totally geared up for the forthcoming tour of

Australia in 1982. It would be his third trip there with England in four years, and he was getting a little stale of international cricket. He did not do himself justice on this trip. He was never mentally attuned to the shuttlecock of internal flights across that vast country; he wanted to stay in Sydney, where Kath had based herself with the family. When Botham is morose, he has a tendency to eat and drink too much and this happened on that Australian tour. Contrary to tabloid innuendo, Ian usually eats sensibly – lots of seafood, vegetables and no potatoes – but he does have a remarkable capacity to hold his drink and keep a clear head. He met Elton John for the first time that tour and Elton's sincere friendship helped alert Ian to a wider world than that provided by cricket. He also struck up a firm friendship with Allan Lamb – like Ian an open, friendly character with a love of outdoor pursuits like hunting, or drinking beside a barbecue. As a result, Lamb and Botham often went off on their own in Australia, a country where tour managements always find it difficult to maintain an intimate team spirit without social distractions. This was the first time that Botham became reclusive on tour, a trend that accelerated in the Caribbean in 1986. He restricted his circle of acquaintances, partly through a series of damaging stories in the press. Once again the *Sun*, Botham's mouthpiece, let him down. It alleged that Botham and his captain, Bob Willis, were not speaking to each other (laughable), that Botham thought the Australian umpires were incompetent – true, but that was a comment not meant for public consumption, and for which he was fined by the tour management – and even more remarkably, that Botham had been seen brawling with Rodney Hogg on New Year's Eve at Sydney's Pier One, a restaurant and nightclub. This particular piece of fiction at least led to an apology in the *Sun*, tucked away inside, occupying three lines. Graeme Fowler, who was with the group at the time, recalls Botham and Hogg indulging in their usual banter as they passed each other, and that was it. Botham talked to Hogg en route for the door, just as the Australian was arriving. Anyone who knew more than a morsel about Botham ought to have been aware of his friendship with Hogg that dated back to the 1978/9 tour, when they bet each other a bottle of any drink that one would get the other's wicket more often. It was bad enough having the other tabloids scouring for Botham scandal but he was now being stabbed in the back by his own alleged supporters in Fleet Street. In vain did Bob Willis and other close friends counsel him to sever his ties with the *Sun*; the money was too good, he countered, and since when did anyone ever take the tabloids seriously? Sometimes

Ian's gullibility is even more astonishing than his thick skin.

So the 'weight' story was dusted down and given another outing – this time with more justification. Ian was photographed sitting beside a pool with Dennis Lillee during the rest day of the Adelaide Test, and it must be said that Ian ought to have breathed in as the shutter clicked. Lillee, six years his senior, looked a good deal trimmer, despite his recent knee problems. Ian's excess avoirdupois now resembled an impressive bay window starting at the chest and sloping majestically down. It did not really matter all that much, except he was not faring particularly well on the field. He kept telling Willis not to worry but the facts are that his top score on the tour was 65 and that, although he took most Test wickets for England, they cost him 40 runs apiece. The batting was not really the problem – during the Perth Test he had completed 1,000 Test runs in a year – and he was such a good, orthodox player that one bad series could be put down to ill fortune or excellent bowling. Certainly the Australian bowlers had done their homework on him after the traumas of 1981, as Geoff Lawson recalls: 'We set fields to contain him, to tempt him. We bowled line and length to frustrate him and he got himself out.' In the dressing-room he did not even watch the opening overs of the match, retiring to the bowels of the room with his pads on to play cribbage with Geoff Miller, and only reappearing when it was his turn to bat. Miller remembers that his friend's usual ebullience began to drain away during that series and he was over-tense when he batted. Botham even went so far as to have a net on the rest day of a Test, a rarity in the Halley's Comet class, and an unwelcome surprise to Robin Jackman, who had to trundle at him for a long time when he had deserved a day off after hours of net bowling.

Yet it was Ian's bowling that was a greater cause for concern. He had lost his timing, he was not releasing the ball at the right time, no longer hitting the seam. His bouncer was harmless, his run-up laboured, and occasionally he was no more than medium pace. He was not getting his body round enough to bowl the outswinger and, with the inswinger his stock delivery, he lacked that variety which had always distinguished his bowling. He was hampered by a strained side, his back trouble seemed to have reappeared and he looked in need of a hard gallop.

Yet Ian at times still had that magic touch. Take the Melbourne Test, that thrilling game won by England by the margin of just three runs – who else but Botham could conjure up a win with his trademark, the wide half-volley? With his first ball of his new spell, Golden Arm did it again with the gentle loosener that has always characterised his bowling;

Jeff Thomson stopped playing like a proper batsman, reverted to type and chased it. There was a snick, a fumble by Chris Tavare and Geoff Miller took the rebound. Willis's desperate solution to a desperate situation had paid off: when in deep trouble, take a chance on Botham. But it was typical of Botham that the man who almost won the game for Australia was using Botham's bat. Allan Border was going through a bad trot and Ian had offered his own bat to see if it would make any difference. It certainly did – Border batted magnificently in the second innings and for the rest of the series. It is also symptomatic of Botham's reputation as the supreme competitor that no one attached any significance to him helping out his friend; on the field of play, he would be after Border's scalp.

Bob Willis, loyal friend of Ian's, admits that he expected more from him on that Australian tour. Their friendship was not strained (they have been through too much for that ever to happen,) but Willis was forced to display the same loyalty as Botham did when his fast bowler was struggling with no-ball trouble in 1980. Willis admits that he and the tour manager, Doug Insole, had many long discussions on how to get the best out of their matchwinner and in the end they agreed that cajolery rather than the big stick was preferable. 'After that tour I gave up trying to change him,' says Willis. 'He had always gone his own way before and been very successful, so I relied on his flair and competitiveness coming through. Unfortunately Ian didn't bowl well abroad during my time as England captain.'

Willis was forced into more public messages of support for Botham in the summer of 1983. It was the year of the World Cup and Botham's failure (40 runs in four innings, 8 for 288 in 80 overs in the seven games) contrasted with the inspirational captaincy and all-round talents of India's captain, Kapil Dev, who lifted the trophy after a surprise win over the West Indies. Richard Hadlee, New Zealand's main all-rounder, performed impressively in the World Cup and, in the four-Test series, outshone Botham with a batting average of 50 and 21 wickets. All of a sudden Botham appeared to be sliding down the ranks of the all-rounders. When England lost the Leeds Test Botham bowled so badly in the first innings (0 for 81 off 26 overs) that Willis did not give him a bowl in the second innings until New Zealand needed two for victory. On the Saturday night press conference during that Test, Willis was put on the back foot by the press, avid for a 'Botham must go' story. It seems a surprise that cricket writers should feel that an England side without Botham – even a subdued Botham – was an improvement, but press conferences during Tests had long concentrated on the world's most controversial cricketer. After Willis explained to the press that he only had one-fifth of the vote at the next selection committee and that he would still want Botham in his team, the press persisted. Willis asked them for suitable candidates, posing the question 'Which two players will we need to take Botham's place?' When the names of Surrey's David Thomas and Hampshire's Trevor Jesty were offered, the captain reasonably pointed out that neither man was likely to approach Botham's overall Test record. That ought to have been the end of it, except that the esteemed correspondent of the *News of the World* rang up both Jesty and Thomas, told them 'Bob Willis says you can't play the game', and then ran the predictable mock-outrage follow-up. Willis was furious and at the next Saturday evening press conference at the Lord's Test we had the extraordinary scene where the England captain replied 'yes' or 'no' to every question put to him. Willis could see no other way of signifying his fury at the *News of the World*'s mischief-making. The feud rumbled on and in the final Test at Trent Bridge, when Botham scored an exhilarating century on the first day, he refused to talk to the press. In such a heightened atmosphere, every reputable cricket writer was being tarred with the same brush of opportunism, a fact regretted by Willis and Botham, but inevitable. Around that time, Botham showed his feelings for the press in a spectacular manner. One evening, while walking across the Taunton ground with friends from the opposition, he suddenly stopped, picked up a deckchair and hurled it through the press-box window, smashing a few panes in the process. As he stood there, mouthing a few choice words at the empty press-box, he was hustled away before anyone saw what he had done. Time has not mellowed Ian's feelings towards the more hostile elements of the national press and even towards those who strive to write merely about events on the field of play. 'So often it's been a case of "we haven't give Botham any stick lately, let's give him a serve now", and all my family have come to the same conclusion. I think the public are now as sick of it all as I am.' But surely Botham's paymasters on the *Sun* are more guilty than any others of trivialisation? 'At least their sports coverage is comprehensive, and no one can say I don't try to be constructive about cricket in my column. I never go out to knock a fellow-professional. Cricket's a very simple game with very simple rules, but many of the pundits don't seem to grasp that fact. When I hear them droning on about David Gower not moving his feet, it makes me mad. Do they ever see where he's hit the ball? Do they know what it's like out there? It's a bloody hard game. A lot of the so-called experts would be clean bowled by my young son wearing a blindfold, yet they tell *us* how to play. They should simply stick to the facts.'

By the Trent Bridge Test, Ian had become sickened by the machinations of the media. As he saw it, attempting to drive a wedge between himself and Willis was bad enough, and he could take the criticism of his cricket abilities, but he was appalled by one personal matter that became public property. At the end of the Leeds Test, Kath learned that she had lost the baby she was carrying. It would mean an induced miscarriage as soon as possible. Ian handled everything, including packing off the children with mother-in-law for an arranged holiday to the South of France. He chartered a plane to fly him down to play in the Nat-West quarter-final at Hove, then to whisk him back straight afterwards. Then he spent the next two days with Kath, sharing in her grief. Kath's mother, Jan, will not forget Ian's strength at that time: 'He was marvellous, an absolute rock. He was terribly upset, of course, but taking charge helped him, gave him something to do. Ian loves all children but this hit him very hard as you'd imagine. I felt awful, going on holiday, leaving my daughter to face that hospital visit, but Ian was insistent and he was right. It was best to leave them alone together.'

It would have been more bearable without the attendant publicity. At a time when any grieving couple want to turn inside themselves, away from the outside world, Kath Botham's miscarriage made front-page news the day after. The BBC's nine o'clock bulletin even headlined the event. One would have thought that other events of a less private nature might have made the news that day, but no. The story had leaked out and the Bothams were denied privacy when they most needed, and deserved, it.

When Ian flew down to play against Sussex, he did not mention Kath's miscarriage to anyone, apart from his close friend, Trevor Gard who, of course, kept the secret. It was an important game and Ian did not want the rest of the players to be distracted. Botham took 4 for 20 on a fast wicket and the game was over by mid-afternoon. Trevor Gard says that Ian was like a man in a trance that day: 'When he bowled Ian Gould, he ran down the wicket as usual to me, but his eyes were a blur, he seemed in a dream. He has never bowled quicker that day when I've kept wicket, he was like a man possessed. I could see he was terribly hurt – whatever you hear, he's devoted to Kath and his kids.'

A fortnight after that Sussex game, Ian won the Nat-West semi-final more or less single-handed. He played an innings of 96 not out that was a model of authority and rectitude. He was captaining Somerset that day in the absence of the injured Brian Rose and victory against Middlesex was clearly of paramount importance to him. Ian still hankered after the England captaincy and he thought the way back was via the Somerset post, with his performances displaying a new maturity under the increased responsibility. Another final at Lord's might at least set him on the road to the first beachhead, the Somerset captaincy. Never was the cliché 'a captain's innings' more worthy of use, although it must be said that, in the Middlesex innings, Ian got his calculations wrong and Joel Garner, the best one-day bowler in the world, did not bowl his full twelve overs. Marks, Oxford graduate and all that, was usually put in charge of on-field arithmetic, but somehow Nigel Popplewell was pressed into service after lunch, and it was he who ended up bowling the last over as Garner looked on quizzically! Nigel was not finished yet; he came out to join his captain at 52 for 5, still 171 adrift. Botham radiated massive assurance and told Popplewell there was nothing to worry about. In 1983 Middlesex had a very strong bowling line-up, yet after Botham hit Emburey out of the attack by lapping him into the Mound Stand for six, they did not seem so threatening. Popplewell just could not believe how relaxed and serene Botham appeared: 'We still had a lot of overs in hand, yet we were a long way adrift. But Beefy was so professional; he was prepared to let me get the runs as well, whereas normally he hits the ball back past you like a shell and you run when he tells you to. His defensive play is so sound that once he decided to stay there, he looked invincible. At tea-time, Beefy just sat there, very quiet – unlike his normal, raucous self. It was the kind of cool, masterly effort you used to see from Clive Rice.'

After Popplewell and Vic Marks had guided their captain to the brink of victory, Trevor Gard came in with seven balls to go, one run to tie the scores and two wickets in hand. Botham was on strike and came up to tell Gard, 'Whatever happens, run and get in at your end'. He did as he was told and, at the end of the penultimate over, the scores were level. Middlesex, however, had lost a wicket more and Botham ascertained from the umpires that Somerset would win if they ended with eight wickets down. Emburey was brought back on and we had the rare sight in the final over of a limited-overs match of seeing all the fielders around the bat. When you consider that the man on strike was one of history's greatest attacking batsmen it was even more bizarre, especially when Botham padded up to the last ball and was perilously close to being lbw. He survived, Somerset had won and Botham ran from the field arms aloft in the euphoric manner of Edgbaston 1981. In the final, Somerset comfortably beat Kent and Botham had won a trophy for the first time as a captain. It was the end for Brian Rose as skipper and Ian got his wish to lead the side. The consequences of that would become clearer two years later.

Botham may have started 1983 in a below-par physical condition, but he ended it looking as fit as he had been for several years. Football training with Scunthorpe United had worked wonders and the lure of a first-team place gave him an extra incentive. To his great delight Ian made the first team and played until a few days before leaving on the England tour to Fiji, New Zealand and Pakistan. That situation brought out all Ian's bloody-mindedness. The Test and County Cricket Board was perturbed that he was risking injury so near to departure by subjecting himself to a contact sport like Fourth Division football, while Botham wondered if the same concern had been expressed to David Gower and Allan Lamb (abroad skiing) and Mike Gatting (also playing local football). Not for the first time Botham thought the TCCB had handled him in the wrong way: 'When they rang me up, I thought "balls, I'll please myself", yet I was going to pack up before Christmas. Because they tried the big stick, I played till December 27. On Boxing Day in front of 18,000 at Hull, I marked Billy Whitehurst out of the game – he later played in the First Division, you know. The next day we lost 5/1 to Preston after being 4/0 down at half-time, so at least we drew the second half! We flew out to Fiji two days later. I've never been fitter for an England tour. I did all the training and came back for extra in the afternoon at Scunthorpe. And I was on the wagon!'

It was ironic that a tour which began with Botham fit and raring for the fray should prove to be the only one to see him bow the knee to injury and return home early. In more than one way, it was to prove an extraordinary tour.

7

Hold the front page!

●

The first day of 1984 saw Ian Botham warding off mosquitos in the oppressive heat of Fiji, and the last one found him in a police station trying to justify why drugs had been found at his home. By any standards, even those of Botham, it was a remarkable year. It was also the year that relations between England cricketers and the media reached a nadir. There were faults on both sides, but the presence of Botham polarised the issue. In 1984 Ian was mostly in the wrong frame of mind to play Test cricket; he should have followed his instincts and taken a sabbatical from the tour to Fiji, New Zealand and Pakistan, even though he felt physically fit at its start. He ought to have prepared sensibly for the visit of the West Indies, the ultimate test for any international cricketer in the 1980s. As Ian's social horizons broadened, touring became more and more of a drag. His decision to opt out of the 1984/5 trip to India came not a moment too soon, otherwise he might have been lost to cricket before his thirtieth birthday.

To traditionalists that tour of Fiji, New Zealand and Pakistan was nothing short of a disaster. It was not simply that England lost both series – sadly that was no longer a rarity – but that lurid allegations placed the players on the front page of the newspapers rather than the back. By the time the party got to Pakistan, investigative reporters were swarming all over the team hotel and alarming allegations were winging their way back to Fleet Street. The scalpel of curiosity was not taken to the blameless reputations of tourists like Bob Taylor, Chris Tavare, Derek Randall, Chris Smith, Neil Foster and Vic Marks. As usual it came down to Botham, and anyone else who happened to be a friend.

When one newspaper said that a group of England players had been seen smoking 'pot' at an Elton John concert, it did not take the acutest intelligence to know who would be under suspicion – the younger, gregarious members of the tour party who were close to Botham, as well as the captain, Bob Willis. Yet Bob Taylor, a generation apart from Botham and a man of unimpeachable integrity, was also there and saw no evidence of drug-taking by his team-mates. When the *Mail on Sunday* alleged that some of the players smoked 'pot' during the Christchurch Test – stuffing towels under the dressing-room door to restrict the spread of that distinctive, sweet smell – it strained the realms of credulity. England may have played at Christchurch as if in a stupor but this was ridiculous. Alan Smith, the tour manager, was in the dressing-room for most of the time in question and scoffs at the allegation: 'Anyone who knows the amount of traffic in and out of a dressing-room will know how ridiculous that sounds. It was supposed to have happened when rain had stopped play – in such circumstances, how many people are knocking on the door, looking for bats to be signed or autographs to be collected? There was nowhere to hide, it was simply not possible.'

The *Mail on Sunday* thundered that 'booze, birds and pot-smoking' had been on the menu in New Zealand and named Ian Botham and Allam Lamb as the culprits. Over the past year, Lamb and Botham had become great friends, and it was inevitable that some of the mud thrown at Botham would hit Lamb as well. The rumours about sexual pranks came close to wrecking Allan Lamb's marriage and, for a long time afterwards, he was bitter about this massive interest in his private life. In the summer of 1984, as Lamb scored four Test centuries, he refused to have anything to do with press conferences. Certainly journalistic curiosity had reached intensive levels by the time the England party checked in at the Hilton in Lahore. The allegations by the *Mail on Sunday* were filtering through, and hard-nosed, foot-in-the-door hacks were pushing for morsels. The regular cricket correspondents were being quizzed by the investigative reporters and, with Alan Smith vainly trying to deflect the torrent of media interest, the scene was like an updated version of Evelyn Waugh's *Scoop*. The proud upholders of the public's right to know would hide behind potted palms in the hotel foyer, then ambush an England player as he got into the lift, firing questions about cannabis, groupie girls and assorted orgies. Bob Woodward and Carl Bernstein have a lot to answer for.

Fortunately for the players' peace of mind, the principal quarry was soon taken away from this madhouse and the remainder of the party could get back to the normal challenges of playing cricket in Pakistan – like stomach disorders, flat wickets, myopic umpires and the dawning realisation that victory was impossible. While his team-mates tried to claw back a one-nil deficit in the series, Ian Botham flew home to have surgery on his left knee. Even in his departure, Botham fanned the flames of cynical media curiosity; it was hinted darkly that Alan Smith had sent him home to get the hacks off his back, so that the rest of the tour could proceed along normal lines. The scenario painted was that Botham would sit in a hospital bed for a couple of days, dodge an operation and disappear for some fishing while the fuss died down. Alas for fond hopes; Botham had damaged his left knee six weeks earlier during the Wellington Test, but the management had kept quiet about it. By the time Botham got to Lahore, surgery was essential if he had any hopes of getting fit for the start of the next English season. Bernard Thomas, the physiotherapist, made the decision to send him home: 'It was a legacy of an old football injury he'd picked up in his teens and there was no question any more of delaying surgery.'

Even while lying in a hospital bed, Ian could not escape damaging publicity. He gave an interview that offered the opinion that 'Pakistan's the kind of place to send your mother-in-law to for a month, all expenses paid.' When that remark was disseminated throughout Pakistan it caused outrage. The Cabinet met to discuss the implications, Alan Smith needed all his diplomatic skills to defuse the row, and Sarfraz Nawaz, that idiosyncratic cricketer-cum-politician was so incensed that he branded Botham as a drug-crazed opium-pusher. Eventually Alan Smith managed to soothe the ruffled feelings of the hosts and the tour reverted to as near normality as is possible, with players dropping like flies. Later Botham was fined £2,000 for his remarks and warned about his future conduct. Here I must declare an interest: I was that interviewer at his bedside. I had popped in to see him, partly for professional reasons, but also to cheer up a friend whose restless nature is hardly suited to having pillows fluffed at regular intervals. I stayed for a couple of hours and in the process recorded a half-hour piece for BBC Radio that ranged far and wide. Botham offered his views on Pakistan in a jocular context, accompained by chuckles from both parties. Anyone who knows Ian's relationship with his mother-in-law is well aware he was only joking. The contentious part lasted about thirty seconds and the rest of the piece was a good deal more serious – dealing with the strain of playing for your country under armed guard, the resilience of the tour party under such enormous pressure, the sportsmanship of the players in the face of controversial umpiring decisions and the utter impossibility of anyone smoking 'pot' in a dressing-room at a cricket ground. Yet my editor in Broadcasting House in London was soon bombarded by demands for an apology by the Pakistan High Commissioner and a request for a formal reply from the editor of the *Mail on Sunday*. Both were denied, but it was another example of the different stances that people adopt when Ian Botham is involved. The views of any other player would not have caused such a brouhaha while the sleuths would not have cared about the alleged nocturnal activities of anyone else but Botham. I cannot believe that an England team-mate of Botham's would have been docked £2,000 for a joke about a country. When Ian is involved, the goal-posts often seem to be moved, a suspicion confirmed by the TCCB's support for Mike Gatting and his players after the troubled England tour to Pakistan late in 1987, when Botham was absent.

If England had not played so ineptly in New Zealand a few weeks earlier, they would have been spared the dubious pleasure of being accosted from behind the potted plants at Lahore by those fearless pedlars of moral probity. The cricket correspondents were rightly appalled at the abject surrender at Christchurch in the Second Test where England collapsed to 82 and 93, losing by an innings in just twelve hours' playing time. Botham especially bowled dreadfully on a dubious pitch ideal for an English-style seamer who could bowl line and length. Willis, the captain, was shattered by the ineptitude he surveyed; 'We all bowled badly that day, but Beefy was worse than anyone. He'd made little effort to get fit for the Test, having done no training for a week and he wasted a golden chance to go one-up in the series. I'm afraid that by that stage I was no longer so inspirational at goading him into bowling with fire.' In England's second innings, Botham was caught first ball at short leg and he walked off the pitch, grinning. This rendered the English cricket writers into near-apoplexy as they came to the conclusion that Botham's smile symbolised that he was not bothered in the slightest about the débacle to which he had largely contributed. They failed to notice that it was a rueful smile, because Martin Crowe had taken a stunning reflex catch to dismiss him off a firm push off his legs. Botham is not the most fatalistic of cricketers – believing that in part you can actually make your own luck – but that catch made him conclude that is was to be neither his nor England's day. No one, not even Botham's harshest critic, can claim that he does not stiffen his resolve for England and his philosophical smile ought to have been judged in context. Yet his poor showing in that Test constituted the blue touchpaper, lit by his reaction to that first-ball dismissal.

The press trawled for reasons why England were playing so poorly. It could not be as simple as a team under-achieving while the opposition all-rounder, Richard Hadlee, was turning in Bothamesque figures. They looked dreadfully passive at Christchurch and press-box pens were dipped into the ink-wells of vitriol. It was too much to bear when several of the team were later seen enjoying themselves with a few drinks as if they had earned a few days off. The presence of Elton John also assumed a significance in the eyes of the scribes. Middle-aged men more at home with James Last and Nat King Cole would have difficulty taking seriously a dumpy little figure in an assortment of garish costumes, whose stage performances were unashamedly a mixture of the camp and the spectacular. It mattered little that Elton John was by now a true friend of the likes of Botham and Willis, a genuine sports fanatic and a passionate supporter of England in any field of sporting endeavour. To those seeking reasons for England's humiliation, Elton John was an unwelcome presence. They felt he belonged to the world of the drug-taking bisexual, where the curtains in hotel suites were still drawn around mid-day. Can it be that England's stupefying performances at Christchurch were influenced by the social mores of the rock world? A whisper or two along such lines to Fleet Street sports desks and the investigative hard men were again wheeled out, while the correspondents cried 'foul'.

It was the corollary to playing international sport in an age of intense public scrutiny, with Britain's most famous sportsman in the party. England cricketers were now earning handsome sums of money and some sections of the media ruled that they were thus fair game for root-and-branch investigations. Heaven only knows what those boot boys would have done to unashamed hedonists like Keith Miller, Denis Compton and Bill Edrich as they wassailed their way through the post-war years. Or to Arthur Mailey, who was met on the steps of his hotel at 8 a.m. by his captain after a night of gambling and drinking during the vital Oval Test of 1926. Or to Bobby Peel, who arrived to play for Yorkshire in an intoxicated state and proceeded to relieve himself on the pitch and bowl at the sightscreen. In recent years, none of the super-sleuths has highlighted the sweet aromas coming from the hotel suites and dressing-rooms occupied by the West Indies players. They, of course, were winning, unlike England in 1984. Elton John was even more intimately involved with the team in Australia in 1986/7, with the blessing of the management – but he was then a harmless fan, because England kept winning.

Amid all the thrashing around by the eavesdroppers, one scoop about Botham was missed. On the last night of the New Zealand leg of the tour, the England players threw a party at Auckland, not in celebration but in realisation that the next few weeks in Pakistan would be hard going, with many creature comforts missing. That night Graeme Fowler contrived to fall onto a piece of glass, cutting his hand so that it needed three stitches. It happened late in the evening, when most of the party were less than sober, none more so than Ian Botham. But it was he who drove Fowler to the hospital and waited till he was treated. Says Fowler: 'He insisted on getting me there, even though he was over the limit. He was taking a hell of a chance in helping me out. But Beefy does those kind of things for his mates. It would have been Beefy in the headlines, not me, if we had been stopped by the police.'

When Fowler returned to England, he encountered an interesting viewpoint on the rumours from someone he had never met: 'This bloke said to me in the street, "Were you on that sex and drugs tour? By 'eck, it sounded great – mind you, it's got nowt to do with the bloody press!" I think the general public feel the same way.' Richard Hadlee certainly does. As the drugs allegations rumbled on, Hadlee felt constrained to write to Botham. He had heard that Botham believed he was one of the sources behind the rumours, and he was quick to scotch any involvement: 'I wasn't the slightest bit interested in what they suggested. I assume Beefy believed me, because he's never spoken to me about it. It's totally wrong for people to pry into your private life, but at the same time you have to beware giving them any ammunition at all. I think Botham's done amazingly well to weather all that stuff and I'm sure it's much worse than I suffer. All credit to his wife for her strength of character as well.' Kath needed all of it, around this time, especially when six-year-old Liam learned that one of his schoolfriends had been told not to play with him because the Botham family were drug addicts.

As the English season approached, Botham shrugged off the vicissitudes of recent months and geared himself for the visit of the West Indies. Before then, he suffered a blow that affected him a good deal more than any journalistic muck-raking. 'Jock' McCombe, his friend, philosopher and odd-job man in Taunton died suddenly of a heart attack. At the time Ian was on holiday at Viv Richards's house in Antigua. The news hit Botham and Richards hard; they had been very close over the past few years and McCombe, who had been around the

Taunton scene for some time, had dedicated himself to making their lives easier by attending to various items of trivia beneath the dignity of two such illustrious figures. He simply adored looking after Richards and Botham, who in turn responded generously to his ministrations. Some officials at Taunton criticised Jock's influence at the county ground, especially when he was appointed liaison officer between players and committee, press and public, but the present secretary Tony Brown is quite certain that he did a very good job while they were together on the staff. Yet there were rumblings that the superstars were beginning to form their own clique down at Taunton, with McCombe acting as a sieve to assess those who should be allowed to get near to Botham and Richards. That feeling may have been born of jealousy or bruised egos, but it would re-surface with a vengeance in the autumn of 1986 when Botham and Richards left the club.

'Jock' McCombe's sudden death also left Ian with a problem that was not satisfactorily resolved. It was Ian's benefit year and McCombe had been charged with getting him to various functions in his honour and keeping tabs on the multiplicity of dates and venues. Unfortunately, he was not a paragon of administration; his filing system tended to consist of pockets full of various envelopes, containing vital information about a boxing evening or a skittles night in rural Somerset. Soon the press was enjoying itself again at Ian's expense – carrying stories about Botham's rude non-appearance at functions for his benefit year. It did not matter that Botham was unaware of them due to his dead friend's administrative inexperience, it was still open season on Botham. The *Sunday People* carried a particularly nasty piece, alleging that Ian had arrived late at a benefit match at Sparkford, that he deliberately got out early and refused to sign autographs, behaving boorishly. Luckily Ian's parents were at the game and can speak the truth – that he was delayed by road works, sat down to sign endless autographs and chatted to all and sundry. Somerset CCC happily confirmed this. On another occasion, he had hosted a shooting day but left before the dinner that was to end the day. As he exited hurriedly, Ian fell face down in the car park. He had enjoyed just two drinks, but they had been 'spiked'. It took him a few days to recover from the experience and it was some time before he could bring himself to take a drink in public again.

He was well aware that he needed more bad publicity like a hole in the head. For instance, David English, a close friend, was with him at a benefit dance in Taunton that year and saw him snuff out a potentially damaging incident: 'Across the other side of the hall, one bloke was trying to bottle another guy. It had nothing at all to with Beefy, but he went over and pulled them apart. "Pack it in – it'll be in the papers tomorrow that I started it", he said, which was sadly true.'

The occasional bouts of snide publicity led to the inevitable cancellation of some benefit functions, but Ian was delighted by the final sum of £90,000. It would have been a good deal more if he had given up his weekends in the autumn of 1984 (soccer for Scunthorpe United took precedence) or if he had taken the selfish way out and not helped other beneficiaries that summer. Jeremy Lloyds, his team-mate and occasional driver, reckons he would easily have made another £20,000 if he wanted: 'He chartered numerous helicopter flights to zoom up and down the country for other beneficiaries and to raise money for Leukaemia Research. Others would've stayed put and feathered their own nest, but Beefy's a genuine, caring man who sticks to his word.'

Most beneficiaries look drained by the effort long before their year is over. Botham, never a man to count his pennies, took a broader view and enjoyed himself. When Derbyshire visited Somerset in mid-August, Geoff Miller expected to find his friend shattered by the travelling and praying for the end. Not Botham. When Somerset batted Botham rattled up 90 in 56 balls, reminding Miller of his promise a few years back that he would never block another ball from the off-spinner. By tea, Miller had gone for 174 runs and Botham, now out, joshed him unmercifully. Soon after the interval, Colin Dredge slammed Miller for six into the home dressing-room. That summer a snooker table had been installed beside the dressing-room and as Miller stood, waiting for the ball to be returned, he wondered what Botham was up to. He soon found out: Botham threw out one of the red snooker balls, shouting gleefully 'One hundred and eighty!' Miller responded by throwing that red into the River Tone.

Perhaps Botham was in particularly skittish mood because he no longer had to face the West Indies any more that summer. With England losing 5/0 under a new captain in David Gower, the press were looking around for scapegoats. They had been deluded into thinking that Gower's whimsical attitude to life would not seep into his cricket, that there would be an iron fist inside the velvet glove. They honestly believed that at 27, Gower would be transformed from a charming, civilised man of wide social interests into a Charlton Heston figure, storming the ramparts of Caribbean invincibility. This ignored the fact that Gower's attitude to nets and physical exercise matched that of Botham and that his time-keeping would have shamed even Shirley Williams or George

Best. There seemed to be a vague concept that a brilliant player who had served under Mike Brearley and Ray Illingworth must have learned a lot about tactical niceties, while Gower's two defiant hundreds in Pakistan appeared to ring with the stuff of leadership (his blatant time-wasting during the Lahore Test could be dismissed as a minor aberration). So a concerted press campaign sought to rid Gower of his Cavalier's ruffs in favour of the Puritan breast-plate. By the Second Test, they had to recognise that Gower's many cricketing talents did not include attention to detail; on the fourth evening, with England looking for quick runs, he failed to keep an eye on the batsmen out in the middle, for the simple reason that he was watching Wimbledon tennis on the dressing-room television. That evening and during the post-match press conference, Gower had his first experience of the glare from thwarted patronage.

Botham sympathised with his chum but generally kept his head down that series and got on with the cricket. His all-round figures were reasonable (second in England's batting averages and most wickets, 19, even if they did cost him 35 apiece), but he would not have been able to stem the tide even if he had turned up the figures of 1978–80. The West Indies bowled very well at him, bowling with accuracy and speed in the off-stump area to make him play at the ball, without letting him swing his arms and crash it through the off-side. The extra pace meant he could not adjust his shot in time and he was gradually worn down. They also tempted him with bouncers, knowing that he hooks in the air. Botham never suggested permanence as a result, but his was always the prized wicket. The delighted reactions from the West Indians at Botham's dismissals throughout that series demonstrated the respect in which he was held. Yet he batted well in three of the Tests. He twice chanced his arm at Birmingham, making 102 in the match, and in the second innings there was a typical exchange of views between captain and outgoing batsman on the Saturday evening:

Botham: 'What are the instructions, leader?'
Gower: 'I think you should hang on for the last half-hour.'
Botham: 'I think entertainment is called for, leader.'

He managed both to entertain and to stay in till Monday morning. After smashing Michael Holding for a six over mid-wicket, we had the bizarre sight of Marshall being warned for bowling too many bouncers at Botham, who was visibly enjoying the battle. Only 'Dickie' Bird, hopping around anxiously, took great exception to the barrage of bouncers. On the Monday, Botham was given out lbw by Barry Meyer; his reaction to the decision was typical, as Meyer recalls: 'He just looked at the line, never glanced at me and went off. On reflection, it was probably going down leg side, but he never said a word to me or caused a fuss. He knows full well that umpires are only human and make mistakes.' Botham was equally charitable in the next Test at Lord's, where Meyer admitted he had a bad match, giving some dubious lbws. Botham and Richards were both given out lbw in unfortunate circumstances but their differing reactions were graphic. Richards stood at the crease, awash with wounded pride and punctured hopes, only to make his way slowly back to the pavilion, expressing obvious disgust at being out 28 runs short of a century. Yet Botham missed his hundred by 19 runs on the Monday, and he was just as unlucky. He was given out lbw, but it only emerged in a chance remark a fortnight later that he had got an inside edge to the ball. No one would have known that from the way he walked off as soon as he was adjudged out. No wonder Barry Meyer says: 'He's a fine sportsman, who has never snarled to me about a decision. When he's bowling he might ask confirmation while walking past that the ball was going down legside just to get it right in his own mind, but he never complains to me. And if he nicks it, he's off like a shot.'

At Lord's Botham also managed to turn back the clock and swing the ball at speed to take eight wickets in the first innings. Yet it was his second innings effort that contributed to England's humiliating defeat by nine wickets. He had tried to talk Gower out of a declaration on the final morning because the wicket was too flat and the opposition batting too powerful, but Gower left them to get 342 in five-and-a-half hours and they cantered home. Botham went for six an over and Gower admits he kept him on too long: 'He asked for a large off-side field for Larry Gomes, then proceeded to go round the wicket to him and spear it in at the leg-stump. And although Beefy kept promising to sort it out, he didn't. That was the lowest ebb with his bowling that summer. On reflection I wasn't that fair to the other bowlers that series because I bowled Beefy a lot when the others wouldn't have done any worse. But Bob Willis was the only other proven wicket-taker and he was in the twilight and didn't last the series. The support bowling was inexperienced and Beefy was always liable to get you wickets.'

After Lord's he bowled badly in the next two Tests but at the Oval he responded to the quickest pitch of the series by running in with vigour to take eight wickets in the match. His reputation for salvaging

The classic lofted off-drive

The bowling action that has endured through so much hard work

A blow in the ribs from a Caribbean flyer, 1986

Left: Desmond Haynes is superbly taken in the slips

Above: Ian and Viv – soulmates in happier times

One of the numerous handshakes of thanks from the public during the Leukaemia walk from John O'Groats to Land's End

Scores of young fans seek Ian's autograph

Move over Paul Hogan!

The triumphant team in Australia, 1986/7

Another argument with the umpire? This time, Liam, Ian's son, gets a ticking off, during Botham's 1986 suspension

Botham's portrait is painted for the National Portrait Gallery – the first cricketer since W. G. Grace to receive this honour

lost causes remained so high that, on the final day, the media was still making optimistic noises as England resumed on 151 for 5, with the victory target another 224 runs away – this against the most fearsome bowling line-up in modern times on a fast wicket that favoured the bouncer. Yet Botham was unbeaten overnight and the memory of 1981 was still fresh. He failed, making only (!) 54 and the innings folded. The 'blackwash' was complete and English scapegoats were sought. Gower took a lot of the flak, just a few months since he had been hailed as the ideal leader to guide his men through the 1980s to greater glory. Odious comparisons were made about the depth of preparation for matches, with the West Indies working out for half-an-hour every morning, while England went through a perfunctory series of exercises that made them look simply aldermanic in contrast to the glistening, sweating West Indians. The press felt that England became fatalistic too soon in the series, although the press-box habitués did not have to go out and face the likes of Marshall and Garner on the unreliable pitches at Old Trafford and Leeds. A chat with Andy Lloyd or Paul Terry might have given some inkling of how it feels to be badly injured against bowling of that calibre. England did look blasé at times. At Old Trafford Pat Pocock returned to Test cricket after an absence of eight years and his delight was sincere. Pocock's off-spin proved about as useful as a barber on the steps of the guillotine, but that was of little account when you consider there was no one else around with superior credentials. Pocock's bubbling good humour and unquenchable optimism would shame any country vicar but he was disappointed to see that some of his England colleagues did not share his pleasure at walking out to face the West Indies. He was dismayed to hear Botham say 'Oh, not another bloody Test Match against this lot!' and when Fowler and Botham indulged in their usual dressing-room prank of throwing cakes and pad-whitener at everyone present, Pocock remained unimpressed. Over a drink he gave David Gower the benefit of his experience but, although the captain thanked him for his interest, Pocock felt he had made little headway. He came from a different generation, where Test matches were not so plentiful, money was more scarce and fast bowlers were not queuing up to knock your block off on unreliable pitches.

The scandal-mongers, fresh from their partial success in New Zealand, did their best to whip up a drunken orgy story during the Leeds Test. One Sunday newspaper worked itself up into a rage that the England players had been spotted drinking at the Junction pub in Otley on the Saturday night. There was nothing unusual in that, I had been there with them on previous Saturday nights during a Test. Most players have a Saturday night out because they know they are not playing next day. Even some of the former players now making a living out of commentating on the game's declining standards used to indulge in the same harmless activity. At least half that 1984 side were connoisseurs of real ale, and the Junction at Otley is recognised as one of the best purveyors of the amber nectar in the area. Were the players expected to cry into their solitary drinks in an impersonal hotel room? Were they denied the normal healthy pursuits in a pub because they had played badly? Would a hand of patience and some elderberry wine equip them to play Marshall and co with greater ease? The England players of 1984 did not drink any more than their predecessors in 1981 – the difference being that Brearley's team won more games. According to the Sunday newspaper, nothing less than a hair shirt would do for Gower's chastened duffers.

Later in the summer, Botham announced he would not be available to tour India in the winter. His friends and most of his England teammates were relieved; he needed a break, indeed it might have come two years earlier. Judging by a comment overheard by Paul Allott, the selectors were pleased for different reasons. It was the Sri Lanka Test at Lord's, the most embarrassing game that summer for England. As the match dawdled to a draw on the final evening, Botham turned to off-spin with the amused permission of his captain. Botham has always fancied himself as an off-spinner, although one suspects the intellectual battles between batsman and off-spinner would not appeal for long to his turbulent temperament. It so happened that Allott was off the field and lying down in the dressing-room after treatment, out of sight of the chairman of selectors, Peter May. When Botham started to bowl off-breaks, May tut-tutted: 'What the hell's going on now? What's he bowling? Something's got to be done, this can't go on.' It did not ease the chairman's peace of mind that Botham took some wickets, but it was clear to Allott that his friend was far from the flavour of the month in the selectors' eyes. His absence from the India tour was probably a blessed relief to them; heaven only knows how often he would have asked to bowl off-spin out there.

So Botham settled down to comparative obscurity on South Humberside, or as near to obscurity as someone of his status can achieve. He played soccer for Scunthorpe with his customary dash and when he failed to break into the first team, he played for Yeovil Town at weekends. His close friends, Richard and Debbie Lines, put him up when he was playing for Yeovil and he even stunned them by occasionally baby-sitting while they went out to the pub! Richard had been a drinking partner of Ian's ever since the days when he used to borrow money to get into the 88400 Club – Richard's reaction to those who castigate Botham is that 'he hasn't got any enemies that really know him'. Yet Botham was soon to discover that he had enemies in influential circles. At 6 pm on New Year's Eve, two plain-clothes policemen knocked on the Bothams' door and asked to speak to Ian. They said that a small packet of drugs had been found in Ian's trousers that had been sent to the cleaners a few days earlier and that they had a warrant to search his house. Kath was flabbergasted at the idea and even more astonished when Ian was asked to go to the police station. Later Ian rang from there and asked if Kath would also go down to the police station. For the next three hours, Kath and Ian were questioned separately and, for Kath, the whole episode resembled one of those 'mistaken identity' melodramas. Just before midnight, the Bothams were released separately and reached home within ten minutes of each other. It emerged that they had both been arrested on drugs-related matters and that they had been released on bail. The police said they had also found a quantity of cannabis in a chest of drawers in their bedroom. The balloon went up and the papers were full of 'Drugs Raid on Botham's New Year's Eve Party', the implication being that everyone was smoking dope at a wild party. In reality it was only a quiet, intimate family gathering which was to have included their grandparents.

Eventually no action was taken against Kath while Ian was charged with possession of 1.9 grammes of cannabis, just enough to put in a cigarette, about one-thirteenth of an ounce. On 14 February 1985 Botham pleaded guilty to the offence and was fined £100 by Scunthorpe Magistrates. Henceforth Botham could be referred to as 'convicted on a drugs charge' as if he were a drugs baron. To this day, the Bothams are convinced they were set up. Their solicitor, Alan Herd, had picked up rumours on the legal grapevine that the police on South Humberside were keeping an eye on Botham, while Ian later confirmed that he was sure he had been followed for a week or two before the police raid. He swears he knew nothing about the cannabis or how it came to be in his socks drawer and Kath confirms she had just cleaned out the drawer and found nothing. In the police notes given to the magistrate, it was stated that Ian had refused permission to search his house until a search warrant was obtained – this was categorically untrue. The Bothams are sure that the police had not forgotten the fraças outside the Scunthorpe night club in 1980, nor the fact that the case against Ian was not carried. Furthermore, on New Year's Eve, there had been no noise from the Bothams' house, no complaints from neighbours to the police – yet they arrived on the door step at six in the evening. It seemed a strange time to carry out a search.

The attendant publicity lost Ian a lucrative deal with a stationery firm, while Saab asked for the return of their car, and confirmed that the company was looking elsewhere to spread its sponsorship budget. Duncan Fearnley remained loyal, so did Nike, the sports equipment company – such faith prompted Botham to suggest they ran an advert for his cricket shoes with the slogan 'Botham's back on the grass again'! It was a rare shaft of humour amid the gloom. For his legions of admirers and many friends, it was a worrying time. His growing number of critics saw the drugs episode as a further drift towards anarchy, that Botham was now too big for his boots. People in high places were growling that something had to be done about Botham. He was about to come a cropper, or so they thought – but they reckoned without his famous resilience and ability to play cricket rather well.

8

Hudson's Hero

•

Even by Botham's standards, the year 1985 contained enough melodrama to satisfy the most demanding of film producers. It began with the drugs case hanging over him, threatening his cricket career and ended with his popularity at its highest peak as a result of his famous walk for Leukaemia Research. In between, he kept the disciplinary committee busy at Lord's, took on a new manager who changed his image, became a father for the third time, took more wickets than anyone else in the Ashes series, and set up a new record for sixes hit in a first-class season.

Botham's first big test was to get back in the England team after his winter break, and there appeared to be two obstacles. First the drugs conviction: could the Test and County Cricket Board sanction the recall of a man who had been associated with drugs, however minimally? Despite the views of a few voluble backwoodsmen that Botham was an anarchic product of the permissive society, sanity prevailed and he was cleared to play for England against Australia, if selected. Would he be selected? As David Gower's squad performed splendidly in India, one or two newspaper stories were filtering back to the effect that it was a much happier party without Botham. A couple of quotes were gleaned from players, who were predictably not named, to the effect that Botham was a damaging influence on morale, that he was just too powerful an individual to absorb into a unit. Scandal was non-existent compared to the previous year, when Botham was in the tour party. Judging by the comments of the cricket correspondents, the relationship between players and media was now almost as mellow as a gathering of hippies and as frank as a marriage guidance council meeting. The experience of

Mike Gatting was offered as evidence – at last the chrysalis of tentative failure had bloomed into the butterfly of prolific Test runs and assertive vice-captaincy. It seems hard that Botham should have been held partially responsible for Gatting's previous failures at Test level over the last seven years: was Botham operating the strings when Gatting twice padded up at Lord's for plumb lbws against the 1984 West Indians? It is not as if Gatting has ever been the shy, retiring sort likely to be bullied by Botham. Perhaps it was more relevant that he at last had a role to play in the tour party as David Gower's sergeant-major, while at the same time he finally got Test hundreds on flat wickets.

Who would have told the press on that Indian tour that they were better off without Botham? Phil Edmonds? He has always enjoyed an excellent relationship with the media, dropping wicked items of gossip into the conversation and relishing his role as the Hedda Hopper of cricket, but he pleads not guilty: 'I don't recall any of the players expressing relief that Beefy wasn't with us. Others grew into the vacant spot, like Gatt, but it's up to the individuals to stand up for themselves when Beefy's in the dressing-room. I've always found him a good man, loyal, not vindictive, generally well-intentioned. Just because he does the occasional stupid thing doesn't mean he isn't popular. All I can think of in relation to the India trip was that if he had been there, Pat Pocock and I wouldn't have got to bowl so many overs, because David Gower had faith in Beefy's Golden Arm, but that doesn't add up to all that much.' The captain agrees: 'I suppose it made a good story, but it was just a case of working with the people you have on tour and forgetting who's not with you. Beefy's a big man in every sense and you always know when he's around. I'm quite sure he would've fitted in perfectly well if he'd been with us in India.'

With the Australians due in 1985, it was time for the press to indulge in their 'Botham at the Crossroads' features. He was compared with George Best, and moralistic sermons about squandering his God-given talent before he had reached thirty were churned out. It was suggested that oblivion was impatiently drumming its fingers for the man who now saw himself as bigger than the game. Such homilies were about as futile as a clock in an empty house; anyone who knew Botham fully expected him to come storming back into prominence because he faced a challenge. Nothing stirs him more than to be written off by people who want him out of the Test arena. He was also well aware that the men chosen to fill the all-rounder's berth in India had failed. In five Tests, Chris Cowdrey had averaged 19 with the bat and taken four wickets at 72 apiece, while Richard Ellison had averaged three and his four wickets in three Tests also cost him 72 a time. Hardly the kind of figures to worry a man with 13 Test hundreds and more than 300 wickets to his name, least of all one who was fully rested after his winter at home. He was fit and a fortnight's cricket in Barbados in April had helped him find some ominously good batting form.

By the start of the 1985 season, Botham had a new manager and a new image. He had engaged the services of one Tim Hudson, a garrulous character who told Ian pleasant things about himself which he was more than happy to accept. For the next year, until Hudson shot himself in the foot with a fatal indiscretion, he provided an amusing diversion in the life and times of Ian Botham. He had a habit of talking in exclamation marks and a feel for hyperbole that would have shamed Phineas T. Barnum. At various times, Hudson marketed Ian as cricket's Errol Flynn, Cary Grant, Lord Nelson and Winston Churchill, and he predicted great things for his young hero when they finally got to Hollywood. Hudson was long on rhetoric and short on facts. He liked to quote conversations with Howard Hughes – even though Hughes had been a recluse since Hudson had been in diapers – and he purported to have made a fortune in business in America. It was hard to take seriously a man who called his daughter 'River' but Ian did for a long time, much to the distress of his friends. To this day Trevor Gard cannot understand why he and Peter Denning worked out Hudson in ten minutes, while it took Ian a whole year. Richard Lines remembers this period as the most strained in their relationship. Ian's mother admits she was taken in initially, although Les was more sceptical once he had quizzed Hudson closely about certain imminent deals with a clothes company. Kath also felt Hudson's intentions were honourable and that Ian ought to be marketed better with an eye on their security; a few months later, when she realised that Hudson had no plans for a wife and family in his grand design, she changed her mind. By this time, Reg Hayter had sadly parted company with Ian because he simply could not see himself working with Hudson and felt that his grandiose schemes were unsuitable for a top sportsman. The rest is histrionics.

In Hudson's defence it must be said that he helped Ian when he was psychologically low. After the drugs case, several influential companies backed away from Botham, in a commercial version of Orson Welles' epigram: 'When you're down and out, something always turns up – and it's usually the noses of your friends.' Hudson did not. Whether from genuine concern or as a long-term financial expedient we shall never know, but he rang Ian and offered a shoulder at the right time. They had met briefly in the United States in the autumn of 1981 when Botham was on a benefit tour and they had got on well enough. This time Hudson told Botham that he could make him mega-rich, that he deserved much more than he had been getting and that cricket was only a small part of his appeal. An acting career would broaden his appeal, an opinion that amused Graeme Fowler, who recalled Botham's attempt at a commercial in Australia in 1982: 'We all turned up to do this commercial for JVC, the electronics firm who were sponsoring the England tour, and the recording took ages, simply because Beefy couldn't say "five speed shuttle search". I could just see him taking screen tests in Hollywood!' It was all good copy for incredulous media folk, even if much of it – like Botham posing as Rambotham with a machine gun in his hand – portrayed Ian in a dull-witted light. Yet it must not be forgotten that Hudson relaxed Botham, broadened his horizons and amused him with his tales of his disc-jockey days in California. It mattered not if they were true, or that Hudson was dining out on his relationship with 'Mr Botham', name-dropping with fervour – Ian liked him and his cricket prospered under Hudson's influence.

By now cricket was no longer the epicentre of his life, even though he continued to play it exceptionally well. Rock music and its unconventional world appealed to him more and more. The friendship with Elton John burgeoned, as did that with Mick Jagger of the Rolling Stones – Botham was astonished at the detailed questions about the game that Jagger fired at him. In 1984 Botham met Eric Clapton, by common consent the greatest rock guitarist of his generation, and a friendship blossomed into an intimate understanding of each other's business. David English, formerly the president of Clapton's record company, introduced them during the Lord's Test against the West Indies – Botham was amused that Clapton had tried to get into the pavilion without a jacket and he loaned him his England blazer and tie to get through the inscrutable gatemen. Such a typically English social convention appealed to both men's sense of humour and they hit it off straightaway. Clapton sees his friend as a thwarted rock star: 'He envies my world because we don't seem to be hassled by the kind of petty restrictions you get in cricket, like being told what to wear. Rock and roll has always been anti-Establishment which appeals to Beefy. He's a buccaneer, a risk-taker and that's why he's so charismatic – he's come through and beaten the system.' Like Botham, Andy Peebles straddles the worlds of rock music and cricket. For eight years he presented a record show on BBC Radio 1 on Friday nights that focused on the close link between music and top sportsmen. 'So many sportsmen understand the pressures these guys are under when they go out on stage, there's a natural empathy there. Every sportsman I know loves music and there's a great mutual respect between Beefy, Elton John and Eric Clapton. Elton and Eric know that Ian's almost a rock music figure in the sense that you prosper if you have an outstanding God-given talent. Cricket is run by some frightfully nice people but they don't really understand Ian, he's a one-off.'

By the summer of 1985, Botham was seen dining in places like Joe Allen's, the chic Covent Garden brasserie where the glitterati of the theatre and the media mingle with the rock world. Andy Peebles went along there one night with Botham, Allan Lamb and David Gower and their companions were Tim Rice and the actor Robin Askwith. The Lancastrians Graeme Fowler and Paul Allott were also part of the group and, as the champagne flowed, Fowler realised he was getting out of his class: 'I whispered to Paul that I only had twenty quid on me, as the bubbly kept coming, but Beefy and Tim Rice looked after the bill, thank God. It was another world, and yet these rock stars are just as awe-struck in our presence as we are in theirs. Earlier that day, Mick Jagger and Eric Clapton came into our dressing-room at Lord's and you could see how chuffed they were to be there. I remember when we first met Elton John in New Zealand in '84: we went out to dinner with him and he said to me, "You know I've been nervous about this all day."'

So Ian was happy with his widening circle of friends, secure in the knowledge that he was admired by leading figures in another branch of the entertainment industry. He no longer saw himself as belonging exclusively to cricket, it was now just a field of endeavour at which he excelled. There were other spheres that would soon attract his boyish zeal but, for the moment, he just enjoyed his cricket, in the process playing marvellously. The fine, warm start to the 1985 summer meant a succession of firm pitches down in Somerset and Botham started off in scintillating form with the bat. A masterful hundred against Gla-morgan and a dazzling 149 against Hampshire, with Marshall bouncing him and being crashingly hooked into the bargain, suggested that Botham's hitting was now more secure, more controlled. Both hundreds were reached off 76 balls and old pros were spreading the word that the winter's rest had done Botham a power of good. By the time he got to Old Trafford for the first of the one-day internationals against Australia, he was in prime form. He was deservedly placed above Gatting in the order and responded by making a thrilling 72.

Only the manner of his dismissal disappointed: he tried a reverse sweep against the off-spin of Greg Matthews and was bowled. Typically Botham credited the bowler with a brainy piece of bowling and for having the courage to continue pitching the ball up, but the howls of disapproval from the press-box went up, especially as England lost a game they were dominating when Botham was in full flow. The views of the chairman of selectors were sought and Peter May let it be known that he had told Botham to cut out the reverse sweep from his wide repertoire of shots. Now that message was about as likely as Dracula giving up blood for Lent. All the chairman said was, 'Do you really need to play it?', but the tabloids preferred to whip up yet another spurious confrontation between exasperated chairman and self-indulgent star. It is not as if Botham had been sparing in its use in recent years. He played it against the medium-pacers in India on the 1981/2 tour, he was bowled by Hadlee trying it in a one-day international in New Zealand in 1984 and it got him out at the Oval in 1982 after he had hammered the Indians for 208. In the same summer, in the Old Trafford Test, he used the reverse sweep on his way to a courageous hundred. No one pestered Peter May for his observations after those innings. One can understand the disappointment at seeing Botham dismissed when he was playing so wonderfully well, but that free spirit within him makes him play with such panache. One weekend in 1983, he was bowled by Ray East trying the dreaded reverse sweep, yet the following day he got off the mark with it at Trent Bridge, and then proceeded to enjoy a rare, long partnership with Viv Richards that is still spoken of with awe by the Nottinghamshire bowlers. Eddie Hemmings (8-0-88-1) says it was 'a fantastic exhibition of hitting, I just couldn't bowl at those two'. Clive Rice remembers throwing the ball to Richard Hadlee with the words, 'Good luck, I'm going to enjoy this.' Richards and Botham added 138 in 13 overs and everyone on the ground felt privileged to have been there. A month later, Ian again got himself out to the reverse sweep, against David Acfield at Taunton, and Somerset lost the match. You win some, you lose some – the kind of attitude that has made him a dynamic performer. He deserves credit for trying to extemporise against the stranglehold of limited-overs field-setting. When the reverse sweep has got Botham out, it has normally been due to picking the wrong length for the shot.

While Peter May told the press that he could not see the stroke in the MCC Coaching Manual (as if that ended the argument, no one pointed out to him that it had been played a hundred years earlier by public school paragons like Sir T. C. O'Brien, A. J. Webbe and A. H. Hornby. K. S. Duleepsinjhi played it in a game in India in 1929, eight years after P. G. H. Fender had trumped Warwick Armstrong's packed legside field in the Old Trafford Test. The Pakistanis, Mushtaq Mohammed, his brother Hanif and Javed Miandad, have picked up hundreds of runs with the reverse sweep, and the Australians David Hookes and the Chappell brothers had all played it with success before Botham's aberration in 1985. It would have been better just to regret that Botham had got himself out when well set while allowing him to make his own judgements about how to bat, something he does rather better than most cricketers who have memorised the MCC Coaching Manual. Such strictures only enrage a player determined to plough his own individualistic furrow.

Botham has never been able to understand why the more idiosyncratic aspects of his game are not accepted, or at least understood. For years he has treated net practice as an excuse to attack low-flying aircraft with a few howitzers from his bat and that enrages those who feel that a Boycott approach is best for all. This ignores the occasions when Botham has throttled back on the macho aggression and played properly in the nets for a purpose, as Norman Gifford recalls: 'I was the assistant manager on the Australian tour of 1982/3 and now and again, if the spinners were on, and the wicket was a little dodgy, he'd shout to me, "I'll show you I can play properly, Giffie!" and he did for about a quarter of an hour. He'd then show you as good a technique as you'd want to see.' Keith Andrew, who has been associated with the game for the best part of forty years and is now Chief Executive and Director of Coaching at the National Cricket Association, based at Lord's, believes that Botham's approach in the nets is absolutely right for a player of his type: 'You *should* practise hitting sixes, especially with so much limited-overs cricket around. A batsman is now required to belt the ball out of the ground in a match, so why not try to get the shot working? It's like saying to Sevvy Ballesteros, "Don't work at your driving because you don't need to hit it a long way in practice; just concentrate on your putting." In cricket, if you want to drive the ball a long way you need to develop a good swing, just as in golf. Ian Botham's the most correct hitter I've seen, with that wonderful follow-through and the excellent position of his head.'

What about his unique stance in the slips? Surely the hands-on-thighs position is not advisable? Keith Andrew again supports Botham: 'It may look bad, but watch where his hands are when the ball is coming off the edge of the bat. If you get too low down, it is difficult to get up and then go down again in an instant, whereas Ian is at halfway house. I was the same as a wicket-keeper, I put my gloves on my knees as the ball was delivered – and people were kind enough to talk about my good technique. Look at the best goal-keepers when they are waiting to face a penalty kick, they don't get down too low. You should graduate to a position, rather than taking up one too early. I find it funny when the commentators and press suggest that Ian's technique is poor – I firmly believe it is orthodox in all facets of his game.'

Botham says he worked out his attitude to slip catching when he was just a boy (one remembers the discussion he had with his father, Len, on the subject) before anyone took him at all seriously as a player: 'I can't understand why slips are told to crouch rigidly because that leads to tension, which is hopeless if you want to catch a cricket ball. Slip catching is all about reactions, about letting the ball hit your hands. I make sure I come up slowly at the last possible instant, so that I am still relaxed and can go with the ball. I'm lucky with my eyesight, of course – I've got 20/20 vision – but that wouldn't be much use unless I was in the right position for the snick.'

Botham continued to take blinding catches from his distinctive stance at second slip during that 1985 summer. Two in the Oval Test will linger in the memory – a high, leaping one in the right hand to catch Lawson and a low one to his left off a McDermott snick. Breathtaking efforts, the product of swift reactions, marvellous eyesight and the comforting knowledge that he was operating in the manner that suited him best. He felt comfortable standing closer than the other slips, confident that he would at least be able to get a hand on the snick rather than take it frustratingly on the second bounce. With the ball, he also defied the orthodox predictions. Rising thirty, with many wearying spells now behind him, it had been generally accepted that Botham's bowling would continue to decline. Botham had read all the forecasts and was ready. At the start of the series he suggested to David Gower that he felt fit enough to be used as a strike bowler, rather than as a stock bowler picking up expensive wickets from long spells. That suited Gower: he had come to the same opinion after concluding that he had over-bowled Botham against the West Indies and now he would be used in short bursts. At Lord's he roared in to take five wickets for the twenty-fifth time in Tests. More startling than that statistic was the manner of its achievement. He bowled faster at Lord's than for several years: one ball that reared up past the nose of Allan Border was the quickest seen in the match. Paul Downton, who kept wicket for England that series, says that after Lord's Botham bowled quickly for the rest of the summer: 'He really got himself steamed up at Lord's and it seemed to inspire him after that. The crowd got behind him and you could feel the adrenalin pumping. He bowled so aggressively, a lot of it short-pitched, and he physically intimidated the batsmen. The Aussies didn't fancy him at all at Lord's, he got them unbalanced. Hilditch started hooking at everything and Ritchie didn't know whether to hook or to duck. Beefy never bowls to a pattern and batsmen don't like that, they never know what to expect of him. They start swatting and swishing instead of just picking him off.'

In the next Test at Trent Bridge, however, his full-blooded commitment landed him in yet another vat of hot disciplinary water. Just after tea on the third day, Botham and umpire Alan Whitehead had what might euphemistically be called a difference of opinion. The end product was a barrow-load of cant and a fuss that was totally out of proportion. I have already written that Botham is on extremely good terms with English umpires, with the notable exception of Alan Whitehead. On the county circuit Whitehead gets consistently good marks, but he is deemed a hard-liner at the wrong times when a spot of tact or 'Dickie' Bird-style humour might defuse a tense situation. That was all that was needed at Trent Bridge that day. Botham had been brought back with the new ball as Australia climbed past 300 with just five wickets down. Gower had asked Botham for one final, lung-bursting effort. With Allott and Sidebottom off the field, there was only one man who could make the breakthrough with the new ball on a flat wicket. Off Botham's first ball, Gatting dropped Wood at slip. He then trapped Ritchie with a nip-backer, but Whitehead turned down the fervent appeal for lbw. Next ball, Ritchie was athletically caught by Edmonds, diving in at third-man. As the fielders ran to Edmonds, Whitehead stood there, with his arm outstretched, calling a 'no-ball' on the front foot. The call had come late, fairly 'sotto voce' and had not influenced Ritchie's stroke. Soon after that Ritchie edged Botham over the heads of the slips. Then he bowled a bouncer, only to be told by the umpire that he had now exceeded his ration – this against two established batsmen on a benign pitch! Then Botham was warned for running down the pitch in his follow-through. By now Botham was furious, his pores were well and truly open and he called over to his captain at mid-on to do something about Whitehead's decisions. He shouted to Gower that he did not want to get involved, knowing full well that he would say something he would later regret. All this was going out live on television, but the foreshortening of the camera made it look as if Botham was shouting and swearing at the umpire, which was not so – he was addressing himself to Gower, making the reasonable point that he hardly ever bowls a no-ball, that the umpire had refused to tell him how far over the line he had gone and that Whitehead said Ritchie had got a bat on the ball that trapped him in front of the stumps, when he had palpably missed it. It looked bad, it sounded bad out in the middle, but Gower did a good job in calming down Botham and the game proceeded along more orderly lines.

On the rest day the papers enjoyed themselves hugely. Peter May admitted he had not seen the incident because he was driving home at the time – yet he reacted to the bellicose moralising by ordering an inquiry. Former players who had never crossed swords with anyone on the field of play vied with each other to denounce the unruly egotist who was making umpires' lives a misery. It was sad that men who had played for their country, who had been out in the middle when flash-points occurred, should show such a lack of sympathy. They, of all people, ought to have understood that the camera definition of the Botham/Whitehead incident was distorted. Even the House of Commons, that bastion of civilised behaviour joined in, with Botham being lambasted for 'petulance and histrionic behaviour': one would have thought those worthies had more important matters to debate than a spat on the cricket field. Six weeks later, on the eve of the Oval Test, Botham was summoned to Lord's by the TCCB's disciplinary committee. The hearing lasted four hours and it concluded that Botham had been guilty of dissent amounting to misconduct on the field, likely to bring the game into disrepute. He was reprimanded and warned about his future conduct. David Gower, who spoke on behalf of Botham at the hearing, felt it was a complete waste of time: 'The whole incident never needed to go this far. I'd sorted it out perfectly amicably, Beefy breathed life back into the game, which I wanted, and we had forty minutes' or so of very exciting cricket, which the public wants to see. You've got to allow for the dynamism of the man, for the fact that he gets pumped up to deliver the goods. Kill that off and you kill the atmosphere and the bloke's magical touch. Beefy wasn't swearing directly at Alan, he was just letting off understandable steam at me, a long way from the umpire. When we got to the hearing, there was a distinct air of cracking down on Beefy for the sake of it, never mind the rights and wrongs of the issue.'

Greg Ritchie offered to speak on Botham's behalf at the disciplinary hearing, but the tour management refused permission. Ritchie told me that he had every sympathy for Botham: 'I didn't get a nick on the ball that trapped me in front and when I got up to Beefy's end, he asked me if I'd nicked it. I told him I hadn't and he went spare. I could understand his frustrations, but he wasn't addressing them directly to the umpire, he was swearing out loud about his bad luck. That's fair enough, he was unlucky and he was giving his all for his country out there. I was amazed that such a fuss was made of the incident.' For his part Botham points out that, in Test cricket, he has bowled three no-balls to his recollection – one when he went wide of the crease and the other two on the front foot, both called by Alan Whitehead. No one would call Ian Botham a disciplined bowler, but since he worked out his run-up on the Pakistan tour in 1977, he has hardly bowled a no-ball. Sometimes he may not appear to know where he is projecting the ball, but he always knows where his feet are landing.

The crowd's reaction at the Oval assured Botham that he was more welcome in the affections of the average cricket fan than with the beaks at Lord's. The punters preferred to remember his all-round skills that summer, particularly his six-hitting. He had broken Arthur Wellard's fifty-year-old record of sixes hit in a first-class season (66) and if he had not injured a toe and missed the last fortnight of the season, he would undoubtedly have improved on his tally of 80. I sought the opinion of 'Sam' Cook, the former Gloucestershire spinner who played against Wellard many times and also enjoyed umpiring games involving Botham. He has no doubt that Botham was the better all-round hitter: 'Arthur could hit just as far straight back over the bowler's head, but he couldn't play the hook shot like Both. Arthur was more firm-footed, with a wonderful eye, but Ian seems to be able to judge the length of the ball better and, with his good footwork, he gets to the pitch of the ball. He is definitely one of the great entertainers of my time – and don't forget I also played with Wally Hammond.'

Two games at Edgbaston epitomised Botham's controlled hitting in 1985. In the Test Match, he was sent out to get quick runs before the declaration. The Australian bowlers were demoralised at the sight of Botham striding forth at 572 for 4, with the crowd baying for something spectacular. McDermott's first ball went back over his head into the executive boxes for six and the third suffered the same fate. In seven balls, he made 18 before Jeff Thomson caught him on the square leg boundary off a full toss and he retired grinning from ear to ear. That night the Australians crumpled, lost five wickets and, in effect, the match, but after a day of prolific English batting and penetrative bowling, all the talk around the ground concerned seven deliveries faced by Botham.

Three weeks earlier he had stayed rather longer at the Edgbaston crease and played a fantastic innings, there is no other adjective applicable. Old hands like Dennis Amiss, Norman Gifford and David Brown vied with each other to pay tribute to him. On the final morning, Somerset led by 118 with just five wickets left when Botham came in at 12.28 pm. The ball was turning sharply and Norman Gifford was licking his lips, the old pro looking for a few cheap wickets. Yet Botham cruised to an astonishing century in just 26 scoring strokes; 94 of his first 100 runs came in boundaries, in exactly 50 balls. In just half-an-hour before lunch, he made 74. In all, he hit Norman Gifford for eight sixes, three off the off-spinner Adrian Pierson and two off the medium pacer, Dean Hoffman. When he declared, Botham was 138 not out off 65 balls in 67 minutes. One of the first to congratulate him as he came off the field was the then Warwickshire manager, David Brown, an England bowler twenty years earlier and a man not given to lavish praise: 'I watched that innings as a fan, once I knew that Beefy had no intention of letting us run away with the game. It was a phenomenal display of hitting. He got into position and played high-class attacking shots at will.'

Botham was not just hitting through the line of the ball, relying on his immense power and innate timing to clear Edgbaston's long boundaries. The ball was turning for the two spinners and everyone else had been in trouble. The bowlers tried their hardest and Gifford and Pierson fully expected to get him every over. Of his 13 sixes all but two of them were hit in the arc between long-off and long-on. Those off Gifford from the Pavilion end would all have been a carry of a hundred yards if they had not struck the building. Gifford, a man who has laboured honourably and successfully in English cricket for almost thirty years, was dumbfounded at Botham's nerve and clean hitting: 'In one over he came down the wicket and hit two sixes back over my head yet I beat him on the outside three times that same over and he just grinned at me and said, "Hard luck, Giffie." Other batsmen would have used their feet and got down to the pitch of the ball and done nothing with it, but Beefy went all the way and trusted his driving on a turning pitch. It takes a lot of self-belief to do that. He can dominate you with one stroke – after he hits you for six, he'll stand there as if to say, "Now what are you going to do?"'

Dennis Amiss, another much-admired cricketer who became a professional at Edgbaston in 1958, finds it hard to remember an innings that made such an impact on him. He stood at slip throughout Botham's *blitzkrieg* and was amazed at the way Botham played offensively and defensively with a consistently straight bat: 'It was powerhouse stuff from a great player. There can't be anything worse for a bowler to bowl a good ball and see it sail out of the ground. I truly revel to see an Englishman play like he does – and I only hope his example will inspire youngsters to bat like him.' As John Hampshire, one of the umpires, remarked whimsically, 'When Beefy bats like that, you need to give the fielders bus-passes to go and find the ball. I've never seen an innings like that one, everyone out there was dumb-struck, apart from Beefy who was his usual cheerful self.'

If Botham's batting was affording him great joy, the same could not be said of his time as Somerset captain. The 1985 season was a disaster for Somerset – bottom of the table for the first time since 1969, with only a quarter-final place in the Benson and Hedges Cup as scant consolation. Botham only played in ten of the county's 24 first-class games, due to international calls and a toe injury, and although he averaged 100 with the bat, he took just eleven first-class wickets. Somerset's poor season was hardly the full responsibility of Botham but it is clear that, if he had not resigned, the captaincy would have been taken away from him. He was a good captain when play began – full of ideas, all of them positive, and he led by example – but he would only bowl when he felt like it, conserving his energies for England or the one-day games, and he was irked by the minutiae involved in the job. Tim Hudson's dictate meant that Ian was often missing from the county ground when important matters needed to be thrashed out on behalf of the players, and to the young professionals who had not grown up with Botham, he was now a distant, awesome figure to whom they found it difficult to relate. Brian Langford, at that time Somerset's cricket committee chairman, says that Ian would have lost the captaincy after his first year (in 1984), but they kept faith with him after the bad publicity of the drugs conviction. 'We didn't want to see Ian being kicked when he was down. We felt we owed him some public support.' In the event, Botham handed over the job to Peter Roebuck in September 1985 with as much public grace as he could muster. Within a year they would have the kind of relationship Margaret Thatcher enjoys with Edward Heath.

Botham asked for just a one-year contract in 1985, rather than the proffered two years, and the negotiations revealed much about Hudson's commercial *nous*. After grandly announcing that he was too busy to travel down to Taunton and that he would be seeking at least £35,000 for one more year with Somerset, Hudson prepared to be visited by the Somerset delegation. The club secretary, cricket chairman and treasurer duly presented themselves at Hudson's Cheshire retreat. Realising that they would not wish to be in his company for all that long, they had taken the precaution of booking lunch at a nearby golf club, with the promise of eighteen holes in the afternoon. They smiled knowingly as Hudson theatrically delayed his entrance in the best Hollywood manner. When he finally swept in and imperiously demanded a fee of £35,000, the Somerset delegation rose to go. Hudson, realising he had been rumbled and fearful of Botham's reaction, backed down instantly. In the end the deal was agreed at a figure £1,000 less than Somerset expected to pay, around half of Hudson's initial gambit. It was an enjoyable afternoon's golf!

By autumn 1985 the own goals were beginning to pile up in the Hudson net. He had unwisely mentioned to Brian Close that Ian's future career would take off in the States as long as he could be marketed as the bachelor sex symbol, breaking the hearts of girls with his smouldering on-screen persona. Hudson confided in Close that he would ensure that Kath and the children would be well looked after, as long as they faded into the background, with a healthy divorce settlement soothing Kath's angst. Close, as befits a close friend of the Wallers and godfather to Kath, gave Hudson a piece of his mind. By now, Kath was under no illusions about Tim Hudson. It was not just that she felt Ian looked bizarre at times in the Hudson range of clothes, it was not just that Ian was always being exhorted to stay at Hudson's house, rather than come home to Yorkshire – it was because Ian seemed to be believing the twaddle that Hudson pedalled. In Hudson's eyes, Ian's social and professional horizons were endless, and Ian began to think he might be right. He started to behave like a mega-star, and anyone who voiced doubts about Hudson's acumen was off the Christmas card list. It was a worrying time for Duncan Fearnley, Ian's bat manufacturer and friend. Hudson told him, 'What you pay Mr Botham is chicken-feed, we will have to re-negotiate.' He tried to buy Fearnley's business to market his bats with the Hudson colours rather than the Fearnley logo. Fearnley would not accede to the summons to Hudson Hall, so Hudson came down to his Worcester factory and hectored him. Luckily Fearnley had

Botham under contract until March the following year, otherwise he is convinced it would have led to the parting of the ways.

Fortunately for Ian, and for all his friends and his family, his great walk for Leukaemia Research interrupted Hudson's Walter Mitty fantasies, and Hudson took himself off to pave the way for Ian's trip to Hollywood while Botham involved himself in more worthy pursuits. Here again Hudson miscalculated his client, making it quite clear that he disapproved of such a venture, that the next few weeks would have been spent more constructively hanging out in Hollywood bars, hoping to catch the eye of someone who knew the sister of a cook who worked for a film producer. Botham took umbrage at Hudson's total misunderstanding of his character. The Leukaemia Walk was important to him, it had been something he had discussed time and again with Kath as they tramped over the Lake District during their annual Easter vacation. It would prove to be the greatest achievement of Botham's life thus far, something that gave him more satisfaction than any other sporting performance. At last Botham managed to do something that made his detractors realise that underneath the veneer of boorishness, there lurked a compassionate, sincere man. Those of us who joined him at various stages of that walk could only wonder at the depth of physical and mental resources needed to get from John O'Groats to Land's End, a total of 874 miles in five weeks. Those who criticised Botham for failing to stop to sign autographs never understood how important a settled rhythm is when you are clocking up around 30 miles a day. The woman who jostled Botham for an autograph as he walked through Taunton was undoubtedly well-meaning but she has no idea of the agony she caused Botham's back. At one stage, Botham had to stop for treatment on the trapped nerve in his back and, for the next few days, he was in great pain. When Botham jostled a policeman on top of Bodmin Moor in driving sleet and rain, his psychological condition must be taken into account. He was still suffering from the injured nerve in his back when he heard that Phil Rance, one of the four who walked all the way, had been moved on brusquely by the police while answering a call of nature in a nearby field. Botham, annoyed that the heroic Rance had been treated unsympathetically, reacted sharply and the incident made worldwide news. The police took no further action and the matter was smoothed over – but it was clear that Botham was expected to have the sweet temper of an angel, while his body was submitting itself to daily, draining torture.

Chris Lander, a journalist who only intended to join the walk on the

first day, offers an interesting insight into Botham's powers of inspiration, and his need for company: 'After the first day, he said to me
over dinner, "If you can walk for 32 miles like you did today, you must
be able to carry on", which struck me as bizarre logic. Next morning
he told me that I would always regret it if I packed up now, I'd wonder
how far I could've gone, that I had a chance to find myself, to dig deep
into my own soul. I lasted the second day, when Ian and I had a private
walk, ahead of the rest for 36 miles. He never admitted how much pain
he was in, but I saw it. After the second day, the physio told him not
to run any more, just to keep walking, otherwise he had no chance of
finishing. His ankles were in such an awful state so early in the walk
that they couldn't take the strain of running. With such inspiration
coming from Ian, I just couldn't leave him, I had to go for it.'

Many others felt the same as Botham's example drove them on. One's
admiration for the four who lasted the whole trip (Botham, Lander,
Rance and John Border, brother of Allan, Australia's captain), remains
immense – it was an unbelievable performance. Some cynics suggested
that Botham was undertaking the walk as a form of atonement for
recent misdeeds – well, that ignores the fact that he had planned it for
years, and that it was a mighty long way to walk just to get some
favourable publicity. Anyone who saw the tears in his eyes as he met
leukaemia sufferers would have stumbled over the real reason why Ian
Botham gave up five weeks of his time. Anyone who saw him wrapped
in blankets after each day's walk would understand how much it took
out of him, how unfair it was to expect him to attend every function
arranged in the evening by a well-meaning but parochial group. There
were times when Ian could hardly climb the stairs at night, when he
could barely lift his fork to eat, when depression overwhelmed him –
yet he was always ready for the fray next morning.

Although the major firms baulked at getting publicly involved, the
rank and file of Britain had no such qualms. Their generosity and
supportive comments kept Botham and his cohorts going. Every day
threw up touching vignettes, whether it was an old lady tipping out the
contents of her purse, a contribution from a school or the harrowing
sight of sufferers from the cruel disease. The effect on Leukaemia
Research is incalculable. The money raised (around £880,000) was,
of course, invaluable, but more important was the raising of public
consciousness about the disease. By the time Ian Botham walked again
for Leukaemia Research in April 1987 there was genuine optimism that
a cure was in sight and Ian was grateful to the late Eric Morecambe for

his suggestion in the late '70s that he should stick to one charity rather than diffuse his fund-raising activities.

By Christmas 1985 Ian Botham could fairly be described as the most popular man in Britain. He had even survived the horrendous experience of being dragged off to Hollywood, four days after the Walk ended, to listen to Tim Hudson's latest monologues and watch his vaunting ambitions wither on the Hollywood vine. Another colourful episode in Ian's life was about to end, as an even more remarkable year dawned.

9

A momentous year

•

Anyone beavering away in a reference library into the life and times of Ian Botham needs a strong pair of arms when the year 1986 is reached – for one reason or another the weight of newsprint is staggering. Botham hardly ever seemed to be off the front page and his many admirers feared that Ralph Waldo Emerson's dictum that 'every hero becomes a bore at last' might soon apply to him. The George Best analogy was again dusted off as Botham lurched from yet another 'sex and drugs' scandal to a ban from cricket for half the summer, to civil war in his county. Finally he became more like the Howard Hughes of cricket, rather than George Best, and his low profile coincided with a triumphant tour of Australia.

The first few months of the year found Botham at the lowest ebb of his career. Along with his team-mates in the Caribbean, he was blitzed by the West Indies pace attack and the 5/0 series result was inevitable as the stuffing oozed out of the squad. Everything that could possibly go wrong did so, and the cautious optimism before the tour began to look foolishly naive. Undoubtedly England played badly, but there were extenuating circumstances. At times the West Indies bowlers were frighteningly fast on pitches that were uneven in bounce, and dangerous. After a pitiless bowling assault in the First Test at Sabina Park, John Woodock, of *The Times*, not a man given to wild statements, wrote: 'I never felt it more likely that we should see someone killed.' Peter Willey's arm would have been broken without an arm guard while Phil Edmonds might have died if the beamer that struck him over the heart had not been cushioned by padding. David Gower concluded: 'It's beyond normal skills', and it is rare indeed that someone of his physical bravery and sharp athlete's reactions would be so negative. By the Second Test in Trinidad, armed guards were patrolling outside the England players' room at the Port-of-Spain Hilton, in case protestors against the South African involvement of Graham Gooch and co. got a chance to convey their hostile views: that excursion to South Africa in 1982 was still fresh in many memories in the Caribbean. The only relief from such confinement at the hotel was facing four balls an over aimed at the head from Marshall, Garner, Patterson and Walsh. Soon a siege mentality settled among the players, exacerbated by the swelling press contingent. England had again broken the golden rule – they were losing, and losing badly – so within a matter of weeks the travelling media party had grown from 23 to almost 60. They included the cynical newshounds and the feature writers in alligator shoes who jet in and out within four days, after penning vitriolic pieces from in-depth research around the hotel pool with anonymous informants and a hefty bill for umpteen banana daiquiris. The assistant manager, Bob Willis, encapsulated the mood of the players when he was asked by a British Airways steward if there was anything he wanted him to take home, and he replied: 'Yes, 34 reporters and two television crews.'

It must be admitted that the players did not help themselves by getting involved with cheque-book journalism. Four of them (Botham, Gower, Edmonds and Gooch) had exclusive contracts with tabloid newspapers and they could hardly complain too vociferously about the prying and snooping that raged on. They would reply that they were happy to talk about just cricket in their columns, but they were sophisticated enough to know that you get between the sheets of tabloid journalism at your peril. Soon the atmosphere was corrosive and much of it was blamed on Botham. By the Second Test, the tour manager Tony Brown had to go to the press-box to refute allegations that the team was unhappy with Botham's preparation and attitude to the matches. He had bowled badly and got out to two very good deliveries but it is hard to imagine that the manager would need to go so far if it had been any other player simply having a bad match. By the time England returned to Trinidad for the Fourth Test, Botham's morale was as low as it had ever been. His team-mates were concerned that they could not get him out of his hotel room to come down to the bar for a drink and he simply became more reclusive and morose, as Kath noticed in the various phone calls she received from him back home. His form was dreadful – four wickets at 53 and a batting average of 13 in the first three Tests and David

Gower was exasperated that Ian was bowling too aggressively at the openers, Greenidge and Haynes, so that they were off to a roaring start far too often. Ian felt he could run in and bowl sharply in the same way that he had against the Australians even though, as he well knew, Gordon Greenidge is not Andrew Hilditch.

Moreover, his batting against the quicks on unreliable surfaces was looking more and more hit-and-miss and he was clearly being dragged down again by the burden of expectation. As long as Botham was still at the crease anything was possible, but he of all people seemed to be finding the responsibility too much. When Botham is down, he can get very negative and mulish, and in the Third Test at Barbados, his colleagues did not see him in a terribly favourable light. He bowled badly, then got himself out twice in a day. The first time he hung on grimly for an hour until he top-edged a hook five minutes before lunch. When England followed on, Phil Edmonds batted ahead of Botham as night-watchman but when he was out, Botham came in and smashed 21 in four overs before getting himself out in the last over of the day. It was not intelligent cricket. In the dressing-room a significant exchange took place when Botham returned after his dismissal. He threw down his bat and said, 'How can you play that stuff on these bad wickets?' It cut no ice with Mike Gatting who, having had his nose rearranged by Malcolm Marshall, and then had his thumb broken, was very frustrated on the sidelines, watching yet another disintegration. He suddenly flew at Botham, saying he was fed up of hearing about the poor wickets: 'You're the most talented player in the team and if you go on about the wickets being unplayable, that does nothing for the confidence for the lesser batsmen in the side who look up to you.' Botham attempted a justification, but it was game, set and match to the vice-captain. Gatting felt better for speaking his mind: 'I couldn't sit there listening to any more of Ian's excuses. I could understand how he felt because I know how important it was to him to put up a good show this time against the West Indies when there was hardly a decent wicket around. But it was all symptomatic of Ian's negative state of mind at the time.' John Emburey was present at the time and feels Gatting's intervention was justified: 'Ian had to stop moaning and looking for excuses, because we needed him to be positive. Trouble is he never thinks he's out – sometimes he thinks the bowler's a chucker, or the bat handle slipped or he just didn't see it. At Barbardos in '81, he was beaten three times in an over by Holding and he threw the bat down onto the pitch and put his hands on his hips as if to say: "How can I play against that?" That did nothing at all for the morale of inferior players like me who had to follow him. On the '86 tour, Beefy was very uptight about again failing against the West Indies.'

For the first time in his England career, serious thought was given to dropping Botham for the Fourth Test in Trinidad. The press had indulged in such fancies since 1981, but this time the selection committee tossed the idea around. They had to consider not only Botham's poor form, but the accumulation of damaging publicity. A fortnight earlier Cornwall Police had issued a statement that they wished to interview Botham about drug allegations during the latter stages of the Leukaemia Walk. They had been fed information by one Simon Worthington, a freelance journalist who had conned his way into the entourage by saying he was writing for a health magazine, when in fact he was sneaking out titbits for the *Mail on Sunday*. With true campaigning spirit Worthington passed on his dossier to the Director of Public Prosecutions and openly boasted about his success. In the event no action was taken, but such subterfuge seemed to be encircling Botham's private life. No wonder he stayed in his hotel room. The next blow came from a friendlier source – Tim Hudson, old clattertrap himself. On the eve of the Trinidad Test, Hudson was quoted as saying 'I'm aware he smokes dope, but doesn't everyone?' Hudson later insisted his remarks were distorted by the *Daily Star* but Botham did not need another 'Drugs Shock' headline. He promptly sacked his manager. Compared to all this aggravation, an hour or so at the wicket dodging the flak from Marshall and Patterson was a picnic.

It was against this background that David Gower asked to see his friend on the eve of the Trinidad Test. The captain told him his position was discussed but that he was happier with Botham on the side. Botham thanked him for his support and went back to his room. It was all over in two minutes. Gower, like the rest of the England party, still hoped for a miracle from Botham, still felt that some vintage heroics were just around the corner. The next bout of lurid revelations rendered that extremely unlikely in the near future. The *News of the World* alleged that Botham's last visit to Barbados had included bedroom antics with a former Miss Barbados, Lindy Field, which also involved drugs. The usual round of allegation, rebuttal and writ for libel followed, and during all this Botham had to play in a Test Match, with his England career hanging in the balance. At every interval, Chris Lander, his ghost for the *Sun*, would bring him the latest published developments and Alan Herd, his solicitor, would offer advice. Lander would also be relaying messages back to Botham's wife in Yorkshire, as she prepared to fly out on a pre-arranged holiday. It was an impossible situation for a Test cricketer yet, paradoxically, Botham found his best form of the series. He batted responsibly in each innings, making second top score both times and took 5 for 71. Viv Richards says he has never seen Botham look so anguished as he did during that Test: 'his eyes were sunken, his cheeks hollow, he looked awful and he just got more and more down as the tour went on.' Michael Holding also noticed the change: 'I saw him in the coffee shop, and he didn't wave and shout "come over" like he usually does. It wasn't the Beefy that we knew. All this prying was none of anyone's business. We don't have this kind of thing in the Caribbean because we are from different islands and there aren't so many cricket writers following us around. The English press just don't appreciate Beefy and I thought then that they were driving him out of the game.'

A couple of days later, Kath flew out and the media had another field (no pun intended) day. Kath was pigeon-holed as cricket's Tess of the d'Urbervilles, the eternal wronged woman, and the speculation about the Bothams' marriage reached extraordinary heights as the couple tried to sort themselves out in privacy on the lovely island of Antigua. The whole distasteful episode encapsulated the brutalising thrust of a section of modern British popular journalism. Having lost its role as a news-gathering force to television and radio, some tabloids had veered towards soft-porn and witless hyperbole with truth becoming the first casualty in a bitter circulation war. Botham was far from blameless. The damaging allegations about sex and drugs romps in Barbados came from the *News of the World* yet Botham continued to give his exclusive thoughts to that organ's Wapping stablemate, the *Sun*. With Tim Hudson cranking up the publicity machine in the past year, Ian's private life was bound to be even more scrutinised if he was setting out his stall to be more than just a cricketer. It is naive to expect the media to attend a news conference that rambles on about Botham's imminent acting career in Hollywood and swallow every word. Hudson ought to have realised that grandiose forecasts have to be backed up eventually by solid achievements. It was Ian's weakness that he ostensibly bought all that gibberish and went along with the rumours. To Ian it was just a laugh, a harmless foray into another sphere of the entertainment business. Many journalists who had been harangued by Hudson and snubbed by Botham were itching to carve up both men. The stench of a lynch mob would not fade away.

The cricket writers did their best to concentrate on the sad events on the field of play – apart from the correspondents who preferred to cover the game from the beach, with the radio commentary their only concession to professionalism. Tony Brown was forced to make more and more articulate defences of his players and their preparation for the Tests. Caustic comments were passed about the alleged scruffiness of the England players at official functions and in the nets, but Brown refutes them vehemently: 'At one function, I was given wrong information that we could dress casually. It looked worse when the West Indies boys turned up in their official gear and we were dismayed that we had been misled. On every Test Match day, we practised in whites, whereas the West Indies boys were in all sorts of colours. I've got a photo of Beefy and Viv alongside each other, and guess which one's in white? I also have one taken by Lawrie Brown, our physiotherapist, which shows our squad exercising in whites, with Viv and his team in shorts and all kinds of tee-shirts.' When the press criticisms were put to Brown by high-ranking figures at Lord's, he felt constrained to offer those photographs as evidence. He remains angry that so much was made out of the compulsory/optional net saga. The cricket writers took a poor view of the alleged indifference to net practice as the thrashings continued. It was felt that the England players should at least be seen to be working hard at their game, inadequate though it clearly was. When Geoffrey Boycott flew out in a journalistic capacity, he lost no time in embarrassing the England management. He announced that he had no problem in finding a place to have a net and, furthermore, that he was available for selection. The press, who had long been used to Boycott's unusual sense of proportion, swallowed that one because it fitted in with the superficial scenario – England losing because they were not working hard enough in the nets, while the veteran opener from Yorkshire showed the tenacity the team needed. Tony Brown, not surprisingly, takes issue: 'We weren't looking for the flat, easy batting surfaces that Boycott loves to have in the nets. We wanted to practise against short-pitched, nasty fast bowling on unreliable surfaces – in other words the kind of wickets we were getting in the Tests. In the end we had to settle for concrete surfaces which weren't satisfactory. I don't believe that anybody could've tried and achieved anything other than what we did on that tour. I was surprised that everyone got so uptight about nets, especially as the surfaces were so obviously sub-standard on many occasions. It all got distorted because we were losing. Both David Gower and Ian Botham attended nets that weren't compulsory – before, during and after the fuss about practice. They had a couple of sessions a day with Fred the bowling machine as well as with the main bowlers and they tried their best to work out how they should attack or defend the kind of deliveries they would face in the Tests. At the start of the tour I told Ian there would be times when he would be expected at nets, and to be seen to be working hard – he said, "I know what you mean, manager, I'll be there." He was as good as gold about that.'

David Gower is even more dogmatic about the matter than Brown. Gower has always been of the opinion that nets are for honing a particular skill. His customary urbanity fades, however, as he considers the sniping about net practice on his final tour as England's captain:

> It was absolute rubbish to say that a squad of sixteen players should do the same thing in the nets, because sixteen human beings are different. It comes down to whether you are captaining the side for the good of the team or for the press – the soft option is to treat everyone the same, but that shows a lack of understanding about individual's needs. There were three decent net wickets on the entire tour, and they were all in Barbados. We went to see Boycott's practice wicket, it was crap – one day it was covered in goat shit the next it had been watered and wasn't usable. The ball didn't bounce above ankle height! It was half a net, useless for sixteen blokes. We were coming second by a long way and we had a lot of spare days: if we'd practised on every free day, we would have destroyed ourselves. When you're losing, you cop the flak even if it is ill-considered.

It is worth pointing out that the new régime of Mike Gatting and Micky Stewart which was so successful a year later in Australia was rather more similar in outlook to nets than the press admitted. Stewart had been taken on to professionalise England's preparations and it is true that he initiated some good ideas in Australia. Yet after the first week of the tour, when everyone worked hard as a unit, the experienced players were given many options to skip nets. Gower, Botham and Lamb often availed themselves of this latitude and credit must go to Gatting and Stewart for their flexibility. They realised that on such a long, demanding tour with so much cricket being played in tense circumstances, a break from nets was at times advisable. When full nets were called in Australia, everyone was seen to be working hard – just as they were in the Caribbean when facilities permitted. The major differences were superior net surfaces in Australia and the fact that England kept winning. The press chose to offer Stewart's alleged iron-rod discipline as one of the main reasons, even though one feels that the quality of opposition was rather more relevant. The sight of Elton John batting in the nets at Melbourne with the England players hardly suggested that Micky Stewart's régime was an authoritarian one.

For Botham, some good at least came out of that West Indies tour, even if his cricket was generally disappointing. His marriage, at its rockiest at that time due to the sheer weight of lurid allegations, grew stronger as Kath developed a new independence, branching out into modelling and writing. Ian decided he wanted to spend more time with his wife and family and the genesis of his decision to end touring for England came in those miserable days in the Caribbean. He also spoke to Allan Border over the phone and agreed to join Queensland as soon as he was available, but they decided to sit on the story until the timing was more suitable. Typically Botham did not want to appear to be bowing to media pressure in stepping off the international treadmill.

On the next tour to Australia, Kath and the children spent some very happy weeks out there with Ian and it was good to see them so relaxed in each other's company. On Christmas morning, as we mingled over pre-lunch drinks in our Melbourne hotel, Kath said to me, 'I wonder what Lindy Field's doing now?' She deserved her new-found serenity, it had been a difficult year for her, trying to keep her family together as one blow followed another. It also looked as if Ian would at last gain some financial security after the damaging efforts of Tim Hudson. At 3.30 one morning he was woken up in the Trinidad Hilton by a call from Brisbane. It was Tom Byron, a sports manager who had met Botham through a mutual friend, Jeff Thomson, eight years earlier. They had enjoyed a few drinks together in the intervening years, usually in the company of the redoubtable Thommo, and unknown to Botham it was a burning ambition in Byron to manage him. When he heard about Hudson's demise, Byron placed a call to Trinidad. Botham liked the language Byron talked and they agreed to meet in England later that year. Byron admits he took a chance. He had just gone through a rather expensive divorce and his coffers were hardly overflowing. He knew that Botham would be taking a long, hard look at him, so he risked all. He sold all his assets, gathered up his remaining savings and came to Britain for a month, with the aim of landing Ian Botham. They spent several days in Jersey, and at no stage did Byron blanch at the hotel prices or the exorbitant cost of expensive brandies. Their casual acquaintance developed into friendship and Byron returned to Brisbane as Botham's Australian manager. The gamble paid off and he is now in charge of

Botham's business affairs in Britain as well as Australia. He smiles as he remembers Thommo's introduction in 1978: 'I hate the Pommie bastards, but this one's not bad,' and the amount of lucrative contracts he has secured for Botham in Australia confirms that the bulk of the populace agree with Thommo. Byron promised Botham that he would make him a millionaire (sterling, not dollars), and he is well on the way, despite Ian's extravagant spending style and immense generosity. It has been a good partnership, with one drawing strength from the other. Byron is shrewd and personable enough to enjoy an amicable relationship with the British press and Botham has a far better chance than ever before of an improved public image.

Although Botham's marriage grew stronger and his financial status at last improved, he knew that the days of carefree socialising were over. His experience in the Caribbean had soured him and he decided he would become more selective in his company. In the West Indies, he was hardly seen in the bar, apart from in Barbados when his father-in-law arrived to cheer him up, and then in Antigua when Kath flew out to the clatter of camera shutter speeds. Botham called his hotel room 'the bat cave' and he would spend hours in there, watching videos, using room service or yarning with his room-mate, Les Taylor, Bob Willis, and his brother David. The grim spectre loomed of Botham turning into cricket's Elvis Presley – reclusive, overweight, morbid and listless. It was a prospect that appalled his friends and saddened those who remembered Ian as a boisterous character full of daft tricks and galumphing humour, but essentially without malice. The day had never seemed long enough for Ian, no jape was ever spurned, no bottle ever left half-full. Now he was wiser, and essentially more cynical. Before the 1986 West Indies tour, he had often found himself in trouble, sometimes without courting it. Mike Hendrick recalls an obnoxious man demanding Ian's autograph in a London pub, then roaring 'Is that it then? Nothing else?' when the paper was politely signed and handed back. Hendrick, one of England's more genial seam bowlers, wanted to sort the chap out, but Botham moved him away. Richard Lines remembers a race night in Taunton for a soccer player's benefit in the late '70s when a brawl developed that did not involve Botham – but soon Botham was on the ground and several brave characters were queuing up to have a kick at him. In 1984, in Hamilton, New Zealand, Botham walked into a bar for a quiet drink with Graham Morris, a freelance photographer and friend, and the atmosphere changed right away. Two men stood behind them, making sniffing sounds and announced 'this place stinks of f . . . . . . Ian Botham!'

They were obviously spoiling for a fight, but the two Englishmen finished their drinks and walked out of the bar. When Morris asked Botham for his reactions to the blatant aggravation, he was told, 'Don't worry about it – no point in spoiling a quiet night out.'

That West Indies tour convinced Ian that no good would ever come from standing around in a bar, as in his more carefree days. 'It just got too ridiculous. It didn't matter where I went, heads would turn, eyes would bulge and press blokes would come out of the cracks in the wall. Some dope would want to bait me and I just had to accept that as part of fame and fortune. But I was very sad about it, I've always been one for the cheerful natter at the bar.'

In 1986, Andy Withers became even more important to Botham. Andy had been working for Ian since 1982, driving him around and acting as a buffer for any unwelcome attention. He had been a drayman, and part-time barman at the Four Alls pub in Taunton, and Ian liked the way he once defused a potentially difficult situation. Andy started to look after Ian in the way that 'Jock' McCombe had for Viv Richards, and he has done an excellent job of it. Ian liked the idea of having a 'minder' – he took to calling him 'Tel' after Arthur Daley's sidekick in the 'Minder' series, one of Ian's favourite programmes – but Andy has become more than just a paid employee. With Kath mostly staying at home in Yorkshire, he spends more time with Ian than anyone else, combining the roles of driver, cook, secretary and emotional punchbag. When Ian is angry, it is Andy who invariably feels the initial blast. It is amusing now to observe the sporting superstar eating the TV dinner that Andy has de-frosted and cooked, watching the videos Andy has selected in the shop and drinking the can of beer handed to him by Andy. The Odd Couple indeed: given Ian's chronic untidiness, he would be ideally cast in the Walter Matthau role.

Ian now likes nothing better than to sit in front of the television, watching a film packed with gore and the kind of action he has managed in his own career. It took Tom Byron a while to come to terms with this side of Ian's personality: 'We'd sit there, watching this bloody film that was an insult to our intelligence and Ian would say, "Good, isn't it?" If I said no, he'd offer to put another one on. Anything, rather than go to bed and get some sleep. At three o'clock in the morning, he'd be sifting through more videos and pouring me another drink. He just hates to be alone.'

For this very reason Andy Withers is an integral part of his life, as he travels up and down the land on cricket business or personal appearances. Andy checks that his shirt will go with the jacket, that the shoes are the right colour (Ian's colour-blindness means that he relies on Kath to buy him the right shades, with appropriate matchings), but more than that, he can talk to Andy if no one else is around. Peter Roebuck used to have fruitful late-night chats with Ian in the days when they shared the same vision for Somerset cricket. They would sit watching videos of Dire Straits in concert and just talk. For Roebuck, that was a sympathetic part of Botham's personality: 'That little-boy-lost thing makes you warm to him. He has a warmth that draws people to him and, by and large, he keeps his friends. This fear of loneliness goes against Ian's one-dimensional, comic-strip image, but it is far more attractive than all that Rambo rubbish. Yet he is very insecure, he has felt threatened by sophistication all his life. Collars and ties perturb him, he likes to think of himself as the average man's hero. In our first year on the staff, he was fooling around in the dressing-room and one chap called him "pig ignorant" – Ian flew into a rage, he looked frighteningly intense, even though the remark was not meant literally. Ian has always wanted credibility on all levels.'

Ian is also touchingly impressionable and it manifests itself in some ways that are amusing to others, but not to him. Graham Morris, the freelance photographer, needs a psychologist's insight into his moods sometimes, when he has been charged with getting an exclusive picture of Botham doing something daft for the pages of the *Sun*. Morris shares Botham's boyish attitude to life and he taps that mutual chord when he knows that a conventional request to Botham will be spurned because a game of cards is in progress, or a nap is called for, or because he cannot be bothered. When Morris took those ludicrous 'Rambotham' pictures for the *Sun* in 1985, he knew that Botham would refuse to dress up in a silly outfit with a gun in his hand, so he resorted to a subtle ploy. The conversation proceeded along these lines:

Morris: 'Tell you what Beefy, that Rambo's a bit of a lad, shooting up all those people.'
Botham: 'Yeh, yeh.'
Morris: 'Can't imagine Lord's liking it if they saw you dressed up like him. They'd say "typical Botham, does he think he's Ché Guevara?" They'd think you saw yourself as Rambotham.'

Once the idea was lodged in Botham's mind, and once Morris had found a cogent reason for doing the picture (i.e. to annoy Lord's), Ian was willing. The rebel with a cause. Morris used the same technique when he dressed Botham up as Crocodile Dundee on his last England trip to Australia. Morris and Chris Lander went to the National History Museum in Brisbane and borrowed an eight-foot, stuffed crocodile. They bought all the other impedimenta: the hat, the huge knife, the crocodile teeth necklace, the faded shirt. They left the gear in Botham's room, knowing that he would not resist trying it all on. Botham had seen the film, loved the character played by Paul Hogan and identified with his rugged, yet sentimental persona. Botham eyed himself up in the mirror, he particularly liked the knife and allowed Morris and Lander to drive him north of Brisbane, to stand in a swamp. The deciding factor was the hire of a Porsche for the journey. Botham liked the idea of a high-speed trip to pose as a macho character, with no one else around to view any possible discomfiture. Morris says of him with affection: 'He's just a small boy, really – but that's not a bad thing. You can get by a lot easier in life if you can get laughs out of it.'

Botham needed all his sense of humour within a month of the end of the West Indies tour. Once again the *Mail on Sunday* had taken aim and this time had scored a direct hit. Botham announced in that newspaper that he had taken 'pot' in his younger days: this was contrary to the statement he had issued two years earlier, when instituting legal proceedings against the *Mail on Sunday* for its sex-and-drugs allegations concerning the New Zealand tour (see Chapter 7). It was an agreed article; by May 1986 the exorbitant legal costs had forced Botham to the conclusion that he could not afford to pursue his action any further. The comment by a Law Lord in the 1930s that 'the law, like the Ritz Hotel, is open to everyone' had grim significance in this case. Despite earning handsome sums over the years, Botham was not wealthy and could not afford to indulge in the legal trench warfare that comes easier to a newspaper than to an individual. In turn the *Mail on Sunday* clearly felt it had some trump cards up its sleeve (for example, testimony from alleged witnesses), and would not settle for a paragraph or two of meek compromise. Botham was in trouble, even though his article carried the fond hope that he and his family would now be left in peace.

Within a day of publication, the TCCB's Executive Committee instructed that Botham should be withdrawn from the one-day internationals squad that had been announced earlier. An investigation was also announced. In vain Botham pointed out that his statement in the *Mail on Sunday* contained nothing new in the way of drugs involvement. Seven weeks earlier, in an interview with Frank Bough for BBC TV's

Breakfast Time, he admitted he had once smoked marijuana. Only a week earlier, his latest book with Frank Keating had been exclusively featured in the *Guardian* and the same ground was covered. Why did the TCCB not act a week earlier or seven weeks earlier? Why wait till now? The fact that marijuana was not one of the prohibited drugs contained in players' contracts under the TCCB's jurisdiction was also curious. Could it possibly be that Botham's name had induced another state of over-reaction? The sight of Botham again hogging the pages of a Sunday tabloid was just too much. The next fortnight was to see the tabloids vie with each other in malignant pomposity, with recommended punishments varying from a life ban to one of three years. On the day after the TCCB banned Botham from the one-dayers, he was given an inkling of the public's attitude during the charity match at Edgbaston in aid of the starving people of the Third World. Botham received an overwhelming reception from the 17,000 crowd when he came on to bowl and when he fielded on the boundary in the rain, he was inundated with offers of umbrellas. Nor did the other world-class players at the game adopt a cooler attitude to him. They pulled his leg genially as they picked over the lurid headlines and Imran Khan summed up the mood when he chortled: 'Beefy, you've made it – you're immortal!'

If this was now the game's blackest episode, someone had neglected to convince a lot of fans and world-class cricketers. The twisted morality of the age seemed to sanction 'yuppies' snorting cocaine to combat the pressures of making small fortunes on the stock market while a great sportsman who had done much for society on and off the field was being pilloried for smoking a joint or two in his youth. Anyone who has read Bob Geldof's explicit autobiography is aware that his capacity for philanthropic deeds does not preclude a self-destructive, illegal streak. Yet Geldof (deservedly) was on his way to an honorary knighthood, while Botham was in the stocks again, taking all the rotten tomatoes the gleeful press could find. When Botham returned to his cottage in Taunton after that Edgbaston game, he was immensely gratified by a telegram from Eric Clapton and Phil Collins, which simply read 'Cheer up – we're all behind you.' That day, as we talked in the cottage, Botham remained bewildered at the fuss. He alternated between rage at the authorities ('if they try to ban me, I'll slap an injunction on them!'), to a bitter tirade at the hypocrisy of the press ('I know for a fact that some of those writers have taken drugs on tour, yet they climb into me, saying I'm a bad example to the young. Did it sound like it at Edgbaston?'). It was all sadly reminiscent of Lord Macaulay's whimsical observation a century ago: 'We know of no spectacle more ludicrous than the English nation in one of its periodical fits of morality.'

The build-up to the Disciplinary Committee's meeting was frenetic and one-sided. Denis Compton called for a life ban and the *Daily Mail*'s headline announced, 'Botham and English Game on Trial'. That paper's cricket correspondent, Peter Smith, thought a year's ban would be sufficient. He had attacked Botham, despite a friendly relationship built up over the years, because he felt the *Mail* readership demanded a draconian stance: 'I was getting letters asking me why I wasn't going for him and in the end I just had to come out against him. Drugs is a very emotive issue and the *Mail* readers were solidly against their use.' One would expect the *Mail* reader to take that stance, yet a *Daily Mirror* opinion poll supported Botham. The meeting at Lord's was billed as the most important since Kerry Packer met the International Cricket Conference nine years earlier. It lasted for seven hours and Botham was suspended until 31 July for bringing the game into disrepute by using cannabis, and for admitting in the *Mail on Sunday* that he had indulged in the drug after having denied this previously. David Graveney attended the meeting as Cricketers' Association representative and, in his opinion, Botham received a fair hearing.

When the verdict was announced on television, I happened to be in the company of a vastly experienced county cricketer of high intelligence and strong moral principles – superficially not the kind of man who would support drug-taking. He burst out laughing at the news. He is fond of Botham, he thinks of him as an amiable rogue, but his derision was directed at the TCCB. His reaction marks a useful counter-balance to the anonymous quotes from county cricketers who had told the correspondents that something should be done about drugs, that Botham could not get away with this one. My companion sneered: 'How can they say Beefy brings the game into disrepute? The punters love him, he's the greatest thing to happen to cricket in my lifetime. I smoked the stuff at university, so will I be charged if someone tells the TCCB?' That opinion was a salutary corrective to the established line that cricket's major sponsors would insist on being associated with a spotless product, that Botham's bad publicity would frighten off firms wishing to sink money into the game. One would have thought that Botham had done more than enough for Test cricket since he and Cornhill Insurance started out together in 1977; no other English cricketer had matched his ability to fill stadia, including executive boxes. He had kept faith with the official version of international cricket during a decade when first

Kerry Packer and then South African Breweries were casting covetous eyes at him. If Botham had gone to South Africa in 1982 the appeal of Test cricket in England would have been undoubtedly diluted. Surely the whole cricket industry benefited from Botham's presence on the field? Why was he never honoured for bringing the game into repute?

Other disturbing issues emerged from the decision of the TCCB's Disciplinary Committee. Was it fair to ban someone by referring to a rule forbidding drug-taking when that rule did not exist when the drug-taking took place? The TCCB had never found evidence of drug-taking despite an inquiry set up in the wake of the New Zealand allegations in 1984, so the committee was considering Botham's own admission. It was tantamount to banning someone from driving under the new seat-belt regulations after the driver had admitted not using seat-belts in 1970, before such practice became illegal. No evidence was offered that Botham's cricket had ever been affected by drugs, or that he had taken drugs to improve his abilities in that field. It was purely a social activity, away from the cricket ground: surely it was therefore a matter for the courts of law, not a cricket court? When Chris Cowdrey was banned around the same time from driving because of an excess of alcohol, his case was judged by a court of law, not by Lord's with that catch-all phrase 'bringing the game into disrepute' being wheeled out. The same ought to have applied to Botham. If it had been a proper legal trial, Botham could have pleaded contempt of court, after the positive deluge of sanctimonious condemnations recently aired over the electronic media and in newspapers.

The crucial factor was that, in the eyes of the game's ruling body, Botham needed his wings clipped. He had to realise the game is bigger than any one individual – an opinion, incidentally, that Botham has never contested. He has never kicked an opponent up the backside like Dennis Lillee, he has never thrown a brick into a crowd, like Sylvester Clarke, he has never run out an opponent at the bowler's end without warning, like Ewan Chatfield, he has never flicked off the bails when dismissed, like Chris Broad, Keith Fletcher, David Gower and Chris Old, and he has never come within light years of Javed Miandad's malevolent, calculating box of tricks. One hopes that Botham's record of sportsmanship was considered just as thoroughly as other cricketers' brushes with authority – but the verdict suggested not.

Botham came within a whisker of retiring from cricket after he was suspended. 'Somehow cricket all came into perspective for me. I had such a good time that a lot of the interest went for me and I was so close to giving it away. I simply couldn't be bothered about playing again, there were more important things to enjoy. I thought the ban was ridiculous. It came from media pressure, the desire to crack down on me. I couldn't believe the hypocrisy of some of the cricket writers – some of them have smoked the dreaded cannabis and even asked me if I could get some of it for them on tour! Then they turn round and give me hell for admitting something way back in the past. That sickened me. Then I thought, "No, I'll decide when to go, I won't let the press drive me out." I'm glad I carried on, because I'm going to enjoy the game as long as things are still functioning properly.'

The ban meant that, for once, he could spend time with his family, taking Liam to the school's parents v. pupils cricket match and fussing over baby Beccy. Right from her birth in November 1985 Ian has doted on Beccy: he realised just what he missed by being away so often when Liam and Sarah were growing up and, to general astonishment, he even took a hand in changing a nappy or two. It was, of course, accompanied by the usual macho grumbles, but the subsequent billing and cooing over the freshly-powdered baby would reveal his true feelings. During that time Ian also learned to fly a helicopter from scratch in just three weeks, cutting an incongruous figure as he shoe-horned his massive figure into a desk to take in the blackboard instructions, but showing his excellent hand-to-eye co-ordination when theory gave way to practice.

It was too much to expect Botham to stay out of the news during this period and twice he hogged the headlines through no desire of his own. At a fund-raising lunch in Manchester, having established that all his answers would be off-the-record and that no journalists were present, then proceeded to deliver himself of some racy observations, all of them deliberately fanciful to get a few laughs. One of them was taken rather more seriously – he referred to the England selectors as 'gin-slinging dodderers'. It was a phrase Botham had used for some time, and it would have gone no further, except that a fearless member of the Fourth Estate had smuggled in a tape recorder. He sold it to a tabloid for a handsome sum and Botham was in trouble again. Mercifully the selectors, some of whom had suffered from the whimsies of previous incumbents when they were England players, saw the observation in the proper humorous context. He was let off with a warning, but it only served to alert Botham to further sharp practices next time he spoke in public. He was completely floored by the next 'exclusive', this time in the *Daily*

Mirror. On the Friday after the Leeds Test, the lead story screamed out, 'England Stars Snub Botham' – the paper's cricket correspondent alleged that none of the England team had turned up at Botham's barbecue that he usually hosts on the Saturday evening of the Leeds Test. It was a farrago of lies and half-truths. Botham had not decided to hold a barbecue this time until he got to Headingley on Saturday afternoon to watch the Test and see some of his friends in the dressing-room. He was well aware that he had left the organisation rather late and fully understood that the bulk of the England team had made alternative arrangements. Those based in the London area would be going home in any event and since the last barbecue they had thrown, the Bothams had moved further north, and were now an hour's drive from the centre of Leeds. The article neglected to point out that several players phoned through their apologies and that it would take a lot to keep Lamb, Pringle, Dilley and Lever in particular away from a social evening with Botham. It was a typically puerile, knocking piece on Botham.

Such piffle was mercifully shelved in the last month of the season as Botham marked his comeback in spectacular fashion. He had not really missed the game, he genuinely hoped that the England boys would re-discover form and confidence against New Zealand and he nurtured hopes that he might get back in the team for the last Test at the Oval. Before then he had to prove both form and fitness. The press provided just the incentive he needed: the general consensus was that Botham would not be picked again for England that summer and that he was also unlikely to make the Australian tour. Perhaps the wish was father to the thought, but Botham relished the prospect of being judged on his cricket ability once more. In his first game back for Somerset, he made a century off 65 balls against Worcestershire. Three thousand came to see him at Weston, and Botham was indebted to the support of Viv Richards as he stepped back onto centre stage. He told him, 'Come on Beefy, you're still the top man – go out there and show you can still do it.' Richards's faith helped him bat with his normal ebullience.

A week later, in the unlikely setting of Wellingborough School, Botham played an innings that was astonishing even by his standards. Significantly, he admitted afterwards to his team-mates that he was very pleased with the effort – a rare self-indulgence from a man who does not dwell publicly on his own deeds. In just 26 overs, Botham smashed Northants for 175 not out, including thirteen sixes. It was a John Player League game, but a Northants attack containing three international bowlers did not willingly succumb. Botham came in at 18 for 2, with the seamers moving the ball around and testing everyone. After an initial reconnoitre, he grinned at the Northants' captain, Geoff Cook, and said, 'You'll have to bowl the spinners sometime, Tosh.' Not before he played one astonishing shot off the fast-medium pace of Neil Mallender: it was an excellent yorker on leg-stump, but Botham dug it out from between his feet and deposited the ball over deep mid-wicket for six. It was the kind of shot that demoralises good bowlers. As hundreds still tried to get into the ground, ninety minutes after the start of play, Nick Cook's left-arm spin was tried. The first ball was played with exaggerated care by Botham, accompanied by a hearty guffaw. The next seventeen went for 27 runs, a rate of nine an over compared to an overall rate of $6\frac{1}{2}$ an over. As Cook later reflected: 'Most boundaries are too short for him. All he needs to do is just hit the spinners straight. He calls us step-and-fetch-it bowlers, and that's all we seem to do against him.'

Wellingborough has seen nothing like it in cricketing terms. Around 10,000 people managed to get into the small college ground and the town was choking with traffic before and after the match, a tribute to Botham's drawing-power. A couple of Botham's sixes crept over the line on this fairly small ground, but the others were authentic sixes anywhere. One of them landed in a depot about 60 yards past the boundary, a carry of around 130 yards. As the Northants players sat shell-shocked in the dressing-room after Botham's innings had ended, their captain told them they had just witnessed one of the great innings in recent times. That may sound a tall claim for a Sunday slog but Geoff Cook is not given to rash claims: 'It was an astounding innings, we just couldn't bowl at him. There were two games going on out there – one when Botham wasn't on strike and we bowled well, and the other when the ball disappeared out of the ground. There was no point in feeling down about it, we didn't bowl badly and we didn't disintegrate in the field. Botham just destroyed us with a cascade of brilliant shots.'

Clearly there was nothing wrong with Botham's batting but his bowling was rusty. Would the England selectors, when they met to select the team for the Oval, take a chance on a man who had bowled just 43 overs after his comeback to first-class cricket? A conversation around that time between Micky Stewart and Botham proved to be significant: Stewart had just been chosen as cricket manager for the Australian tour and he wanted to find out from Botham if he really wanted to be involved again in the big-time. A lot had happened in Botham's life since his last England appearance and Stewart approached him with a completely open mind. He was pleased with Botham's response: 'I was very keen on creating an environment on tour which kept everyone happy. I simply wanted to let Ian know the way I worked and what contribution I was expecting from him if he toured. I pointed out that certain things had to be done together on and off the field and that he had to accept them, even if some of them went against the grain. Mike Gatting and I very much wanted him to go and I was reassured that Ian still wanted to be successful for the side.' So while the press were speculating that Botham's England career might be over, the new England manager was sensibly keeping his fingers crossed and trusting to the country's best player to rediscover his pride in performance. Meanwhile Mike Gatting was pressing Botham's claims to the England selectors and they agreed that the team at the Oval would be stronger with him in the side. They picked the best-balanced England team of the summer and Botham fitted right back into the fray, as Gatting recalls: 'As soon as he walked into the dressing-room it was a cheerier place. In cricket terms, Beefy remains a very big piece in the jigsaw puzzle and we were delighted to have him back.'

Not even Botham's most devout followers would have predicted that he would take a ball with his first delivery in his comeback match. Yet Bruce Edgar was mesmerised by a wide half-volley he need not have played, and the catch was safely pouched at first slip. After Botham had gestured his pleasure expansively, Gooch asked drily: 'Who writes your scripts?' Botham was not yet done – Jeff Crowe edged the next ball low past John Emburey at third slip and in Botham's second over was trapped lbw. That wicket took him past Dennis Lillee as the top wicket-taker in Test cricket: only someone with an innate sense of theatrical timing could have stage-managed such a return. John Wright, New Zealand's opening batsman, watched it all from the bowler's end and afterwards he paid tribute to the man who never seems to think he should settle for a maiden: 'He bowled really well in that first spell. He attacked and seemed to exert a psychological control over our batsmen. Bruce Edgar didn't need to play at that loosener but somehow he was drawn into it. The ball he got Crowe with was a good nut. What I admired about Beefy was that he never compromised, never tried to bowl just line and length. There must have been great pressure on him in his comeback Test to bowl sensibly at the start, just feeling his way back like all sensible professionals would do. But he's so positive even when not in the best physical shape to bowl.'

Botham agrees that the fates had intervened on his behalf:

Everything was set up for me, wasn't it? That must have been the best first ball I've sent down in a Test – you know how I need to get loosened up with a few long-hops! The ball was swinging in the heavy atmosphere and I loved the support from the crowd. When I got that first wicket, I turned to the pavilion and gave it my usual chest-swelling gesture, with the hands clenched above my head. I looked at the selectors – the only one looking up and smiling was A. C. Smith! Somehow I don't think they all wanted me back, because I reckon if it had been left to the public, I'd have been in for the previous Test at Trent Bridge, even though I wasn't match-fit. Next morning, I had two special telegrams – one from Jeff Thomson and the other from Dennis Lillee, congratulating me on passing his tally of wickets.

In truth, Ian looked heavy and in need of some long bowling spells. His subsequent spells were not as good as the first one, but he demonstrated that he had not lost that 'Golden Arm'. When he came in to bat on the fourth morning, he was a good deal more impressive, routing Hadlee with the new ball before storms washed away the Test. Botham hit 59 not out off 36 balls and when Hadlee took the new ball, he conceded 26 in 17 deliveries to Botham. In all Botham scored 47 off 32 deliveries with the new ball. It was interesting to see Hadlee's reaction to the devastating hitting; he had no hesitation in dispersing his field to all parts of the Oval, even though he had a new ball in his hand, and Botham made him look like a Sunday League hack just interested in keeping down the run-rate, instead of the best new-ball practitioner in the world. 'I was pleased to win that little challenge. Of course I respect Hadlee for his talent, but I've always felt he might buckle when the heat was on. He ended up bowling three bouncers an over at me that day just to get 'dot' balls – this with a new ball! I thought I was the only one who wasted the new ball! Even though I wasn't fit to bowl at my best at the Oval, I was in good nick with the bat. Before my ban ended, I'd got 90-odd up at Jesmond, then when the convict was let out of the cage I couldn't do a thing wrong and smashed it out of sight for Somerset. By the time I came to the Oval, I was certain I'd get some runs.'

Hadlee agrees he went into his shell that day: 'I was wrong to agree to a defensive field with the new ball because all my inclinations are normally to attack the batsman. But we didn't want to give away too many runs and Botham was rampant. It was just his day. He is one of the few batsmen I have known who likes to hit you for a boundary off the first ball you send down at them. Only Greg Chappell and Viv Richards have also been like that against me. With those three, you can see the disdain in their eyes, that hint of arrogance: it's a matter of pride that they won't be tied down.'

It was Botham's inner drive, that knack of making his own luck which had allowed him to influence a Test Match when he was still not physically ready. Once again he had demonstrated in thrilling fashion that a positive outlook is invaluable. He simply loved the idea of ramming the sceptical comments down the throats of the press and he gleefully contemplated doing it again in Australia. For within just a few days, Botham had removed all doubts about his playing credentials to tour that winter. Would they never learn that normal cricketing conventions must be shelved when Botham is involved? Why did the press believe it understood more than Mike Gatting, the selectors and the England players about Botham's capabilities? The prospect of metaphorical hats being eaten amused Botham for a fleeting moment, but he was soon concentrating on more serious issues. During that Oval Test, his attention had wandered to Taunton, where a momentous decision had been taken and an illustrious era was drawing to an acrimonious close.

10

The split with Somerset

●

If Allan Border had fulfilled his two-year contract with Essex, Ian Botham, Viv Richards and Joel Garner would all have carried on playing for Somerset. That salient fact stands out amid all the blood-letting of Somerset's civil war that lasted a painful eleven weeks. Ian Botham's loyal support of Richards and Garner has been well documented, and although many feel that the club wanted Ian to leave, this seems unlikely. For Conspiracy Theory read Cock-up Theory. The club did not handle the matter at all well, not least of all in its public relations, but the decisive catalyst came in a ham-fisted way which underlined that the harassed club officials were never quite in control of events.

Somerset knew that a decision had to be made on Richards and Garner as the 1986 season passed the halfway mark. Their contracts were both up at the season's end and, with Garner's knees in a problematical condition and Richards looking stale, the siren song of sackings was irresistible to some influential committee men who had found Richards more and more overbearing. Garner was incidental to all personal attacks – no one on the club's side has anything but good to say about this decent, honourable man. Yet Somerset would have delayed a decision for at least a year if Allan Border had not unwittingly muddied the waters.

In his first season with Essex, Border was finding the daily grind of county cricket hard going. He was seeing little of his wife and family and the Australian selectors were also pressing him to come home for a rest. Border was due to lead Australia to India for a series before England arrived to do battle for the Ashes from November onwards.

An exhausting five months beckoned, and Australia's selectors had many qualms about Border being shattered after giving his usual professional commitment to some Pommie county side. So Border agreed to ask Essex for his release before the season ended, so he could prepare for Australia's various challenges; he also intimated he would not be back in 1987 for his second year of the contract. Essex expressed regret, but they did have a rather handy replacement lined up – Martin Crowe. Since his highly successful first season with Somerset in 1984 (when he stood in for Richards, on Test duty in England), Crowe had developed into one of the best batsmen in the world. His ambitions kept pace accordingly and he was no longer content to kick his heels in Somerset's second eleven while Richards held sway. Crowe told Somerset that Essex had offered him terms for the 1987 season and that he was inclined to accept. That was the time when Somerset woke up to the fact that they had to make a decision about Richards. Garner was irrelevant, but a tightening up of registration of overseas players meant that both West Indians would eventually be replaced by just one overseas player. No longer could a county sign two overseas stars and play them both in the first team at the same time. It came down to a straight choice between the great West Indian and the great New Zealander, with the ten years' difference in age an influential factor. With Somerset having another poor season in 1986, the decision was a vital one.

Somerset gain no points at all for foresight in all this. They hoped to keep all parties happy for as long as possible, but they must have known that Crowe's professional ambitions would not be thwarted much longer at the age of 24. Yet if Border had stayed with Essex in 1987, the civil war at Somerset would have been delayed as the club bided its time and floated a few heretical thoughts among the membership. With the West Indies due in England in 1988, Crowe would have been a straight substitute (if he had been amenable) and it may be that the club would have finally looked down the gun barrel with the 1989 season in mind. By this time, Richards would have been 37 and Garner would surely have been past his peak at the same age, so the club might have been spared the ticklish job of showing them the door. Instead, by August 1986 they had to make up their minds within a matter of weeks, otherwise they would lose Crowe to Essex.

In the first three weeks of August, as Botham returned triumphantly after suspension, urgent discussions were taking place about Richards's future. Viv says he was aware of that: 'I started off that season magnificently, but soon I sensed that something was up. All of a sudden there weren't so many smiling faces and I felt I was on quicksand. I lost heart and confidence in the men around me. I wasn't coasting, I was simply jaded and I felt there was little support for me as the season went on. 'In mid-August, Richards clashed with Peter Roebuck in front of other team-mates at the start of the match against Surrey. The captain had ordered the groundsman to shave the grass off the Taunton wicket and Richards accused him of physical cowardice because he did not fancy facing Sylvester Clarke on a green flyer. A few days later Roebuck visited Richards to try to glean his state of mind. The captain knew that the cricket committee would be making its decision in a matter of days and Roebuck wanted to see if there was any room for compromise. Richards drove him from the house, threatening physical violence if he stayed any longer. Richards does not regret his hostility towards Roebuck: 'He was running around talking to everyone about my future, plotting my downfall and then he came to me looking for help. He is a very ambitious man, there was no way he wanted to be in charge of a dressing-room containing me, Beefy and Joel – he'd rather dominate a side that finishes bottom of the table.'

Roebuck had kept quiet about that stormy meeting because he felt it was a personal matter, but after I told him that Richards had revealed its contents to me, he discussed the contretemps for the first time. 'I went to Viv before the decision was made to see if there was any common ground. I also felt he had been very unfair calling me a coward after opening the batting for a few years now, and I wondered if his hysterical outburst had stemmed from a sense of unease, rather than from hatred of me. I wanted to raise that matter, then the broader issue of how keen he was to carry on playing for Somerset. It seemed to me that Viv's inclinations might have been relevant with the decision about to be taken, but after a minute or so it became clear there was no room for compromise, that the middle ground had been completely removed.' It was a bitter finale to a relationship that had contained a good deal of mutual respect in previous years, based on Roebuck's keen intelligence and broad perspective on life, and on Richards's wonderful ability and proud personality.

That tense meeting in Richards's house at least nails the perception that there had been no contact between him and club officials before the decision was taken to sack him. When the cricket committee met on Friday 22 August, the crux of the matter revolved around Viv Richards or Martin Crowe. By a comfortable majority the committee voted to sack Richards and Garner and offer terms to Crowe. The likely reaction of Ian Botham was discussed, but the unaminous feeling was that the committee should not be blackmailed over a decision that had to be judged on its own merits. The following morning, the two West Indians were called to the ground and told their fate. Later in the day Ian Botham thundered his first broadside from the Oval – 'If Viv and Joel go, I go'. That was Ian's big mistake: the issue did not involve him, even though he was close to Viv and Joel. Ian overestimated his popularity at Taunton in his last years with the club – his captaincy had not been a success, his bowling had not won many games and there was a feeling that he was becoming a 'big occasion' player, despite his excellent batting form in recent seasons. Jeremy Lloyds, who had left Taunton for Gloucestershire two years earlier, feels that Ian had just got too big for the small-town mentality: 'Many just wanted to return to sleepy tranquillity and they resented Beefy's larger-than-life exploits.' David Foot, a keen journalistic observer down there for many years agrees: 'The glamour stuff didn't suit Taunton. All those television cameras and hordes of reporters packing out a small ground ruined its intimacy for many people and Botham was held responsible for that, rightly or wrongly. Ian had a tenuous relationship with the Taunton crowd over the last few years – don't forget he had threatened to go before, in 1985.' There is the other side of the story – that Ian was simply expressing solidarity to his friends whom he felt had been badly treated. There is no doubt that the whole matter was carried out in indecent haste and that the club's public relations had been dreadful. Viv says bitterly, 'All of a sudden I'd gone from being King Viv to Viv the Coaster. Beefy's gesture was magnificent, he's a strong man – he knew that we'd been mucked about.' The club says that there was no other way to have handled it; if they had told the West Indians about their options and the resulting dilemma, they could have complained that world-class cricketers were being put on trial.

Ian's parents remain very bitter about the whole episode. Marie says she was told by a committee member at the start of the 1986 season that some influential people wanted to get rid of Ian plus the two West Indians – Ian was told the same thing in the 1985 season. What is not in dispute is the poor relationship that existed between Somerset players and committee for several years before the crisis of 1986. Les Botham remembers how difficult it was to have a quiet, private word with his son in the dressing-room area as committee men tramped through, showing off their illustrious players to impressionable sponsors. One day, Viv Richards was so annoyed by the invasion of his privacy that

he threw them out with the words, 'This is our area – leave us alone.'
Such actions would linger long in the memory of influential committee
men. Roy Kerslake, a Taunton solicitor and former club captain, seems
to have been the only cricket committee chairman who had the confidence and respect of most of the players, even though the anti-Botham
faction at the club maintains that he gave in to the players far too often.
For their part, the players were still bitter at the way the club had
muscled in on lucrative deals organised by Wyvern Sports, a company
set up to capitalise on Somerset's success in the late 1970s, with the
cricketers having a say in the marketing of scarves, banners, sweatshirts
and all the other paraphernalia that seems *de rigueur* to support a team
these days. Nigel Popplewell, the former Somerset player who was to
have such an influence on the special general meeting of members in
November, confirms that there had long been an uneasy relationship
between players, officials and committee members: 'The management
was usually appalling in my time at Taunton. Too many people wanted
vicarious success from what we were doing out on the field. Many were
jealous of the big stars.'

Perhaps that semi-feudal relationship had something to do with
Botham's decision to enter the public fray on behalf of his two friends.
He had become suspicious of Roebuck since handing the captaincy over
to him: Roebuck had told him that the captain normally goes down
with the sinking ship as Somerset lurched to the bottom of the table in
1985, and Ian suspected some shady manoeuvres. At the start of the
1986 season, Roebuck heard that Ian was referring to him as 'Hitler'
and after the cricket committee's decision, Botham hung a sign marked
'Judas' above Roebuck's peg in the dressing-room. He was incensed by
Roebuck's apparent volte-face after writing to Richards in the winter,
offering him the vice-captaincy and assuring him he had a future at
Taunton 'until your legs turn to jelly'. Roebuck justifies that by saying
that the situation changed once he realised that he could not make it
work, that the team was unhappy and not playing well. 'I wrote to Viv
because I know Ian was feeding him with all that conspiracy stuff, and
I wanted to reassure him. After that I was too caught up in a busy
season to stand back and work out all the complications. It was only
after Border left Essex that we realised we had to do something. Before
that there was no aim to get rid of them, and there was never any official
intention to get rid of Ian, least of all by me.'

Yet Ian Botham remained central to the controversy over the next
eleven weeks, even though he was not directly involved. He had verbally

accepted a one-year contract for 1987, but that lay on the table while the wick of outrage was turned up. Around that period, Ian was in a highly charged state, brooding in his cottage, firing off occasional salvoes in the direction of the cricket committee and vowing solidarity with his two friends: 'Roebuck is a very ambitious man. How can he justify replacing two players with one, especially as Crowe can't bowl? How many matches have Viv and Joel won for Somerset?' At the ground the atmosphere of suspicion would have been recognised by Titus Oates, as claim and counter-claim chased each other round. Ian could see no further than the simplistic notion that he owed complete loyalty to Viv in particular: more than once he used the emotional phrase 'blood's thicker than water'. He was initially certain that the rank-and-file of membership would rally to the flag on grounds of personal revulsion at the manner of the sackings, the popularity of Viv and (especially) Joel, the massive role they had played in Somerset's history and the fear of losing their third world-class player. Ian thrives on controversy and challenge, and despite entreaties by friends to stay out of the row, he was convinced that his involvement would decide the issue. Like a political leader at General Election time, Ian kept insisting that the news from the hustings was good, that the opinion polls were running his way. Yet a month before the members were due to vote, Botham knew the game was up. He held a party at his Taunton cottage for just a few close friends and his general demeanour indicated that he knew he would never return there. Richard Lines remembers the significance of the evening: 'Beefy was off to Australia and he knew that it was over, that the vote would go against him. We had a lovely, mellow evening and, at the end, he was in tears as he stood there with his arms around our shoulders. We all knew it was the end of an era.' Trevor Gard, Ian's closest friend in the Somerset dressing-room, also suspected as much after the last away trip of the season, to Old Trafford. 'Ian said he wanted to take me, Vic Marks and Colin Dredge out for a meal. I lost the toss and had to drive – the best toss I've ever lost because he got the other two paralytic and I was dead sober. Next morning, with Vic and Colin in a dreadful state in the dressing-room, Beefy bounds in and asks what's wrong with them! Looking back on it, Beefy should've stayed out of it all because he was not as popular in Taunton as he thought. He thinks everyone's his friend, he's so trusting, yet people keep letting him down. Many think he's too big for his boots but they are the people who don't really know him.'

On Saturday, 8 November, Ian Botham's Somerset career ended in

the huge show ring at the Bath and West Agricultural Ground at Shepton
Mallett. The bucolic connection seems appropriate, since the quality of
debate rarely rose above the level of the farmyard. Out of 5,000 members,
around 3,800 turned up to vote, so Botham could not complain about
a lack of democracy when the news filtered through to him in Western
Australia, where he was on tour with England. The club was supported
by around two-and-a-half votes to one, and mercifully the verdict was
accepted with good grace by the leaders of the pressure group. Botham
rang Richard Lines from Perth a day later, to be told it was clear he
was no longer wanted by Somerset's members; it was harsh but accurate.
Joel Garner attended the meeting – queuing in the cold with the
members, a typically common touch that showed why he was so
popular – but he did not speak. He was driven there by Robert Burston,
a close friend who had paid £300 for a plane to fly over the ground with
a message of support for Richards, Garner and Botham in the last
Sunday League game of the 1986 season. Burston, who has known
Botham since his days on the MCC ground staff, says that Garner finally
realised that Botham was a reliable ally in their last month or so together:
'Joel didn't say a word in the car either to or from Shepton Mallett, but
you could see he was hurt by it all. He had always called Beefy "mad-
man" and shook his head affectionately whenever we talked about him,
but he usually kept his distance from the daft antics. Now, at the end,
Joel had come to understand that Ian was far closer to him than he
thought.'

Although many came to Shepton Mallett with their minds made up,
the doubters were swayed in large numbers by a two-minute statement
by Nigel Popplewell that stood out as a beacon of articulacy amid the
fog of polemic. Popplewell had left the staff in 1985 to pursue a legal
career. He was basically fed up of county cricket at the age of 28, and
wanted to tackle other professional goals. Popplewell was an ally of
Botham while on the staff but, although he still feels warmly about Ian,
he felt it was time to speak on behalf of the younger players in the
Somerset dressing-room. In his allotted two minutes, he said that
Botham and Richards had become self-indulgent and slapdash in their
attitude to the rest of the side and that both factions had lost respect
for the other. In Popplewell's opinion, the atmosphere had been deterior-
ating since 1983 and the cancer was spreading wider and wider. It was
a devastating intervention, and it carried more weight among the open-
minded at Shepton Mallett than contributions on behalf of the rebels
by former players Peter Denning and Graham Burgess, because

Popplewell had been a recent member of the Somerset dressing-room.

Popplewell does not regret speaking out, although he does not understand why the media made such a fuss about his intervention: he did
not have to make notes of the other speeches, wondering if the point
would ever be reached! He says that he made exactly the same points
to the committee when he retired a year earlier and that his friends,
knowing how depressed he had been on occasions, persuaded him to
make his views public. He was not a Roebuck disciple, he has a greater
personal affection for Botham, but he still thinks it was right to side
with the club:

> I must admit it felt strange to support many of the old buffers I'd
> criticised when I was a professional, but it was one of those times
> in one's life when you can actually influence something that you feel
> is very important. I had moved from justifying Viv and Ian's
> temperamental behaviour because they were great artists to a
> conviction that ordinary human beings and players should not be
> treated so badly. I noticed that particularly in the three weeks of the
> World Cup in 1983 when the three superstars were away – Dasher
> Denning played the elder statesman, some of us wandered around
> like wurzels and the younger ones came out of their shell and began
> to enjoy their cricket. When Ian became captain, he couldn't quite
> get it right with the younger players, he wanted them to be happy
> but they couldn't lose their awe of him and he'd also explode at
> them over something trivial. It was all very well Ian buying them a
> drink in the bar afterwards and placing an arm around their shoulder
> but young players don't always react well to that.
>
> Beefy was wrong to take a public stand on the Viv/Joel issue. All
> he had to do was say to Viv, 'Look, I'm with you all the way and
> I'll leave if it goes against you, so disregard anything I say in public.'
> Instead the spectre of Botham hung over the matter, even though
> he was irrelevant. Some committee men did want to get rid of Botham
> and they must have been aware of how he would react but Beefy
> shouldn't have tossed his hat into the ring. He gets surrounded by
> all sorts of guys who tell him what he wants to hear and don't give
> him balanced advice. I'm still genuinely fond of him, but I wish he
> would be a little more discerning at times.

Vic Marks had also tried to talk Ian out of public statements, but to no
avail: 'I said that inflammatory remarks would be counter-productive

but Ian answered, "These are my mates, I have to stick up for them."
My emotional gut reaction was the same as Ian's and I admired his
consistency. There was also immense media pressure on him to come
out against the committee and he did not resist it. If he had managed
to avoid an issue like Botham versus the Establishment or a player-
power scenario, then the rebels might just have won the day, but not
with Ian wading in. In a sense, Viv and Joel were punished for some of
Ian's extravagances. When he was away on Test duty, they trained with
us and prepared perfectly professionally for the games but when Ian
returned, Viv saw that he was laid-back in his approach and followed
suit.' Marks still misses Botham at Taunton. Trevor Gard, too, found
it very hard to adjust to life after Botham in the dressing-room: 'I can
see him now, waiting to bat, with his pads on and a cheroot in his
mouth. When it was his turn to go out, he'd hand me his cigar and say
"ah well, here we go". I miss those early days on the staff when everyone
seemed to be playing for each other. Viv and Joel were Somerset boys
as far as we were concerned, and we felt we were representing our
county against all-comers. We were local boys getting stuck in, we'd all
grown up together. I don't think there's the same feeling now in the first
team.'

Shepton Mallet cost the club around £10,000 in administrative costs,
half the profit a county can expect to make in an average season. Civil
wars do not come cheap. Membership for the 1987 season was down
by 184, but in the previous three years membership declined on average
by 500. The club lost no major sponsorship deals over the departure of
Richards, Garner and Botham. One of Somerset's new signings delayed
his decision until after Shepton Mallet and he made it clear he would
not join if the club lost the vote. This alienation of young players
by Richards and Botham was a major plank in the administration's
argument, as unattributed leaks were dished out to the media in the
run-in to voting day. It is hard to judge the veracity of the claim but, in
a debate about a club's future, the welfare of young players is often
a powerful, emotional lever when the alleged behavioural defects of
established stars are being dissected. The whiff of bullying usually brings
out support for the underdog in the British sporting breast, even if the
young, downtrodden players were lucky to be on the staff in the first
place. There is no doubt that Ian had lost touch with the younger players
on the staff – in the 1986 summer he was either suspended, playing at
the Oval for England or a brooding presence under Roebuck's captaincy.
He has always been a supportive man in the dressing-room, but his

hatred of failure sapped him of his inspirational juices once he lost the Somerset captaincy.

Botham and Richards had lost contact with the grass-roots at Taunton. In their early days, they used to spend more time at the ground than any others, playing snooker, watching television, larking around, having a drink. They were safe there, no one would try to pick a fight with them to get their name in the papers. After the golden years of 1979–82, they were not so prominent around the county ground. Their fame meant more money, a wider circle of friends and greater leisure pursuits – an entirely understandable development. Except that the hangers-on and name-droppers would now feel thwarted by their absence: tongues would wag, temples would be tapped knowingly and hints would be dropped that Botham and Richards were getting above themselves. Dr Jacob Bronowski once observed, 'The world is made up of people who never quite get into the first team and who just miss the prizes at the flower show' – Botham and Richards would never come into that category, but many of their ill-informed detractors with the small-town mentality should recognise themselves in that observation. They failed to understand that the county could not return to the days when Botham and Richards were hungry for success, when the team was gelling together excitingly and you had to set the alarm clock to get into the ground on the day of a big match. Essex and Middlesex may have had the knack of grinding out consistent performances to win trophies in the past decade, but Somerset were never going to follow suit – partly through tradition, partly because their matchwinners were also erratic. The thrill of climbing a mountain for the first time is always more rewarding than going back down to base camp and starting the ascent all over again.

Somerset lacked the kind of players to achieve such consistency, and after their first triumphs in 1979 they also lost solid performers like Graham Burgess, Peter Denning, Phil Slocombe, Derek Taylor, Hallam Moseley and Jeremy Lloyds, the kind of underrated cricketers needed to support the stars. As Botham, Richards and Garner got wearier through the strain of playing all round the year for their countries, they found it harder to fire regularly for Somerset. Their detractors would say they were into the star syndrome, where they needed the stimulus of a Lord's final to galvanise them, yet that ignored the fact that it takes a very special cricketer to switch on the razzle-dazzle every day when he has become used to playing Test cricket. When Martin Crowe made such a deep, favourable impression on the faithful at Taunton while replacing Richards for a year, they conveniently overlooked that he was just 22 at the time, and hungry to absorb all the fundamentals of playing county cricket week in, week out. Crowe was well aware that English cricket could help him return at some stage and belt the daylights out of English bowling, while wearing his New Zealand cap. Viv Richards was no less keen to better himself and the team when he arrived on the staff in 1974. It is perfectly understandable that he and Botham would eventually get jaded by county cricket, just when a weak playing staff meant they were expected to work the miracles they had managed when young. Amid all the mud-slinging at the time of Shepton Mallett, the Establishment did Martin Crowe no favours by depicting him in such glowing terms. It will be interesting to see if he is still touchingly considerate of the young players and still churning out pedigree centuries when he has ten years of county cricket under his belt. The white charger may have picked up a few strains in the fetlock by then.

Inevitably a man with Peter Roebuck's gifts of communication was bound to get embroiled in the struggle. He deplored the personalisation of the matter, resented the media pigeon-holing of the major characters, and accepts that he lost three friendships that meant much to him. Joel Garner lived just two doors along from Roebuck, but they did not find themselves borrowing too many bottles of milk or bags of sugar off each other during autumn 1986. Roebuck hopes that one day he and Botham might resume their friendship, but accepts that Ian is a good hater. When questioned about his role in the civil war, Roebuck painstakingly but wearily lists the crucial items as he sees it:

> We were facing years of decline at Somerset. Three captains (including me) had not arrested it. It was a case of planting a new tree after a magnificent old oak had been rotted by age or disease. Ian needed a fresh challenge because his batting was so extraordinary that he was becoming a performer rather than a cricketer. I did not want him to go, and I believe most people on the committee shared my view, and at least the ructions arrested his decline and galvanised him into a new career at Worcester. He's a far better player when motivated or upset. We had been rivals since 1983 when he instigated the removal of Brian Rose as captain. He believed that Rose had been given too much credit for Somerset's success and he thought he could regain the England captaincy by making a good job of the Somerset one. When Ian sets out to get something, he's a formidable opponent and that is why his wonderful innings against Middlesex

in the Nat-West semi-final was so important to him. He conjured victory from an improbable position and that made it inevitable he'd get the Somerset captaincy in 1984. I told Ian that Vic Marks should have been appointed and I was never a rival until I was appointed at the end of the 1985 season. I had never given it a conscious thought because so many other contenders were ahead of me, but things were never the same again between Ian and me.

You must realise that 1986 was not a one-off. We had been awful in 1983, good in 1984 and awful again in 1985. Clearly something had to be done: do you act as an individual or as captain of a club with young players, members and hopefully a bright future? You have to act according to your role and mine had changed. Ian is an extraordinary man with a dynamic force in him that manifests itself in a bullying tendency. He is good at joining groups against an individual, and his fierce loyalty blinds him and affects his judgement on individuals. I've never believed all that puppy dog stuff, he's dangerous when roused and he set out to wage a vendetta against me. He was too late in trying to isolate me in the club, because he'd lost contact with most of the players on the staff who hadn't seen him at his best.

When the decision was taken to sack Viv and Joel, I was well aware that it was momentous, emotional and difficult. I didn't think Ian would leave over it, but within a week it was inevitable because he said so much in public. I think it's rather arrogant to accuse me of jealousy. Their contributions were wonderful, but we are all dust in the end and it's only cricket we're talking about, not war. I have never been the slightest bit jealous of Ian or Viv, I wouldn't swap my life for anyone else on earth. My only ambition in cricket is for Somerset to win the championship, but I couldn't give a stuff who is the captain! Ian has never really heard my side of the story, even though I went to see him a couple of times in Australia to sort it out, but he wasn't there. I resent being cast as a Judas figure: I make decisions on reason, whereas Ian relies on emotion. You have to be as clever as he is when you're his enemy because you lose popularity if you take sides against him.

Botham still maintains that all he wanted was to play for Somerset for the rest of his career, but that he could not stand by and see his friends let down without a fight.

Peter Roebuck underestimated me again, he thought I wouldn't carry out my threat. Good luck to the new régime and all my mates down there, but I couldn't have lived with myself if I'd kept quiet. When I look at the way we all knock around together now at Worcester – even down to playing golf or having a barbecue on days off – I think back to the days when it was just the same at Somerset. It was great, growing up together and winning trophies, but time marches on. I'm amazed they could say that Viv had got stale – try telling that to the Warwickshire bowlers he hit for 322 in a day in 1985! He was still a great player, but all the back-stabbing undermined him. Is it the responsibility of Richards, Garner and me that we got more publicity than other players at Taunton? It wasn't our fault that we played the game better than others. Roebuck didn't like all the coverage and he manipulated the situation into a publicity stunt to secure his power base. I was never going to stay at Taunton after what they did to Viv and Joel, but Roebuck didn't seem to have worked that out. If he really means what he says, that he wanted me to stay, it shows how little he knew about me, even though we had played cricket together since we were fourteen.

Viv's final words remain bitter: 'I hope they find it difficult to sleep at night.' For a man of his pride, it was a massive blow to spend the 1987 season plying his trade with Rishton in the Central Lancashire League. For Ian Botham, Somerset's decision turned out to be just the fillip he needed.

11

For Worcestershire and England

•

Ian Botham arrived in Australia a Somerset player in the autumn of 1986 and he left a Worcestershire player – but he could easily have been the new captain of Warwickshire. In November he had agreed to come to Edgbaston if the money was right. That proved no problem. The stumbling block was a matter of two votes on the Warwickshire committee. If just a couple of committee men at Edgbaston had chosen to ignore the damaging publicity about Botham and trust the judgement of the cricket management, Botham would have been playing in Birmingham in 1987, rather than in the shadow of Worcester's famous cathedral.

When it became clear that Botham was leaving Somerset, Warwickshire's cricket manager David Brown was determined to sign him. In this he was unanimously supported by the captain, Norman Gifford, and all the players. They knew that Botham's presence would inspire the side and they had enjoyed enough good times with him to ignore the press distortions and hints from Somerset that he would be a bad influence in the dressing-room. Anyone who has ever seen Botham in the Warwickshire dressing-room would know that he has always got on very well with their players, whether talking racing with Andy Lloyd or Norman Gifford, discussing stocks and shares with Dennis Amiss, or sorting out Aston Villa's problems with the younger players. Brown had been in business with Botham, part-owning a racehorse and he had absolutely no qualms about signing him. Money would have been no problem to a club that has always been efficient at fund-raising. Jim Cumbes, the then commercial manager, was convinced that he would have doubled their income in Botham's first year. Having done his sums, he informed Brown that the club could afford to offer £50,000 a year and still be comfortably in the black. In the end, Brown offered £40,000 and Botham was happy. With the Worcestershire countryside just twenty minutes' drive away, Botham's fondness for trout streams and green pastures would have been easily satisfied by the club, and with Bob Willis living just around the corner from Edgbaston, he would not lack company. The offer of the captaincy, with Gifford's full support, was another attractive part of the package.

David Brown had surmounted all the obvious obstacles except one – the committee. On 4 December, his hopes were shot down by eleven votes to nine. Bob Willis, commentating in Australia on the Ashes series, might possibly have swayed a couple of doubters, but that is mere conjecture. The rationale of the dissenters was predictably superficial: one believed that the other players would be devastated if Botham picked up a salary four times that of senior players, while another felt that Botham's image would deter likely sponsors. In vain did Brown point out that the players would be delighted to have Botham, in vain did Cumbes report that sponsorship would double. The men in suits decided that Norman Gifford and David Brown would not have been able to get the best out of Botham, a devastating indictment on two vastly experienced, highly respected men of cricket. A year later, Gifford was no longer captain and Brown had lost his job. The level of debate reminded one of H. G. Wells's remark that 'moral indignation is jealousy with a halo' – judging by some of the personal remarks about Botham he was a combination of the Yorkshire Ripper, Javed Miandad and President Gaddafi. It was deemed infinitely preferable to drift along with a mediocre side rather than inject new vigour into a stultifying structure. The committee members, traditionally those unerring experts on the game's more subtle nuances, had decided that their judgement on dressing-room matters was superior to that of the players, the manager and the captain. The biggest fish in the game got away because the angler threw it back in the water.

So the running was left to Worcestershire and Duncan Fearnley, the club's chairman, completed the signing in a Sydney hotel early in January 1987. Ian's brother-in-law, who farms in Worcestershire, had sent him a copy of the Good Beer Guide for that county and although that hardly tipped the scales, Botham knew many people in the area and had no problems settling down in a lovely cottage amid rolling hills and reliable locals who would respect his privacy. Membership of the county doubled, so did gate receipts and John Osborne, Jim Cumbes's equivalent at Worcester, wore a harassed look all summer that stemmed from an inability to please all the sponsors who were clamouring to pour money into New Road. The Warwickshire committee might also like to know that when Botham was away on Test duty during 1987, he was greatly missed by his new team-mates. As Jack Turner, the Worcestershire dressing-room attendant, put it, 'We have a lot more fun when Beefy's around.'

Worcestershire struck a very good deal when they signed Botham. He received no more from the club than any other senior player, but a deal with Carphone, a Frome-based company, brought him a further £50,000 over three years. So Botham was being paid around £30,000 a year at Worcester from all sources, chickenfeed when one considers what he did for the club's finances. Graham Dilley reached a similar type of understanding with the club and Carphone and, although injury affected his season, there is not a shadow of doubt that the highly publicised capture of Botham and Dilley was a great success for all parties in 1987.

Before that summer, Botham was enjoying his happiest tour with England. Quite apart from the joy involved in beating Australia, Botham managed to keep his name off the front pages. Early in the tour, at Bundaberg in Queensland, Tom Byron, Botham's new manager, had been alerted that a Sunday newspaper from England had flown out an investigative team with a blank cheque and the sole aim of trapping Botham in a compromising situation with two scantily clad lovelies. Byron was taking no chances from now on: Botham would stay in executive suites in the hotels, paid for out of his own pocket. Many sybaritic delights (sophisticated stereo equipment, video cassettes, complementary wines, superb food from room service), were included with the suites and Botham entertained his friends royally, but in private. The suites were usually at the disposal of the other members of the England party, and twice in Melbourne Botham staged memorable parties, at Christmas Eve and then a few days later when England retained the Ashes and Elton John acted as disc-jockey, to the delight of everyone present. Sometimes Botham's increasingly opulent lifestyle clashed with the more homespun existence of the rest of the team, but he was now earning excellent money through Byron's agency and none of the tour party begrudged his luxuries. It did look rather bizarre to watch the team arrive at Melbourne Airport: the rest of the party carried their own luggage onto the bus, while Botham walked off the plane wearing dark glasses with a grey-suited chauffeur in black leather gloves carrying his briefcase! The players would get to the hotel via courtesy cars or a bus while Botham would ease himself into a stretched limousine, containing a cocktail cabinet and a television. Ian, the *nouveau riche* of cricket, was living the type of life that the rich amateurs used to enjoy, with cricket fitting into the social whirl. Elton John spent a lot of time with Ian on that tour and there was no doubt that Ian wanted to keep up with the Johns, rather than the Joneses. When Ian's mother flew out to Sydney, Elton bought her a Cartier bracelet that must have cost a small fortune – so Ian decided he was going to visit Cartier's as well. He bought several gifts for Kath and entrusted Tom Byron with the responsibility of looking after a bracelet, diamond earrings and a necklace for the next few weeks. By now Ian had dispensed with vulgarities like cash; like the Royal Family he would rely on others to deal with such fripperies.

The other England players knew very well that he was the same chap underneath the new image. He was usually one of the first to organise trips and, if he was invited anywhere, he invariably brought team-mates along, who loved a glimpse of a more glamorous world. When an invitation came to visit the White Crusader club in Perth during the Americas Cup, Botham packed his limo with team-mates, and took great delight in asking Chris Broad to fetch a bottle of bubbly out of the fridge and crack it open as the car purred along. It was something new to Ian, he was happy flitting from cricket to rock world, and the other players were just as excited to spend so much time in the company of Elton John, an entertainer revered by many of their generation. By the time the tour ended, Elton was more or less the unofficial thirteenth man in the England dressing-room and his presence there was wholly beneficial. All credit to the management team of Peter Lush and Micky Stewart for their forbearance: they realised that Botham had so much to offer if he was in the proper frame of mind and the general ambience on that tour was a stark contrast to the defeatism of the Caribbean disaster just a few months previously.

Stewart paired Botham off with Phillip De Freitas early in the tour and it proved a masterstroke, as the young Leicestershire all-rounder confirms: 'He was fantastic to me in the first fortnight of the tour, especially as he had been on a pedestal in my eyes. When the press rang my room, Beefy would answer it for me, telling them to leave me alone, to stop building me up. He told me he had been in exactly the same position ten years earlier and that he wished he'd been sheltered from all the media attention. I had only been in the game five minutes, yet he was so thoughtful to me: later in the tour he'd ring up asking if I was bored, and I'd take Liam and Sarah to the shops, or go to Beefy's room and just talk. He and Kath treated me just like one of the family.'

When De Freitas returned to England, he found out that a second season in the limelight is often the hardest of all. His form slumped, he was dropped for a time from Leicestershire's first team and there were rumours of a split between him and his captain, Peter Willey. One player at Grace Road told me that de Freitas was now above the ordinary disciplines of county cricket and that he had been led astray by Botham. De Freitas says this was nonsense, that Botham had been nothing but a positive influence on him, getting him to approach the game more professionally. Judging by one conversation I witnessed during the 1987 season, it did appear that Botham was taking a great deal of time to get De Freitas to bowl more consistently and professionally. He had opened the bowling against Botham in their county game, who noticed that he was falling away in his delivery. During the over he shouted to him, 'Come on Daffy, get your shoulder upright and put your back into it.' That night, over a few beers, Botham began a master class of seam bowling, in company with Les Taylor, a man who also knows a thing or two about the art. Botham gave De Freitas a strongly worded lecture, every now and then saying, 'Am I right, Les? Listen to Les, Daffy, and you'll not go far wrong.' It hardly sounded like an incitement to self-indulgence and De Freitas agrees: 'A lesser man would have creamed a few boundaries off me that day, but Beefy genuinely wanted to help. He had warned me I'd be under greater pressure when I got back from Australia and he told me to keep working at my bowling. I'll be lucky if I'm half the player he's been and I've been privileged to get such good advice from him.'

De Freitas was not the only seam bowler to get sound advice from Botham in Australia. In the final Test at Sydney, Botham suggested to Gladstone Small that the impressive Steve Waugh was vulnerable early on to a ball around his rib cage. Small's first delivery to Waugh found the exact spot and he gloved it for a legside catch to the wicket-keeper. During team meetings in Australia, Botham's observations on opposing batsmen were always thoughtful and he left no doubt in anyone's mind that he wanted to end his England touring on a high note. He was one of the first to conceive the possibility of a treble on that tour – the Test series, the Perth Challenge Trophy and the Benson and Hedges World Series – and his competitive streak was fired by the fact that no other side had achieved that. Botham was very influential in that last month, inspiring the side by personal performances and expecting a high standard in the field. During the Benson and Hedges Final at Melbourne, Botham got very annoyed at that great professional, John Emburey, when the bowler failed to get behind the stumps in time to take a throw from Botham at cover. Botham held his fire, in case of overthrows, but he and Emburey had a lively discussion about an area of fielding where Botham does not usually shine either. This time, he felt, it was different: the Australians had to be beaten, fatigue or no fatigue.

Statistically it was not one of Botham's vintage tours, yet his influence was massive at the crucial phases of the tour, those moments when the success of the trip was hanging in the balance. In the First Test at Brisbane, Botham scored a hundred that was a model of sensible aggression. He rates it as one of his best Test centuries because of its significance. Having agreed to play for Queensland for the next three years, he wanted to impress the crowd and any potential sponsors, while the state of the match demanded a Botham hundred. In addition, this was the vital First Test, the time when the pattern of a tour is often set. Australia was strongly fancied while England had looked awful in the first month of the tour. There still seemed to be something of a hangover from the West Indies disaster and the team needed inspiration from somewhere to turn morale around. Botham provided it. Mike Gatting says he had never seen Ian so keyed-up before that innings. After playing himself in (often the prelude to a great Botham innings), he destroyed Merv Hughes with the new ball. David Gower, batting at the other end, came up to Botham and said, 'I ought to be telling you to calm down – but I'm just going to enjoy it instead.' Botham laughed heartily and carried on napalming the bowlers to reach 138. It was a vital innings in the context of the series, and thereafter the Australians always expected something out of the ordinary from Botham, as their initial cockiness drained away. Botham also managed to coax a few wickets out of a docile Brisbane pitch to force them to follow on, and victory was achieved against the odds.

A bad rib injury restricted Botham's bowling after the next Test at Perth. Anyone else would not have bowled for two months, but all he missed was one Test, in which he fretted about not being able to cash in with the bat on a perfect Adelaide wicket. Botham was only around 60 per cent fit for the Fourth Test at Melbourne, yet two days before, he had looked at the green wicket and told me, 'See if you can get some odds on me taking seven wickets in the match. You'll clean up.' Such was the Australians' respect for Botham's 'Golden Arm' that no one would give me odds and, in the end, Botham only took five wickets, all in the first innings. He operated off a short run-up and swung the ball. With his fifth delivery, he got Geoff Marsh out with a good bit of bowling; after an innocuous bouncer, he put more shoulder into the next and it was on Marsh before he got into the right position for the hook, so he edged it to Jack Richards the keeper. He also had Allan Border caught behind, chasing at a wide one after tying him down with uncharacteristic meanness. Although many pundits thought Botham was his usual lucky self to force batsmen into mistakes, that was not the general consensus of the men out on the pitch. 'You can't get all the wickets he's picked up without being a thinking bowler' is Border's verdict. Rodney Marsh, a former team-mate of Border's, agrees: 'That was a good bit of bowling at Melbourne. Injury often forces a bowler to think more and that's what Botham did. When you think you've got the big bugger, he's at his most dangerous – just like Gordon Greenidge when he starts to limp!' Graham Dilley points out that good judges have written off Botham's bowling since 1980, yet he has taken around 200 Test wickets since then: 'I envy his confidence. He's always on at me to enjoy my cricket more and it certainly works with him. He imposes himself on batsmen in a way the rest of us don't. He makes them play differently and they get themselves out. You don't always succeed by bowling a perfect line and length for twenty overs.' Peter Roebuck was out there as a journalist but his recent spat with Botham did not blind him to his skill as a bowler that day: 'He gets people out by getting under their skin, he's mates with them and he winds them up.'

So Botham kept on taking wickets in his own way, much to the chagrin of the purists. He kept muttering about Tom Cartwright and the virtues of line and length – as fanciful a notion as Mae West embracing chastity – but it was good enough for the Australians. It seemed strange to watch Botham turning in immaculate displays of accurate slow-medium bowling in the limited-overs games, but he did so and played a vital role in the tense final games as the treble became a reality. With the bat he consistently gave the innings an explosive start; time after time he proved invaluable in those situations that demanded guts and stern competitiveness and he gave the innings a positive start that had been lacking. For most of the tour, his left ankle was strapped up and the rib injury restricted him for over half of the trip, yet he would not give in. Nor did he forget the efforts of others. When James Whitaker missed a horrible skier off Botham's bowling at an important stage in the World Series Finals, Botham came over and consoled him; he was fully aware that no one fancies one of those as soon as he comes on as substitute fielder. When Chris Broad and Jack Richards scored their maiden Test hundreds at Perth, they found a bottle of champagne in their rooms, courtesy of Botham. He did not confine his sympathies to his team-mates. After Michael Holding injured himself while catching Botham off his own bowling, it was the dismissed batsman who helped carry Holding off the field.

Australia has always been a favourite tour of Botham's and this time he saw a good deal more of the country under Tom Byron's guidance, as they made several personal appearances. At one of them, Botham showed his genius for sincere public relations. He came to Berri, on the Murray River, a citrus-growing area about 200 miles from Adelaide. The populace are dour, hard-working and unlikely to be over-enthusiastic about a cricketer with a taste for flamboyance and streaks in his hair. It looked as if Botham would have to work hard to gain the audience's interest and support. Before he took the stage, an eight-year-old asked him to sign an elaborate card he had made in his honour. Botham was greatly moved by the care and attention to detail on the card. He ascertained the boy's name was Matthew, asked for some paper and spent ten minutes writing a long message to the lad. Later, as Botham started to address the audience, he suddenly stopped and said, 'Hang on, where's my little mate, Matthew?' and brought him up on to the stage with him. Young Matthew sat alongside his hero for the rest of the night and Botham had won over the audience with that single spontaneous act. After the deserved standing ovation, he said, 'Listen I've got nowhere else to go tonight – why don't we stay and tell a few more stories?'

At the end of the tour, with the Ashes safely in the bag, and the one-day trophies too, there was just time for a few days with friends on the Queensland coast. Here Botham unwittingly gave a fresh insight into that intense, competitive urge which has never left him. He was lolling around in his chalet, watching videos and cat-napping when he was woken up by an impromptu cricket game involving Chris Lander, Graham Morris, Tom Byron and David English. He watched their stumbling efforts and finally said, 'You lot are bloody useless – let's have a proper game.' In a trice, he had worked out how many runs you scored if the ball hit the trees or the chalet. Botham agreed to take all four on, in a two-innings match. Off his shorter run, he dismissed them for twelve. Then it was his turn to bat. He kept score and soon he had made 130 not out. Instead of declaring and winning by an innings, he elected to bat left-handed and, by the time it was dark, he had made 190 not out, without giving a chance. 'All right you buggers, back here tomorrow and I'm 190 not out,' said Botham, and he took the game seriously. Lander remembers: 'I was on my knees keeping wicket and the others were too shattered to bowl at the end, but Beefy wouldn't give it away. It was just a joke game of beach cricket to us, but not to him.'

That inner drive served him well in his next major public appearance, the walk from Belfast to Dublin in April for Leukaemia Research. Botham was aware of the remarkable generosity of the Irish during Live Aid in 1985 and it was his idea to cover the 150 miles between Ireland's two major cities. For those of us who completed the distance, it was an emotional, rewarding experience that gave us a hint of the kind of challenge posed by his earlier Land's End to John O' Groats odyssey. Compared with that, 150 miles in seven days was a gentle stroll, but to we lesser mortals it was exacting enough. At various stages, we were joined by such sporting luminaries as Willie John McBride, Mike Gibson, Alex Higgins, Barry McGuigan, Pat Jennings, Mike Gatting and Bob Willis. It was fascinating to observe that steely resolution was not confined to the head of the Botham household, as Kath was driven on by Liam to finish the whole course. It was instructive to understand Botham's attitude to pain – 'this is fun, this does not hurt!' he would roar at us – and his relationship with Mike Gatting became even warmer on that trip. Gatting had already won Botham's respect on the cricket field, but the England captain proved an excellent travelling companion on the winding roads and steep contours of the Irish countryside. To Gatting's intense disappointment he had to give best to a massive blister that had dogged him for six days. Just before Drogheda, his foot simply exploded, blood pouring everywhere. He had not trained for the walk and only his self-respect and professional sportsman's guts had got him through the first hundred miles. Botham appreciated Gatting's strength of character and the way he refused to hog the limelight. Invariably Gatting would be found at the rear of the walking group, signing autographs or passing round the collection box. He was a popular figure on that trip and even Botham gave up pulling his leg about his legendary appetite.

Amid the laughs, there were touching moments that reminded us all of the point of our endeavours. One night in Lurgan, we met little Elizabeth Gibson, a blonde charmer who presented Ian with a cheque for the fund. Just two months before, three-year-old Elizabeth had been

Even a cricket cavalier sometimes feels the tension – hardly surprising in this Test, the Melbourne one of 1982 that ended in such a gripping fashion.

Fiji, 1984 – en route with the England team to stormier waters in New Zealand and Pakistan.

Flashpoint in the Trent Bridge Test of 1985. Umpire Alan Whitehead waits for the storm to blow over as England's captain David Gower soothes the highly charged emotions of his bowler. Meanwhile Australia's Greg Ritchie wonders when the next ball will be delivered.

In the Caribbean on the West Indies tour of 1986 – the lowest ebb in Botham's career.

The Oval, 1986 and New Zealand's Jeff Crowe is trapped lbw to give Botham the record tally of Test victims on his comeback after suspension.

Botham's idiosyncratic attitude to his stance in the slips has offended the purists for years – yet he still manages to pluck great catches out of nothing.

Australia, 1987 and Botham helps the West Indians carry off Michael Holding after he tweaked a hamstring. The fact that Holding was injured in the process of catching Botham off his own bowling at a tense stage in the match underlines the Englishman's sense of sportsmanship that rarely leaves him.

To be as selective and consistent a hitter as Botham, the head must stay down at the moment of impact.

A classic example of Botham's orthodox batting technique: the still head, the leading left shoulder, the straight backlift, the balanced footwork. Keith Andrew, the National Cricket Association's Director of Coaching believes this picture encapsulates the perfect way to play the off-drive.

In the field, Botham is as
great a competitor as when
he has a ball in his hand.

Two men who can see the funny side
of cricket, despite the tensions:
'Dickie' Bird is wearing the white coat.

our legends from the rock world pop into the county ground at Worcester to see a
ricket legend who also happens to be their friend: from left to right, Jeff Lynne of
e Electric Light Orchestra, George Harrison, Eric Clapton and Elton John.

Iessing about on the river with Eric Clapton (standing) and David English, near
otham's cottage in the Worcestershire countryside.

Botham shares with Dennis Lillee a love of outdoor pursuits.

Not the kind of pose that would have entranced Hollywood or Botham's erstwhile agent, Tim Hudson – but a graphic example of the fun that Ian still gets out of cricket.

a perfectly normal child. Now she had leukaemia. She had picked up a cold that led to bruises on her body. After hospital tests, her parents were told that at best she had two years to live, unless she had a successful bone marrow operation. They suffered with their little girl through the initial treatment as she lost over a stone in weight. Elizabeth faces daily hospital visits and chemotherapy treatment for the next two years if she is to survive: she has a fifty-fifty chance. When Ian presented Elizabeth with a Bunbury bunny, a few pairs of eyes misted over in that room. Two minutes later, when she ran back into the big man's arms from twenty yards away, grown men wept openly and unashamedly. Botham's many detractors might have found that experience an enlightening one. Elizabeth Gibson's smile illuminated many a dark corner of the mind over the next couple of days as we complained about such trivia as sore feet, painful blisters and aching calf muscles.

With the Leukaemia Research Fund richer by around £150,000 Botham left the Irish salmon in peace for a few months and clocked in at Worcester to start a new county career. He found a club beside itself with excitement. Advertisers were queuing up to be associated with Worcestershire's cricket fortunes and more than a thousand turned up at Edgbaston to see Botham bat in a pre-season friendly. The Worcestershire players were intrigued to note that Botham out-hit Graeme Hick in practice out in the middle; such competition between them could only be good for the team. As it turned out, Hick rarely got a chance for a long partnership with Botham, to their mutual disappointment. They never seemed to find each other out in the middle at the same time, but it will be fascinating to see if Botham tries to outscore Hick in the same way he did with Viv Richards.

As a counter-balance to Warwickshire's pessimistic forecasts, no more than a dozen resigned their membership at Worcester and not every one of those did so over Botham's arrival. With membership doubling so that many cars could not get into the ground, Worcestershire's courageous management received just reward. As for the alleged disruption in the dressing-room, Basil D'Oliveira, the coach, says that it's almost as if Botham has been there for 25 years. Phil Neale, the captain, had always refused to entertain negative thoughts about Botham's influence, a mature response from an intelligent man who had known Botham for years. Neale was delighted with Botham's support and performances: 'People get such a distorted view about him from the media, they don't hear about the stacks of good advice he used to give me as we changed places between overs. They didn't see how his confidence rubbed off on the rest of the boys. As for nets, he actually had two sessions in successive days because he was concerned about his batting! He got rather uptight about not scoring enough runs at one stage, and that was purely because he was trying too hard. I never used to agree about this, but I now realise that you have to give a little to highly talented players in return for their flair. This goes against the grain in soccer, I know, but cricket is different and great players like Beefy have to be given some leeway. Yet if I ever asked him to come to the nets, he was there like a shot, helping others as well as working hard.' Botham volunteered to open the innings halfway through the season when no one else fancied the job and it was a great success in the Sunday League, which Worcestershire eventually won. His influence on his opening partner, Tim Curtis, was obvious. Botham has long rated Curtis as a fine, well-organised opener and he encouraged him to play some shots on Sundays.

Nor was he supportive of just his Worcestershire team-mates in 1987. David Capel has good cause to be grateful to Botham after surviving a nerve-wracking first hour of his England career in the Leeds Test against Pakistan. After just one hour's play on the first morning, Capel came down the pavilion steps with England in total disarray – five wickets down, the ball seaming and swinging and Imran Khan with his tail up. Botham met the debutant – who had been billed by the tabloids as the umpteenth player to usurp the all-rounder position from Botham – and immediately calmed him down with the reassuring words: 'Don't worry about getting out, Capes – just play your natural game.' Capel is grateful that he clearly wanted him to do well: 'Another player would've concentrated on his own game in such difficult conditions, but he made me feel at home right away. Beefy made sure I hardly had to play a ball in the opening overs and he settled me down. He never stopped encouraging me between overs.'

When Botham and Dilley signed for Worcestershire, there were wildly optimistic forecasts that a county championship was a near-certainty. This ignored the fact that the two players would only be available for eleven championship games through England calls (in fact Dilley only played in six of them through injury), and that the loss of Dipak Patel and David Smith would be sorely felt. A one-day trophy was always the best bet and, if Botham had been used more imaginatively in the batting order, success in the Benson and Hedges might also have been achieved. They got there in the 40-overs Refuge Assurance Sunday League and Botham's part in this was incalculable. His batting invariably gave them a good start and, off his short run, he regularly gave masterful displays of accurate seam bowling, with enough swing to get the good batsmen out. He called himself 'Mr Economy' when he bowled on Sundays and again the name of Tom Cartwright was invoked as he turned in eight-over spells in which he went for around $3\frac{1}{2}$ an over. Several times he was not fit, having pulled a groin muscle in early August, but he kept plugging away in the manner of the last month of the Australian tour.

He admits he was never fully fit in the 1987 season. 'That rib injury I picked up at Perth took me longer to shake off than any other in my career. For the whole of my first season at Worcester, I was never confident of letting the ball go, because I knew that I might be putting extra pressure on my back. I felt very frustrated at times but the line-and-length stuff worked in the one-day matches in Australia, where the ball just didn't come on to the bat, and also in the Sunday League for Worcestershire. I'll bowl the same way on Sundays in future, but I'm not finished with my long run-up!'

He kept telling his team-mates that they would win the Sunday League with a month to go, and his confidence was not misplaced. The penultimate game against Surrey epitomised Botham's influence. On a slow, bounceless pitch at Hereford, he made 80 off 74 balls. The pitch was so slow and low that of Surrey's 154 in 40 overs no less than 97 of them were singles – yet Botham managed to put bat to ball. He hit the spin of Medlycott for 18 in one over and one six over extra cover landed forty-five yards past the boundary ropes. You have to possess exceptional timing and strength to bludgeon an attack on such a pitch and no one could match his stroke play. He then took a superb low catch at mid-wicket to dismiss the dangerous Alec Stewart and when he came on to bowl (rusty after recent injury), he took a wicket with his second ball, ending up with 3 for 24. It was an all-round performance of great authority, even if it was only a Sunday League match, and after that Worcestershire just needed to beat Northants to win the trophy. Botham spent the last week telling everyone it was in the bag, and after relaxing half the Northants team the night before in his cottage, he proceeded to dominate the match. Once more came the legendary Botham generosity – he picked up the £200 tab for the celebratory Indian meal for twenty friends.

Keen trawlers for disruptive influence in the dressing-room might like to know that Botham received as many appalling stink bombs in his jeans as the rest of the players, that he organised a strippagram for Phil Neale's thirty-third birthday, that he gave the younger players stacks of advice and that a day off often brought an open invitation to Botham's cottage for a barbecue – wives and children included. The players to a man felt he was a magnificent addition to life at New Road, both socially and professionally, and having spent a good deal of the summer at that most delightful of grounds, I saw no evidence to the contrary. Botham also spread the gospel of Leukaemia Research, bringing sufferers into the dressing-room, getting bats signed for them and spending a lot of time with sick children. Sometimes their plight was too much for one or two players, who were overcome at such suffering, but that only increased their admiration for Botham's unselfishness.

Ian thought that it might take the best part of his first season to feel fully at home at Worcester, but in fact it took him about a fortnight:

> I thought it would feel a little strange after all those years at Taunton but with Graham Dilley also joining at the same stage, that helped me settle in. There are so many great lads in that dressing-room I already knew so it was always going to be just a matter of time before I felt at home. I can honestly say that after just one season at Worcester, I know more of the committee than I ever did at Taunton, even in the good times. It's a pleasure to go into a committee room and be able to talk freely and about other things than cricket. Even though some of the committee have experience of playing first-class cricket, they don't earbash you about what's gone on that day and they stick to what they know best. Nobody tells you how to play the game, everybody thinks and talks constructively and we all have a laugh. It's brilliant, I love it. I've never been happier in county cricket – a great set of lads, a bloody good team, a lovely part of the world and excellent cheap beer! What more could I want?

There was another addition to the benign atmosphere at New Road in Botham's first season. To the great delight of the players, legends from the rock world used to pop in and watch the cricket. In June, the first day of the Leicestershire match was watched by Eric Clapton, Elton John, George Harrison and Jeff Lynne of the ELO: afterwards it was difficult to work out which stars wanted whose autographs! That night, Clapton and Harrison played guitar at Botham's cottage and for those of us there, it was a magical evening which could not even be spoiled by Bob Willis route-marching us through his Bob Dylan repertoire, with George Harrison accompanying him on the guitar. All the while, Botham sat back, aware that his tone-deaf attempts at singing would have cracked several windowpanes – he was content to sip an Australian red, delighted he had thrilled his old friends with some string-pulling. He is a great social organiser and it gave him a particular buzz to provide such entertainment from two giants of rock music. Botham was even prepared to smile tolerantly at the sight of Mike Gatting swigging some very expensive Grange Hermitage straight from the bottle!

When one of Botham's old mates heard that he was laying on George Harrison at the cottage, he replied, 'Knowing Beefy, he's probably brought John Lennon back from the dead to accompany him!' Well he could not quite manage that, but he organised an impromptu performance by Eric Clapton at his local pub. It was a bizarre evening, standing in that sweaty, cramped room, listening to the world's greatest rock guitarist while the locals wondered what all the fuss was about. As far as they were concerned, Eric Clapton might have been someone who had wandered in off the streets, even if the likes of Graeme Hick, Steve Rhodes and Neal Radford had tried to disabuse them. Clapton had agreed to play there after winning £180 at three-card brag in the Worcestershire dressing-room earlier in the day. After Botham had asked him for that favour, he agreed – provided Botham scored a hundred next day against Essex. He did. Clapton bought a speaker with his cards winnings and a memorable night was had by all. That was not the only favour Clapton accomplished that day for Ian. After he had given Clapton the bat he had used in Australia, Eric racked his brains for a suitable gift in return. He came up with his Statocaster Fender guitar, custom-made, one of only two in the world, worth around £10,000. That was the guitar Eric used that night in Botham's pub, the one that Ian would desperately love to be able to play, except his fingers are not supple enough after picking up so many injuries over the years. The guitar now occupies pride of place in Botham's cottage, with a sentimental value far higher than anything Ian has ever collected in his career.

Ian also treasures the memory of meeting the legendary rock singer, Tina Turner, during the 1987 summer, although he keeps quiet about the sting in the tail. On the Saturday of the Lord's Test, Eric Clapton took Ian to see Tina Turner in concert, the realisation of an ambition for the cricketer, who shares the view of millions that the indestructible Ms Turner is one of life's true originals. Towards the end of the concert, Clapton was called up on stage to help her with a couple of numbers and by this time Botham was ecstatic, waving at Eric from the special enclosure. Afterwards he said to Eric, 'I've got to meet her! She's fantastic!' Eric eventually effected an introduction back-stage: 'Meet

Ian, he's a famous cricketer,' to receive the devastating riposte: 'What's cricket?'

Lest it appears that everything was sweetness and light for Ian in the summer of 1987, it has to be admitted that he made a fool of himself at Chepstow early in May and the subsequent hostile publicity was all of his own making. A bottle of whisky on an empty stomach unleashed the dark forces within him and his behaviour in front of many sporting luminaries and influential people tarnished a day in which he had helped raise generous sums for charity by playing golf. At one stage Ian verbally abused a waitress and then head-butted a waiter. It took Tom Byron a week to douse the fires of indignation and persuade the injured parties to drop thoughts of legal action. It was just the kind of incident Ian had avoided recently, and his manager warned him that a repetition of such conduct would see a parting of the ways. Under Byron's management Ian seemed to have gained a new maturity, apart from the Chepstow incident, with the keen antennae that enabled him to duck trouble before it smacked him in the eye. At a barbecue at a Worcestershire pub around the same time, he had spent three hours, chatting happily to all and sundry and signing autographs, when he suddenly scented a change in the atmosphere. 'I'm off – I smell the press here,' he said and left abruptly. Most of the predominately male gathering had been delighted to observe the growing phalanx of desirable young ladies, but Botham was so wary of a 'stitch-up' that he did not wait to discover if they were genuine cricket supporters or in the pay of certain newspapers.

Byron lost a £40,000 deal and several one-day personal appearances from the Chepstow incident and, for once, Botham sheepishly accepted the dressing-down. The story was broken by the *Sun*. It was felt that a blind eye had been turned to Ian's other allegedly anti-social activities in the pages of the *Sun* over recent years and that this time they would not ignore it. Once that decision was reached the *Sun* threw panzer regiments of dirt-diggers down to Chepstow and they ran a two-page feature the day after, splashing the story ahead of anyone else. The rest of the tabloids were slow off the mark and the *Sun* had the story to itself for a day. As a result Botham felt there was a vendetta against him at the *Sun* and his relationship with Chris Lander was placed under its greatest strain.

Chepstow was an example of how Ian can occasionally be thrown off kilter for no apparent reason. That day he had decided to join Ian Woosnam and Max Boyce in a drinking competition and although all three ended up the worse for wear, only one failed to remain jovial. Yet

Ian is the drinker with the greatest stamina. Perhaps it is the dark drinks like rum, brandy and whisky that let loose unpleasant vapours in a man of immense kindness and good nature. Complex tensions swirl around the corridors of his psyche and his behaviour on the rest day of the Edgbaston Test afforded another clue about those tensions. Ian went to Worcester to watch his new county play his old love, Somerset. He took up position in the executive suite, where he could watch the play if necessary and proceeded to demolish a goodly proportion of vodka. He was surrounded by friends and his parents, but it was not a pleasant ambience. There was a recklessness about his drinking that was disturbing, a bravado that surfaced in a message he sent to the home dressing-room: 'Tell the lads the vodka's going down a treat and that it'll go down even better when you've stuffed those . . . . .!' Around six o'clock, Ian was getting louder in front of many others who were not in his social circle and finally Richard Lines managed to calm him down and he was taken back to the cottage. Ian's father was shocked and upset and Eric Clapton had to play the guitar for three hours to relax Ian before they returned to their Birmingham hotel for the next day's play. Les Botham was angry at what appeared to be Ian's relentless desire to get drunk that Sunday: 'He should've relaxed at home, not in public. It's fine for his friends to egg him on, but I'm sure they don't drink when they've got a big business meeting early the following morning.' Ian was sixteen not out on Saturday night and many were anticipating a feast of batting from him on the Monday morning. Perhaps that was the problem – the burden of expectation again. Perhaps deep down Ian knows that his powers are in decline and yet he does not want to acknowledge that inexorable fact. Possibly the drink helps to ward off that fear of failure. He has always been a prodigious drinker when the mood takes him, and usually he handles it extremely well, but once or twice he gets trapped by the *in vino veritas* syndrome and his inner conflicts warp his behaviour.

After Ian was dismissed within half-an-hour on the Monday morning, Eric Clapton talked about the schizophrenic side to Ian's character. Having survived and prospered in the mad world of rock music for more than twenty years, Clapton is better qualified than most to understand the problems of stardom. 'Deep down Beefy's terrified when he goes out to bat, terrified that he'll fail. All that bravado is just a façade: there are times in the day when he shrivels inside and he needs that hard exterior to protect the soft inner core. His arrogance can trip him up sometimes. He's still very young, operating in a restricted world and he can't get far without Andy. It took me a long time to stop people doing things for me – now I can get my own fags, check myself in at an airport and be a proper human being. Beefy is the equivalent to me in cricket terms, yet he's now distanced from reality. He has to mature and get out of that narrow world. I know what it's like: I nearly killed my manager ten years ago by harrying him with my ego. We all have to learn humility, mustn't think we're Jack the Lad all the time. He's at a difficult age in difficult times, there's so much hype behind him – but I think he's got the capability to come through it all. Certainly he couldn't have a better partner than Kath, she's so strong.' Caring words from a man who is now one of Botham's closest friends. They spend long periods together on fishing trips, comparing their respective worlds, and Eric is one of the few people who can shout Ian down when he is in one of his raucous, aggressive moods. He will be a staunch ally over the next few years as Ian comes to terms with new roles in his life.

Perhaps Ian's occasional manic outbursts in 1987 stemmed from an insecurity about his future England career. By midsummer the press were sniping at him for low scores and a lack of bowling. In the lead-up to the Edgbaston Test, a lot was made of a series of niggling injuries that prevented him bowling all that much. From 30 June to 23 July, the first day of the Edgbaston Test, Botham did not bowl in first-class cricket, yet he was still able to send down 48 overs over the next two days and bowl skilfully on the final day as England almost forced a win. The press tried to suggest that Botham was making a fool out of Micky Stewart by turning up at Muirfield to watch the Open Golf rather than proving his fitness in the nets – this despite the fact that persistent rain had ruined any chance of a proper outdoor net. We had the usual spectacle of the press demanding punitive action over Botham, despite medical confirmation that an ankle injury and a septic elbow had prevented him bowling recently. The press felt it knew better than Botham about the physical demands of bowling in a Test Match, trotting out the boring utilitarian line that Botham ought to be subjected to the same disciplines as anyone else. They ignored the fact that Test cricket is now a commercial enterprise, with Botham the principal attraction. No amount of puritanical moralising would place Botham in jeopardy because he is simply different from the rest, with a cricket talent that does not flourish amid the daily grind of net practice.

Around that time, support for Botham came from a surprising source. Bob Taylor was the complete professional during his quarter of a century in the game and no one would ever accuse him of shirking the duties of preparation. He used to get annoyed at Botham when he called him 'OAP' (short for 'Old Age Pensioner'), and told him he would not be around in the game at Bob's age because he would have made his pile, but Taylor feels that Botham is always the best judge of his own fitness: 'You can never criticise Both's attitude to training because he always goes out there on the field and gives everything. He's like the old players like Fred Trueman who got fit by bowling and bowling – if Both was around in those days, he'd have bowled just as many overs as Fred, and not break down either. Ian didn't really need to do all those stretching exercises before play started because he has always been very athletic and flexible in his body. How many times has he been injured due to a lack of preparation?' One can only imagine how Trueman and Botham would react to being bracketed together, but the views of a man with Taylor's experience and long memory might have interested the press.

Even Botham's most virulent critics had to choke on their bile in the last Test at the Oval. It had been billed as possibly Botham's last Test, although the England captain and manager certainly hoped not. Botham went for more than 200, one of the most expensive spells in Test history, as Pakistan piled up a huge score. Yet he did bowl 52 overs, picked up three of the first four wickets and had Javed Miandad dropped off a mishook. His zest for the fray continued through his marathon spells and the brilliant manner in which he ran out Imran Khan on the second evening was a tribute to a great trier. On the Monday night, with England facing a ticklish final day on a wearing wicket, Botham and the England team relaxed at the Groucho Club, at a party thrown to celebrate Botham's 5,000 runs in Test cricket. He sat in a corner seat for a while with Mike Gatting and promised that the Pakistanis would not get him out next day. It is fair to say that Pakistani cricketers rank some way down his scale of affections and he had been incensed by their churlish, quibbling, unsportsmanlike attitude all summer. At Leeds he had been driven to a finger-wagging confrontation after Salim Yousuf, the wicket-keeper, claimed a catch on the second bounce. Typically, Botham went into the umpires' room as soon as play ended that day and apologised for any embarrassment. It was not his fault that the Pakistanis seemed to view an appeal as a basis on which to start haggling negotiations.

On the final morning in the nets at the Oval, Botham told the England players he was going to whack the bowlers around and make them pay for the frustrations suffered by England that summer. Something happened between the start of play and Chris Broad's dismissal, because

Botham then embarked on a self-denying ordinance that belonged in a Trappist monastery. It must have been the most boring innings Botham has ever played, as he kicked away Abdul Qadir's leg-spin for hour after hour when he must have been itching to hit him back over his head. He took 22 deliveries to get off the mark and, after 72 balls, he was three not out. Botham's defensive technique against the spinners is, like the rest of his batting, founded on the most orthodox of principles and, to avoid the risk of an lbw, he was cunning enough to look as if he was playing a shot when the ball hit his front pad, even though he was determined to keep his bat out of the way. Qadir got more and more frustrated at this, while Botham enjoyed the spectacle immensely. It was not until he was into his third hour at the crease that he trusted himself to strike the ball with any conviction – and even then the boundaries were rationed out frugally. When the game was left drawn, Botham walked off with his captain, having batted 252 minutes for 51 not out – by his normal scoring standards, that ought to have been about 150. In the dressing-room afterwards Botham had the happy air of a man who had won a Test with an unbeaten hundred: once again he had shown the knack of coming up with the unexpected.

Although Botham's remarkable exercise in patience seemed totally out of character, he had shown that cussed side to his nature many times before. There was that long haul with Randall at Sydney in 1979, when he batted 90 minutes for six; the masterful innings at Lord's in 1983 that won the Nat-West semi-final; and countless other occasions when he has 'milked' the spinners for singles rather than risk getting out to them with a rush of blood. Botham's batting has never been just an exciting amalgam of nerve and brilliance: a man who has scored so many Test hundreds does not always play flamboyantly. That Oval knock was more an example of Botham's capacity to surprise rather than a sudden maturing or a fork right to the Road to Damascus – yet that innings offered an intriguing prospect as he approached his cricketing middle age.

12

'Bonjour Tristesse'

●

If degrees were ever awarded for shooting oneself in the foot, then Ian Botham would by now have graduated *summa cum laude* from the University of Life. His short-lived stint as an all-Australian hero either side of Christmas 1987 would constitute the thesis that brought him the glittering prize. In the space of four months, Ian turned his back on a fortune in an ingenious manner – he managed to alienate some Australians by rowdy behaviour in public. One does not need to be a devotee of Barry Humphries' more basic material to realise that a court appearance for rowdy behaviour almost constitutes a campaign medal in the eyes of many Australians, but Ian chose the wrong time to assimilate himself into the Ocker culture. It was fun to be cricket's Ned Kelly as long as he ignored Ned's eventual comeuppance.

Such is Botham's schizophrenia that he managed to turn the trauma of Australia into the triumph of Turin in the space of three weeks. Only a man of colossal self-belief and willpower could have brazened out the first sacking of his cricket career and eventually forced reluctant praise from a press corps that came to the South of France in the hope of seeing Botham buckle under pressure that was largely self-imposed. His march from Perpignan to Turin in aid of Leukaemia Research was, in my view, a greater performance than his epic trek from John O'Groats to Land's End. Botham's professionalism as he approached Turin was as impressive as his inspirational qualities to the other walkers, his determination to stay out of trouble and his insistence on rising above the petty squabbles and hassles that made this latest odyssey an unsatisfactory experience for many veterans of previous hikes for Leukaemia

Research. A lesser man would have been dragged down by the goldfish-bowl nature of the task, by the realisation that even the supportive members of the travelling media party feared he might not walk 450 miles in 21 days, that the slightest social indiscretion would be gleefully publicised. Yet by the second week of the walk Botham was warning some of the more boisterous sections of the walking group to tone down their antics in public. In some jaundiced eyes, such strictures would be tantamount to President Reagan extolling the virtues of a hard day at the office, but Botham knew the score. In his own way, he had framed the rules of the game, yet no one was going to catch him offside. This the man who had just picked up a record fine from the Australian Cricket Board for bad behaviour, a man whose coarse language had succeeded in shocking that most unshockable and long-suffering of characters, the Australian female. An enigma variation of some stature.

By the time Ian Botham landed in court in mid-March for his behaviour on a flight from Melbourne to Perth, he was fed up with Australia. This is not to excuse the public misdemeanours that landed him in a police cell and led to his sacking by Queensland, simply an explanation of his state of mind. He had become bored – always a dangerous time for Botham when he sometimes teeters over the edge of self-indulgence. Months spent in hotels and rented accommodation contrasted with the lifestyle he had imagined a year earlier, when he had signed for Queensland on a three-year contract and pointed out the site of his proposed luxury house as he flew over Brisbane with his England team-mates. When he arrived to play for Queensland, the house was not available, nor – despite the purchase of all the necessary furniture – was it ever ready during Botham's stay in Australia. His relationship with Allan Border had become strained by March. It was nothing that two such close friends cannot patch up over a beer in England this summer, but by the time the Queensland players boarded the plane for Perth, the captain was not the most popular player in the squad. That accolade probably went to Botham and he took it upon himself to climb into Border on the flight. Border had recently admitted to the press that he had become 'Mr Grumpy' in recent weeks as he had seen Queensland's marvellous early start fade away. Western Australia had overtaken them in the Sheffield Shield table and had earned home advantage in the Final. Border probably felt that Queensland was again due to miss out on the Shield, once more failing to break the duck in 56 attempts. The wheel had come off on the southern tour of Victoria and Tasmania and an early departure from the McDonald's Cup, the one-day competition, had done nothing to improve the captain's mood.

During the trip from Melbourne to Perth, Border became involved in an argument with Greg Ritchie, Botham's room-mate and a fine batsman. Ritchie felt he had been harshly treated by the Australian selectors that season and finally, fortified by a few grogs, told the Australian captain so. As the argument continued, Botham weighed in. Now when it comes to sheer compulsive force in an argument, Botham has no peers and soon his annoyance at Border's recent moodiness and his sympathy for Ritchie's frustrations led to a considerable rise in the decibel level, and the use of a certain Anglo-Saxon adverb. The other passengers in the economy-class section had already endured a fair amount of the explicit conversation that seems to be common to all sportsmen who have drunk heartily for several hours. They had also listened to a tape which parodies the cricket coverage of Channel 9 in a wickedly funny way. Although that tape is now of about five years' vintage, it remains very amusing in an earthy fashion. When played among friends over a few drinks, it is a delight; on a plane with the sound turned up, and strangers seated nearby, it is rather crass. When a man turned round and finally suggested a modicum of self-control, Botham turned the stranger's head back to the front and suggested in the frankest of terms that he should mind his own business. Worse, he directed a volley of abuse at a woman a few seats in front.

After the plane landed, Botham made a point of apologising to both parties. The matter might have ended there if he had not left behind an enraged waitress at Melbourne Airport as the Queensland players changed planes. Greg Ritchie had to apologise to the waitress for Botham's behaviour and when the police were called, they were annoyed to find the plane had just left. When other passengers complained to the airline at Perth, the local police, armed with the views of their Melbourne counterparts, just had to take action. The following day, as the Queensland players relaxed after training around the pool at the Merlin Hotel, they were visited by the police. Botham was taken to a cell and charged with assault and offensive behaviour. He faced a night in the slammer unless someone who resided in the state of Western Australia would furnish the necessary £2,000. Finally, Dennis Lillee was tracked down and, armed with a crate of beer, Botham's old adversary came to the cell and bailed him out. Next day, he was fined £320 after pleading guilty. He was lucky that his solicitor Alan Herd had just flown in with Kath Botham (ostensibly for a holiday interspersed with a spot of work), because Herd performed wonders in court, not least of all by siphoning off the full text of his client's advice to the lady in the plane.

With Greg Ritchie also charged with offensive behaviour and Allan Border just managing to escape with a charge, it was hardly surprising that Queensland lost the Final. So many statements were taken by police in the Queensland dressing-room during the match that the players did well to escape for a bat. A few days later, when Botham was fined $5000 by the Australian Cricket Board, the matter appeared to be closed. True he was still under fire for his part in a spot of vandalism with Dennis Lillee in a dressing-room after the Tasmania game, but that was no worse than the usual antics on tour of rugby union internationals, who include men of high academic attainments and professional distinction yet are allegedly imbued with the amateur ethos. It has never seriously been suggested that any of those paragons should be suspended for letting off steam. Botham had also been fined £250 for swearing at a spectator as he walked off the field at the Melbourne Cricket Ground. According to the Queensland players, that spectator had subjected Botham to a torrent of foul-mouthed abuse all day, and they felt they themselves would have replied in similar manner. In any event, the Tasmania and Melbourne incidents did not appear to be all that serious in terms of Botham's future with Queensland.

Certainly Botham did not expect to be sacked when he flew into Perpignan on March 27 to prepare retracing the Emperor Hannibal's footsteps over the Alps, complete with elephants. He talked enthusiastically of boosting the coffers of Leukaemia Research by around £5,000,000 and seemed relaxed, passing off recent vicissitudes as so many storms in so many tea-cups. On the morning of March 29, the eve of the walk's start, he conducted a press conference with his usual bravado. When pressed about his future with Queensland, he initially blustered ('I don't give a stuff about what's going on 12,000 miles away'), then opted for intimacy ('I'll let you into a little secret, I had a meeting with them a week ago, and as far as I'm concerned, there's no problem'). I winced as Ian played out his role and hoped that his words of insouciance did not come back to haunt him. We all knew that the executive of the Queensland Cricket Association was meeting in Brisbane at that time, and that several reactionary forces in Australia's most reactionary state were less than impressed by I. T. Botham.

Ian Botham's Queensland career ended as he tucked into a meal with friends and family in a Perpignan restaurant. Every member of the media party back at the hotel was soon aware of the decision and the rush to phones and the build-up of cameras were sadly familiar to veteran

Bothamologists. Poor Andy Withers, Ian's loyal personal assistant, had taken the call from Botham's solicitor and had to stand for two hours at the end of the hotel drive, waiting for his boss to return and steeling himself to pass on the wise message from Alan Herd: 'Don't say a word until you've talked to me.' The elements of another Botham own-goal were all there; Ian had told me a few hours earlier that he was off to get 'Brahms and Liszt', a perfectly understandable desire in the context of what awaited him over the next three weeks, yet a potential disaster once he heard he had been sacked and the cameras started whirring on his return to the hotel. Mercifully, Kath and a couple of girlfriends returned early from the meal, learned of the decision and tracked Ian down at the restaurant as he lingered over more drinks. Geoff Taylor, close friend and business associate, talked some sense into him, told him to drop the bluster and carry out Alan Herd's instructions. An hour later, he breezed into the hotel, announced to the media entourage that he would be making a statement in ten minutes and retired to his room. Half an hour later he appeared to utter a terse statement which promised subsequent revelations that would 'make your hair stand on end'. For now, all would be silence except for discussions about the Walk.

Despite Ian's breezy self-assurance, he was shocked by his sacking. Nobody, especially someone with his ego, likes being sacked. It suited Ian to blame Greg Chappell for stabbing him in the back, to accuse Chappell of furthering his ambitions to become Australia's top cricket administrator by grasping the Botham nettle and making an example of him. Certainly a homily on behaviour from any member of the cricketing Chappells seemed as laughable a notion as a book on fair play by the Borgias, but Ian did not help himself. If Chappell was out to nail him, then Botham fell straight into his hands just before the Shield final in Perth. Botham had skipped the final practice session at the Gabba in favour of opening the new airport terminal at Brisbane – this after a six-day break in which he had enjoyed himself up in the Northern Territory. Chappell phoned him and told him he was disappointed with his approach to Queensland's vital game. He expected Botham to play a major part in the Final and Botham reassured him that he was experienced enough to turn on the tap when it was really necessary. A day later, the eventful trip from Brisbane to Perth cast a shadow over the team's eventual performance in the final and Botham's fate was sealed.

Although Allan Border pleaded Botham's case with the executive of the Queensland Cricket Association, he did not have a vote and Botham was sacked by twenty votes to nil. The Queensland players were shattered, local radio switchboards were jammed and the state's newspapers also lined up alongside Botham. He had been an immensely popular signing, his team-mates thought the world of him, but he had misread the tea-leaves. The state of Queensland is hardly the most enlightened area of Australia, and old knee-jerk responses died hard. Some fairly reactionary figures were on that executive committee, men who saw no harm in the police feeling a few collars if more than a couple of people gathered on a Brisbane street corner after dusk. They were not the kind of men who would go into the social jungle with Ian Botham. The punters who saw Ian as a fair dinkum Aussie, a larrikin, understood the man's popular appeal, but they were not present when the executive sat down to decide his future.

Certainly there was no criticism of Ian's all-round performances. He was the country's best all-rounder, batting very responsibly, bowling long spells at an economical rate and holding some stunning catches. In his first game, at the Gabba against Victoria, he held three blinding catches on the first day, batted commandingly the following day (58 off 34 balls) and picked up three wickets at important times. Nearly 11,000 saw Sunday's play, and throughout the season the gates were doubled whenever Queensland played. Ian bowled off his long run, looked fit and sharp and competed fervently. It was his kind of cricket – fiercely competitive over four days, then a week's rest before the next match – and his performances were highly satisfactory. He was disappointed not to get a hundred but he insisted on batting at number six when Border wanted to promote him and, as a result, often ran out of partners. Invariably he would bat in the approved manner – watchfully, gradually unfurling some glorious shots – and his bowling was never less than tight and usually full of menace. In purely cricketing terms, it was hardly Ian's fault that the Queensland jinx in the Sheffield Shield was not broken.

Ian insists he was used by Chappell, but it does appear that his judgement let him down at various stages and the dark forces that occasionally envelop him proved his undoing. If only he had shown the same shrewdness as he did a few weeks later on the Hannibal Walk, he would have still been on Queensland's books. A word or two of sincere contrition might not have gone amiss either. Yet Ian finds it hard to say 'sorry' and genuinely mean it. Significantly it was the first time he had been sacked in his career. At other times (the England captaincy in 1981, Somerset's in 1985), he had read the signs correctly and got out in face-saving time; now his failure was writ large, doubly so in that the sacking had nothing to do with any waning of ability. Ian was galled at his dismissal, and annoyed that he had not exercised his option before the executive committee met. I am certain that he would have broken his contract with Queensland and ended the Australian experiment after just one season. Quite simply he was bored with Australia and was desperately homesick.

> I loved the cricket, the best of its type I have ever played. But I was hardly ever in the right frame of mind. I missed everything about England – the sense of humour, the green countryside, the fishing, the football, the beer. Around Christmas, I had the family around me in a fabulous, remote island off the Great Barrier Reef but I kept thinking how lovely it would be to transport us all back to our home, with the snow piling up outside and the log fire crackling away. I'm very fond of the Aussies and the country but there's a feeling that it will soon be like America, full of go-getters and millionaires, with the crime rate soaring. I really love England, even the wintry weather, and my spell in Queensland brought it all home to me. I wanted to be back there all the time, seeing Liam score a few tries on the rugby field, encouraging Sarah in her exams and listening to Beccy picking up new words. For the first time in my career, I was preparing to break a contract. I wanted out and Greg Chappell did me a favour.

Now it is true that Ian's ability to rewrite history would impress the most ardent Kremlinologist, but he was often depressed during his four months in Australia. Within three weeks, I had seen that at first hand. I had popped into his hotel at Newcastle in New South Wales for a chat and we spent the afternoon yarning in his room with Greg Ritchie. 'Glamorous life, isn't it?' he said as he and Ritchie tucked into hamburgers, milk and racing on the television in a cramped hotel room. Already Ian seemed disenchanted, despite all the hype attending his arrival. A few days later, he returned to England for a week to publicise the Hannibal Walk and film a baked beans commercial. The day before he was due to fly back, he was very morose. He slipped away from a gathering of friends at his home and sat by the lake with his dog and close friend, Joe Neenan. He did not want to go back to Australia and he had to be more or less pushed onto the plane. Although Kath and the children came out for Christmas and his parents joined him for a time in the New Year, he was still yearning for home. In March, he phoned Kath and asked her to come out for the Shield Final. She would only be there for ten days, a ludicrously short period considering the horrendous journey time, but it was indicative of Ian's depression that Kath complied. Within 24 hours, her husband was hauled off to a police cell.

It seemed aeons since a mellow evening in November when a group of us gathered at a swish Brisbane restaurant during Ian's début game to toast his success and that of Queensland. Allan Border stood up and said the appropriate things and all concerned nodded approval, as Ian basked in the certain knowledge that he was embarking on an illustrious stage of his career. I am sure that Border and Botham will restructure their close friendship, but the Queensland episode only underlined the conundrum that is Ian Botham.

It was highly typical of Ian's chronic contradictions that on the day he was sacked for boorish behaviour in public, he should receive a warm eulogy from a section of society that he admires cravenly – the Royal Family. As the media mob-handed its way through the foyer of the Novotel Perpignan in search of Botham, a letter from the Duke of Kent was pinned up on the notice board. In his capacity as president of the Leukaemia Research Fund, the Duke of Kent paid fulsome tribute to Ian's dedicated work and wished him every success on the Hannibal Walk. There we have the enigma that is Ian in one vignette: he will surely never get the summons to Buckingham Palace for a gong, yet one facet of his life wins unqualified Royal approval.

Ian's close friends on the Hannibal Walk feared the worst that day. Despite his outward bonhomous appearance, he was uptight, concerned about the size of the media entourage and fighting a desperate battle with himself to control his public utterances. Early on, Geoff Taylor, Alan Dyer and Richard Lines all attempted to give him advice that owed everything to practical businessmen's experience of the outside world and immense affection. Each time Ian passed it all off, saying he was fine, that he had been stitched up by Chappell and that there was nothing to worry about. Somehow Ian managed to deal with the next three weeks triumphantly. Invariably he was early to bed after propping up his legs for some hours after the day's walking was over. He would be up early to prepare himself, applying all the appropriate lotions and performing all the necessary stretching exercises. He was a model of courtesy to the police who escorted us all the way, he said all the right things via his interpreter to the various civic dignitaries who greeted him at the start and finish of each day's walking. Botham simply gritted his teeth and got on with the job of walking, a task that proved too much for all but seven of the 23 who began at Perpignan, bright-eyed with optimism, flexing themselves in their smart new tracksuits. The pace – around four miles an hour – even broke two supremely fit young Frenchmen who had been assigned as Botham's bodyguards. They were top-rated kick-boxers, used to displaying their lithe flexibility in the ring, possessed of a pugilistic skill that Botham greatly admired – yet within three days, they were staggering around like Glaswegian drunks. The strain on their calves and knees was immense, but to their credit they rallied after treatment and returned to form a touching bond with their leader.

Somehow Botham managed to detach himself from the tensions and pettiness that invariably attend any gathering of around a hundred people of varying personalities who have all been thrown together for three weeks. General Portfolio, the walk's sponsors, were at all times a supportive presence, but the accumulating tensions were not eased by the defects of the organising team, led by Mervyn Edgecombe. Edgecombe's idea of making everybody happy and smoothing the path ahead was to tell everyone about his own problems, to reassure us that we had no idea how difficult all the planning had been for him. Just to underline the point, the press release (which incidentally featured at least eight factual errors), referred to Edgecombe's 'dogged determination' in setting up the whole project, while ignoring the rider that he was not in it for philanthropic reasons. When a press release cannot spell Greg Ritchie's name correctly, and devotes more lines to biographies of the project director and producer than to Ian Botham, one fears for the success of the campaign. As the days unfolded and the estimated daily total of miles to walk seemed to get longer and longer, the walkers angrily recalled the guff in the press release about the detailed studies of the terrain carried out by Edgecombe and his intrepid band of experts. If they could not get the exact mileage right of every stage – a vital piece of information for a walker racked with pain and dark doubts – what else would go wrong? The promised crossing of the Rhone by raft did not materialise, due to the reluctance of the French Army to help out, and a man-made lake that we were assured was a wonderful sight proved to be almost dry – both major disappointments to film crews who were counting on such spectacles to foster interest back home.

Edgecombe's behaviour, combined with the relaxed air of an auction-eer, succeeded in alienating large sections of the party. His attitude to the majority of the media at the start of the walk was an object lesson in provocation. As a former investigative journalist himself, he seemed surprisingly hostile about the presence of the men with smart overcoats, generous expenses and hard eyes. He was concerned about any member of radio or television getting more than a 'good morning' from Botham because he had signed up TVS to do a documentary on the walk. On the first morning, we had the ludicrous spectacle of Edgecombe ordering the serried ranks of the media into a pen while the TVS crew were allowed to get on with the task of interviewing Botham and looking up the nostrils of the elephants. Hard-nosed camera crews used to more taxing assignments in places like Belfast, Moscow and South Africa did the sensible thing and ignored Edgecombe. After a while it dawned on our hapless project director that you cannot make an exclusive of an event that needs the support of the public, but the franc took a long time a'dropping.

Not that the majority of the press corps deserved sympathy. Many of them were there for an unashamed knocking job and when we entered Turin, they must have been galled to realise they would soon have to justify their expenses to their masters for such a derisory return. One of the elephants went lame after a few miles, which prompted a disgraceful piece from one news agency reporter that all three elephants were now out of the walk. Not true, there was never a chance of that. Another tabloid flew in Bill Travers of the Zoo Check organisation to allege that the elephants were being maltreated. He joined Botham for a five-minute chat along the way through Montelimar, but failed to turn up at the press conference when the day's walk had ended, after Botham had invited him along to air his views. It was conveniently ignored by that particular tabloid that the elephants had just been paid a surprise visit by French animal liberation members, who had been so impressed by their welfare that they had made a substantial donation to Leukaemia Research. Another reporter who had filed a piece in favour of Kathy Botham's gritty determination to finish the Easter Sunday stage despite back and groin problems was told to rewrite it along the lines of 'Selfish Botham Snubs Heroine Kath and Goes Back to Hotel Before She Finishes'. Such an angle ignored the need to get a hot bath as soon as possible after walking 25 miles in the rain, that Kath was in good hands as she staggered in, and that an hour earlier Ian had roared encouragement at her as his car stopped alongside. A week later, in the small town of Die, some harmless horseplay with water pitchers in the hotel bar was reported as 'Botham's Hooligans Rampage Around French

Town' even though Botham was not involved and the manager bought all the party a drink that same evening.

Botham knew that many were willing him to falter, or commit some social peccadillo and that the priority was to get him to Turin. It grieved him to keep his distance publicly from his mates, it amused him to be the one to play the stern taskmaster whenever the pranks started, but he kept his eye on the ball and made it. As usual his body toughened up after some difficult early days and by the time he got to Turin, he was game for another 400 miles. Phil Neale, his captain at Worcestershire, walked for three days over the Easter weekend and he confirmed that he had never gone through such pain barriers in that period – this from a man who had played professional sport all the year round for the previous decade. Botham's indestructibility was awesome, according to our travelling doctor, Steve Carroll, who has seen service for Tottenham Hotspur and Brentford Football Clubs. 'I can't believe there can be a stronger, fitter cricketer in England at the start of this season,' was the doctor's verdict and anyone who watched Botham breeze through about thirty hairpin bends while going over a mountain 1500 feet higher than Ben Nevis would surely agree.

So Botham returned to England to face yet another challenge. He says his priority is to help Worcestershire win the championship, but he has never been one to broadcast what he really wants. Botham wants to play for England as long as possible, he fancies being the first bowler to 400 Test wickets, he is quick to remind me of a forecast made in December 1987 in Newcastle ('If Richard Hadlee gets an injury it'll take some time to heal at his age, because you can't shake them off so easily. He might be some time in passing my number of Test wickets'). He knows, along with the West Indian tourists and the experienced county pros, that the pretenders to his all-rounder's crown in the England side are not fit to lace his brandies, never mind his boots – provided he stays fit and in form. After the Australian winter and the Hannibal Walk, he is fitter now than at any time since the West Indies tour of 1986, and that will be most evident in his bowling. Ian Botham is not done yet with his cricket career, despite such a fervent desire on the part of many influential members of the game's hierarchy. His capacity to surprise (both pleasantly and sadly) has not been diminished. Those of us who care about him, who wish that his inherent good nature would finally drive away the startling malevolence, the irrational outbursts, must hope that he will soon get himself organised. Otherwise, the words of F. Scott Fitzgerald, no mean hellraiser himself, will become painfully appropriate: 'Show me a hero and I will write you a tragedy.' Better Botham as Falstaff than Julius Caesar.

13

The greatest all-rounder?

●

No other period in cricket history has enjoyed Test all-rounders of the class of Ian Botham, Richard Hadlee, Imran Khan and Kapil Dev. It has been a good, running story for the media as the quartet jostle for prominence. It is impossible to make precise judgements about their respective status: form changes, injuries are picked up, the opposition fluctuates in quality and the wickets are variable from tour to tour. In 1982, one could say that Ian Botham was the top all-rounder, having seen off Kapil Dev and, to a lesser extent, Imran Khan in England. A year later, Hadlee was named Man-of-the-Series in England – as Botham's bowling declined. That same English summer saw Kapil Dev captain India to World Cup triumph by personal example, when a Botham at the peak of his powers might similarly have inspired England. In 1984, Richard Hadlee became the first player since 1967 to perform the 'double' of 1,000 runs and 100 wickets in an English first-class season. In the following year, Botham was the top all-rounder in the Ashes series in England, while Imran Khan and Hadlee started to turn in consistent all-round performances abroad. By 1987, it was a toss-up between Hadlee and Imran for the title of world's best all-rounder. It is a fascinating contest and the case for one all-rounder's pre-eminence over the past decade is still not proven.

In statistical terms, Ian Botham reigns supreme, even though his bowling record has been in decline recently (Appendix A). One guide to true all-round quality is to assess how many times a player scores a hundred runs and takes eight wickets in a Test. Botham has done this three times and only Imran Khan (twice) has managed it more than once

(Appendix B). None of the other three comes anywhere near Botham's tally of 14 Test centuries, an amount that would please any specialist batsman, never mind a front-rank bowler and prolific catcher. Yet Botham's great attraction has been that he is not consumed by ambition for statistical greatness: if so, his figures, especially those of his bowling, would have been greater. In comparison, Hadlee is the filofax cricketer, a calculating machine who seems driven by a hunger for records. Botham, however, will have none of this:

> Hadlee will probably beat me to 400 Test wickets, but so what? He's a good deal more obsessional than me about such matters. It's more important to me that he is definitely the best white fast bowler in the world, rather than how many wickets he ends up with. He won't get fourteen Test hundreds, though! I've never agreed with all this fascination with landmarks. What's the difference between 99 and 100, apart from one run? Apart from my first hundred for Somerset and for England, I've never been concerned about getting the century. If you look at my record, you'll see that I'm rarely out in the 90s because I keep playing my natural game, and don't get tensed up. I see blokes coming back to the dressing-room, seething because they're out in the 90s, but you'd settle for 90-odd at the start of your innings, wouldn't you?

Of the illustrious quartet, Botham has certainly won more Test matches. With the bat he has often retrieved an innings and the amount of times he has taken five wickets in an innings is only beaten by Hadlee. Yet Hadlee has never batted higher than seven for New Zealand, and he remains a batsman likely to hammer a quick 60 rather than go on to a decisive large total. Imran Khan and Kapil Dev have batted around six and seven in their Test careers, both being hampered by a strong batting line-up, whereas Botham has rarely enjoyed that luxury. As a result, he has had more chance to shine in the middle order because of the greater responsibility. In his early years in the Test team, Botham was also fortunate to have fine bowlers at the other end who exerted the kind of pressure that he turned to his advantage – yet he still had to take the wickets, with Willis, Old and others striving to fill their boots themselves. In later years, Botham has had to contend with an accumulation of injuries, a weaker cadre of support bowling and a decline in England's fortunes. As a result his figures have deteriorated in recent years, compared with the other three (Appendix C). Kapil has had to carry the burden of India's seam bowling more or less on his own shoulders in an era when his country has turned its back on its traditional strength of spin bowling – so his percentage of victims in the first five of the batting order is doubly impressive (Appendix D). Imran missed two years of Test cricket due to Kerry Packer, and then another couple of years through injury, just as he was approaching his peak at the age of 30. As for Hadlee, he has had to operate with mundane support at the other end, with due respect to Ewan Chatfield and Lance Cairns. In their different ways all four have performed wonders to keep going so long.

In Hadlee's opinion, only Imran of the four could now hold down a place in a Test side as a specialist batsman or bowler. Certainly Imran has lacked regular opportunities to demonstrate the unruffled technique he was fortunate to absorb on the excellent surfaces at Aitchison College, Lahore and in the Parks at Oxford. When the occasion demands, he is a devastating hitter with a penchant for the lofted drive, but he sells his wicket more dearly than the other three. He would be the one to bat for your life, unless Botham felt your life was worth saving. Imran is also a great bowler, with the priceless asset of swinging the ball late at speed and the knack of bowling an outswinger from the edge of the crease which the batsmen think will dip in. Hadlee, too, is a great bowler but he would make less runs if more bowlers concentrated on tucking him up with some short-pitched deliveries around his leg-stump, rather than giving him room to swing his arms in the off-stump area. He is not the bravest of batsmen, but a dangerous player likely to enjoy a productive hour if he is not nailed early on by the 'throat ball' from a quick bowler. Kapil Dev's bowling is now in gradual decline after years of stirring solo performances, while his batting remains delightfully mercurial. During two Test series against England in 1982, he scored at around a run a ball with beautiful timing and exotic strokes, but the obverse side came when he was dropped during the 1984/5 series for rash batting. Kapil hardly ever seems to countenance the need for defence and his relaxed attitude to batting at times makes Botham look positively Boycottian.

In terms of technique, Botham is easily the best batsman of the great all-rounders. When you peel away the frightening power, the six-hitting and the flamboyant follow-through, you have a very correct player. You cannot play the way that he has done for so long without having a solid foundation. Botham is potentially England's best batsman and many good judges in cricket believe that should be his next aim. Mickey Stewart, the England manager, gets positively rhapsodic about Botham's batting, praising the basic simplicity of his technique. Stewart wishes he could have worked with him at Somerset in his early days: he feels that he could easily have been Test cricket's highest run-scorer – if he had been hungry enough. Keith Andrew, the director of coaching at the National Cricket Association, who has used Botham as bowler and batsman in a coaching video, says that Ian is the most correct hitter he has seen. 'The basic positions he gets into are all orthodox, and the position he takes up for the front-foot drive is wonderful. He puts his front shoulder to the ball, not worrying about his feet, because he knows that the head and feet follow automatically if the shoulder is leading properly. His backlift is excellent, the bat comes down vertically, the head remains perfectly still and he generates enormous power from that uninhibited follow-through as he throws his arms at the sky. Agreed he hooks in the air, but that's because he likes to hit sixes. He doesn't guide it, he likes to take on the fielder. That's the only shot he plays that doesn't seem to be controlled and he could soon cut that out if he wanted to. In defence he is very straight, with the head magnificently still. Look at what he did at the Oval against Pakistan, that was the innings of a specialist international batsman.'

So the England coach and the man in charge of coaching this country's best young players agree about Botham's immense capabilities as a batsman. That view is shared by almost every other international crick-eter I talked to, with the obvious rider that he still gives the bowler a chance because of the nature of his approach. Phil Edmonds spotted Botham's potential with the bat in the early 1970s when he was just a loud extrovert on the Lord's ground staff: 'I went over to the nets to get some bowling practice and Botham was batting. He kept smashing me over long-off, with a lovely high blacklift and the bat coming down straight. Everyone had told me he was just a slogger, but he looked magnificent. He'd have been an even greater player if he'd concentrated on his batting, but two strings to his bow have helped him approach cricket in an uninhibited way.' When one flicks through the memory bank, some of Botham's greatest innings have defied description. It has been given to few men to play like he did at Old Trafford in 1981, at Brisbane in 1986, or for those hundreds at Edgbaston and Wel-lingborough against good county bowlers when the wicket was tricky. That record number of sixes in 1985 was no fluke: he made them in just 27 innings. No other English batsman since Dexter reduces good bowlers to total disarray with just a few strokes and the presence of such a powerful personality. At Old Trafford in 1986, Botham scored a century off 60 balls in what proved to be his last away game for Somerset. On the second morning, after a convivial evening with Vic Marks, Colin Dredge and Trevor Gard (see chapter 10), Botham walked out to bat at 163 for 5 – he only stayed 82 minutes for his 139! It lasted 79 balls and Jack Simmons thought he had seen everything in cricket till that innings: 'I was certain he was going to get 200 before lunch. He was blocking me for fours!' Perhaps Botham might be the next to hit six sixes in an over: he has the nerve, the eye and the power. All he needs is a spot of luck and a demoralised bowler. Certainly he is only sur-passed as a consistent hitter by Gilbert Jessop in cricket history (Appendix E).

Tom Cartwright is the most powerful dissenter to the notion that Botham's next step is a specialist batting role. Ian's old mentor feels he should never bat higher than number six: 'It's bunkum to suggest that he could be a number four, he'd never be consistent enough. You have to build and manoeuvre an innings there, whereas Ian is purely a spontaneous, natural performer. If we had tried to develop him as a specialist batter at the age of fifteen, you'd never have heard of him.' In Cartwright's opinion, Botham needs to keep bowling to maintain his interest in cricket. Botham agrees that his low bore-dom threshold does not exactly equip him for the role of specialist batsman and in this he is supported by Richard Hadlee: 'On the rare occasions when I haven't been fit to bowl and played just as a batter, I've been very bored. I was frustrated because I felt I wasn't in the game enough. I knew how Botham felt when he's been restricted through injury.'

So how will Botham maintain his interest if his bowling continues to decline? Is he fated to move up the order and become a partnership-breaker in the Greg Chappell/Doug Walters mode? Almost everything depends on his attitude. He is still in his early thirties, younger than either Imran or Hadlee, but does he want to keep bowling? He is as optimistic as ever about that but, more importantly, he appears keen to keep going. 'People don't realise how tired we all get from playing round the year. When Worcestershire won the Refuge Assurance I sat in our dressing-room as all the celebrations were going on and I felt the events of the last few months just coming out of the back of my head. I was exhausted, physically and mentally. But there's a lot of bowling left in me. I haven't been really fit for almost a year because I had the ban, then the rib injury in Aussie, then a recurring groin problem with Worcestershire. When I had my rib injury, I was bowling as fast as anyone else in the side and I reckon I can do so again. Look how sharp I was against the Aussies in '85 after my winter off. Cricket will always be a part of my life but as you get older, you develop wider interests and don't talk all that much about the game. I think that's healthy: Boycott's the only one to succeed by being completely absorbed in himself and cricket. But I've still got aims – like a hundred against the West Indies and a championship medal with Worcestershire.'

Perhaps Botham is happier as a third seamer of attacking bent, rather than as a nagging medium-pacer in the Tom Cartwright mould. He is the only self-indulgent bowler to take 300 Test wickets: he has consistently fed batsmen with their favourite shots and got many out in the process, even though they cost him a few runs. When Botham bowls three bouncers in an over, there is a purpose to it, even though not readily apparent. Among England players, he is acknowledged to be the quickest at dissecting opposing batsmen, even though his suggestions sometimes carry an incitement to bravado that seems unwise in the context of the game. At times he has undeniably lost Test Matches through captains over-indulging his whims, but he has never stopped trying to dismiss batsmen in the way he thinks is right. Of all the major bowlers, he is the one who is prepared to look second-rate if his strategy comes undone. Ideally he needs a mean bowler like Hendrick or Emburey at the other end to allow the team to keep a steady hand on the tiller if his experiments go wrong. Yet he is the man most batsmen fear when they have got in on a flat wicket that is chockful of runs: Botham will always attempt some sort of imaginative strategy.

I expect a batsman to get after me and I really don't mind it when he does. The game is meant to be entertaining and if I'm on the wrong end of it one day, there's a good chance I'll get my own back later on. People forget that the game is played in sessions. I can have a bad couple of hours, but come back in the last session of play with a few wickets. I always forget what has happened in the previous session and concentrate on the one to come. You can't play the game looking back over your shoulder. What's done is done. I admit I do clown around a bit when I'm bowling. If it's a mate, I'll run in with my eyes closed or my tongue sticking out and try to get him to laugh. But everybody who knows me will confirm that I try my hardest when the game demands it, even though I just can't maintain my concentration if it's drifting. That's when I like to make things happen.

It must be galling for splendid bowlers of yesteryear who see Botham garland all those wickets in such a cavalier way, but they are wrong to believe he just runs up and sprays it anywhere. They are also wrong if they think his figures have been inflated by cheap wickets by bowling at the tail. Every strike bowler has normally had that chance (Appendix F).

Botham's main problem in the eyes of his bowling critics is that he was too successful too soon. He then had to build on that success, even though he was getting older, more vulnerable to injury and the West Indies were cropping up far too often. His record against the West Indies will remain the blot on his escutcheon. It is the least impressive of the four great all-rounders (Appendix G), although I would not bet against an improvement in that record before Botham retires. He is undeniably infuriating in the way that his opening over is usually an exercise in locating the stumps, with the first delivery often a free hit, but that is one of the paradoxes of Botham; he defies normal criteria. He has turned the uncertainties of cricket to his advantage by his mental resilience.

I don't go out of my way to intimidate a batsman, but I do like to impose myself on him. I'll play the game according to the rules and there's nothing to say I can't give a batter some verbals to unsettle him. Many other players have done it, although funnily enough the Aussies never bothered doing it to me, even though they were past-masters at it. Some batsmen I'll try to irritate by bowling them boring line-and-length stuff when I know they're itching to smash a loose one. Others I'll tempt with a few long-hops. If I suspect a batsman doesn't like a few choice words, I'll try it on with them. I remember when I first bowled at young James Whitaker in county cricket in 1986. James is a public school lad, from a fairly comfortable family who own a chocolate business in Yorkshire. I knew that, so when he smashed me for four, I said to him, 'not a bad shot from a chocolate tycoon – try this one.' All credit to him, he smashed the next lollipop to the boundary and I gave him the stare. I eventually bowled him and shouted, 'Now you can . . . off and play with your chocolate box, you public school. . . .' He was really upset, even though I didn't mean it and was just testing him out. Next time I saw him we were alongside each other six weeks later on the plane to Australia! I explained to him that I was simply just testing out a new boy, that it wasn't personal. As far as I'm concerned, that goes on all the time out in the middle and you've got to steel yourself to be the top dog. Getting wickets isn't just about bowling the right deliveries, you've got to stand up for yourself and make them wary and unsettled.

Botham has never had the kind of sinuous, wiry build that fast bowlers traditionally possess. His bursts of speed have come from sheer animal strength, but they have largely been absent since 1985. He once shared with Dennis Lillee, Malcolm Marshall and Imran Khan the ability to swing the ball devastatingly late at high pace, although his decline in speed means that the ball now swings earlier. Yet his action has always been naturally high and he still has the priceless ability to hit the seam. If you have command over the seam, you can also manipulate it through the air because the seam is the axis of such movement. Ian also bowls from near the stumps, which is the ideal place for a swing bowler and his hand action is subtle enough to move the ball both ways off the pitch. When injury and lack of match practice reduced his pace in 1986, he started to give some fine displays of medium-pace bowling. At Leicester, I saw him bowl 43 overs on the trot to take 6 for 125 and no batsman was ever happy against him because of his variety and habit of slipping in the occasional quicker ball. His work in Australia after incurring his rib injury was notable. On the first day of the Melbourne Test, he asked to bowl even though he was nowhere near fit enough and, after convincing a sceptical Mike Gatting, he took five wickets, putting it on exactly the right spot on a green wicket. In the Perth Challenge and the Benson and Hedges Cup, he would come on when the batsmen were looking to slog him and bowl his overs right through at an economical rate. In his first season at Worcester, his experience and natural gifts were vital, especially in tight, limited-overs games. Jeremy Lloyds told me how well Botham bowled against Gloucestershire in a three-day game at Gloucester in 1987: 'It was the same old Beefy that I remembered at Taunton. He bowled the lot – the inner, the outer, a slower ball, the sharp bouncer. He simply made batsmen do silly things because he surprised them.'

There seems a remarkable imbalance between those who see Botham's bowling at first-hand and those who sit in judgement on him, with the aid of action replays. It seems *lèse-majesté* to pick up so many wickets by unorthodox means but that is one of his secrets. Batsmen are conditioned to expect the unorthodox. Against seam bowlers who are short of killing pace, they expect to be subjected to a strategy spread over a number of overs, whereby a stock delivery will be occasionally relieved by something different. Like a boxer lining up an opponent with a series of jabs, the crucial big punch is the end result after a good deal of groundwork. Botham will have none of this: he aims for the knockout punch in his first over and will always try to keep the batsman guessing, even down to whether he should hit the bad ball for six or four. Yet the traditionalists remain baffled and exasperated by his success as he appears to mock the precept that hard work and concentration are the vital ingredients for bowling eminence.

Not everyone in the commentary box is that dogmatic, however. Botham's methods are supported by a man who took over 1,000 first-class wickets as a seam bowler, who has been associated with the first-class game for almost forty years and is now building a deserved reputation as a pundit without the blinkers of preconception. Jack Bannister has covered sixty of Botham's Tests since 1980 and he has great respect for his bowling abilities: 'Of course he gets carried away and I've seen him bowl badly, but I'm convinced he never just runs up and plonks it down. His hand action is excellent, he thinks people out with variations and he has the courage to try out experiments. Since his injuries I've been even more impressed as he's cut down his pace and seamed it around as well as swinging it. I've talked bowling with him in depth and found his ideas fascinating.'

Keith Andrew agrees about Botham's hand action: 'You can see his action is almost identical for the inswinger and the outswinger. It's like the difference between a googly bowler and a leg-spinner and normally you can tell the difference a mile off – but not with Ian. He's also got that inbuilt aggression which is vital for a bowler of his type.' Tom Cartwright, Botham's biggest influence as a bowler, helped him develop that aggression as a youngster, but now he is pleased that he seems to be coming to terms with the advancing years: 'Ian's action and build were never suited to high pace and I always preferred to see him as a fast-medium bowler. He should settle now into a medium-fast role, filling in at one end: that's more interesting than trying to knock someone's head off. The slower you bowl, the less margin of error – but has Ian got the temperament to change his entire outlook in terms of bowling?'

Botham is too old now to become another Cartwright, one of the greatest bowlers of his type. His action is not quite economical enough and he lacks the patience to indulge in long, tactical battles with a batsman. He is Alex Higgins with a ball in his hand, not Steve Davis. Botham would prefer to bowl fast-medium again: he likes that role and it also gives him the chance of bowling himself fit, rather than doing all those boring exercises. He is at a time of life when middle age in cricket means his age is showing around his middle, but that is nothing that another walk for Leukaemia cannot cure. People underestimate the man's mental strength; if he wants to get himself fit to bowl like an authentic third seamer, he will do so. Both Mickey Stewart and Mike Gatting want him back in the England side, if fit and in form, and that is a challenge which Botham relishes. Gatting has managed to avoid being pilloried in the press about his ample girth because he has played very well since getting the England captaincy, but he is sympathetic about Botham's fitness dilemma: 'He's done almost everything he's set out to do and it's now going to get even harder. If he can lose weight he'll be up there again with Imran and Hadlee. He's still young enough to come back.'

A personal view is that Botham will want to keep playing and that his pride in performance will drive him to a more acceptable level of fitness. Although he bubbles with ideas for later business activities, there is nothing specific that would make him want to retire. Botham knows that Tom Byron's business acumen will ensure financial security for himself and his family, so he can continue to devote himself to what he does best – enjoying himself. Although he is a talented man in other areas – like driving, fishing, flying and other contact sports – Ian knows that it is cricket that he does best. He is also well aware that retirement lasts a long time. He is not completely cavalier about statistics, but he would rather achieve certain goals than set up personal records. A championship medal has eluded him in his career and he badly wants to recover some prestige against the West Indies. I would not bet against Botham accompanying England to Australia in 1990: he will only be 35 then, admittedly a fairly lived-in 35, but he could make the physical effort to last the course if he so desired. I believe he does desire that, for the simple reason that he has nothing better to do. He is not the sort of man to stay home all week with his family and Kath knew that when they first married; their relationship flourishes when they are not under each other's feet all the time.

Ian still loves cricket, despite occasional weariness, and above all he loves what the Irish call 'the crack'. He is genuinely welcome in any dressing-room around the counties. He has never lost the common touch with the ordinary pros, despite his famous acquaintances, and he knows that he will greatly miss the camaraderie of the game when he retires. Even if he does not play many more times for England, he will still enjoy the different challenges presented by Queensland and Worcestershire.

I'd love to help my two sides to honours. That is now more important to me than getting a 100 against the West Indies or being the first to 400 Test wickets. Funnily enough, if I relax and don't worry about statistical landmarks, they tend to come rather easier than when I'm tensed up about it all. But, for the good of the game, I genuinely hope that guys come along and beat my records. The only one that really meant much to me was getting 3,000 runs and 300 Test wickets because I thought that represented a fair amount of sustained success. After that, everything else was a bonus. I suppose it will all mean a lot more to me when I reach for the pipe and slippers in a few years' time, but now I have to struggle to remember anything about a game that comes on the telly at random when rain has stopped play. They all seem to merge into a mass, apart from a few outstanding days.

Clive Rice, a great admirer of Botham, feels that his attitude to fitness will be the biggest decision of his career. Rice has closely observed the way Richard Hadlee has rationed his resources over the years and although he acknowledges that Botham would never be such a per- fectionist, he is convinced that he could last as long as Hadlee, if he so wanted. 'When Richard said he was finished with county cricket in 1980, he was 29 and exhausted in mind and body. But he changed his decision and worked very hard to keep going in his middle age. I believe that Beefy is so strong and so talented that he could play till he's forty if he wants. You have to do the training all the time, though, because natural ability won't get you through for very long when you're in your thirties. I'd hate to see him disappear over the horizon while comparatively young. If Beefy only half-applied himself to his fitness, he'd leave the other bowlers in the England side for dead. He has been a great all- rounder and I've got a feeling that he wants to re-affirm that before he finishes. I hope so, because no other Englishman I've seen clears the bar like he does.'

Hadlee has enjoyed that extra edge which comes from rivalry with one particular player. It meant a great deal to him to be named Man- of-the-Series ahead of Botham in 1983 because he wanted the pressure of competing with him. With typical thoroughness, Hadlee told John Wright he ought to try to outshine Graeme Fowler that summer and he told Martin Crowe to have David Gower in his sights. He does not believe he was any threat to Botham until that year, and although he will not admit it, he feels that his all-round effectiveness has been more beneficial to his side than has Botham's to England in recent years. Imran Khan has particular respect for Botham's batting: 'He should be given more responsibility in the team's batting order. I wasn't at all surprised by that Oval innings, because I had seen him play with great restraint at Lord's in 1982 when we were pressing for victory. He's a fine bat – it's a miracle he's sprung up through the English system that grinds players down into mediocrity. As a bowler, he's now a luxury if his team have been dismissed cheaply. He's at his best when he has a big total to play with and he can attack and experiment.'

Despite all the caveats, Ian Botham has to be ranked as a great all-rounder. He has influenced so many Test matches and occupied the thoughts of the opposition for so many series that he cannot be denied his rightful place in history, despite a recent deterioration. If you assessed the great all-rounders at their peak, few would rival Botham. Mike Procter would possibly have eclipsed Botham if he had been able to play more Test cricket. In just seven Tests he took 41 wickets – although it has to be said that Botham took 40 in his first eight Tests. Procter was a high-class batsman who scored 47 first-class hundreds. Although not terribly comfortable against pace after his spell with World Series cricket, he usually destroyed the slower bowlers. He was definitely good enough to play either as batsman or bowler and as a captain he led from the front, as Botham would wish. Procter performed wonders as a matter of course for Gloucestershire, but then he was not exhausted or distracted by Test calls: like Clive Rice, he ardently wished to shine in county cricket in the absence of international combat. That lack of regular Test Match cricket must be decisive when comparing him to Botham or the others.

Keith Miller is generally held to be the nearest equivalent to Botham along other leading all-rounders in history. With his charismatic good looks, natural sportsmanship, flair for the unexpected and supreme natural talent, Miller would have been the greatest draw card in the game if he had timed his entry into the world a little better. Today's obsession with heroes and superstars would have forced agents to form a long, orderly queue to get to Miller. In the age of the video cassette, the action replay, the tabloid hype and the demand for lucrative personal appearances, Miller would have been a millionaire in no time. His zestful, Bothamesque attitude to social activities would have attracted the attention of the prurient and it would have been interesting to see how such a free spirit managed to overcome the constraints. Unless dragged down by fatigue, he would have dazzled as an all-rounder: like Botham, he bowled with great heart and occasional eccentricity, he fielded brilliantly at slip and his batting was dashingly handsome. Richie Benaud, no mean all-rounder himself, puts Miller just behind Botham, but there is little in it: 'Miller was the best I ever played with. He was marginally better technically as a batsman than Botham, although not so flamboyantly powerful. Miller was the fastest bowler, he was as quick as anyone when he wanted. But Botham has been a marvellous performer for a long time.'

At the head of Benaud's list is Gary Sobers. 'He was just the most versatile cricketer I ever saw. Apart from his superb batting, he was three bowlers in one, and a great fielder.' Such an assessment finds equal favour with Botham also – Sobers has always been his favourite cricketer. There are many similarities between the two – an unimpressive captaincy record, a chivalrous attitude to the game's basic principles, immense fielding ability in any position and an expensive bowling average in Tests. Sobers was obviously more costly when he bowled his spinners (especially the 'chinamen'), but he shared Botham's fondness for experiment. As a new-ball bowler, he could be deadly, with deceptive speed off a short, loping run-up, and with a ferocious bouncer used sparingly. His batting, however, was on a different plane to Botham's. Although Botham has shown he can prosper on bad wickets, Sobers was in a class of his own because there were more dubious pitches around in his day to test him. He had a wonderful temperament and used to get West Indies out of trouble from the number six position as a matter of course. Gary Sobers was one of the greatest left-hand batsmen in history and few good judges dispute his claims as the game's supreme all-rounder.

Equally, few can argue with the choice of Ian Botham as England's greatest all-round cricketer. He has flourished in an age when the game has got harder, with physical intimidation going hand-in-hand with a relentless whirligig of Test tours. Botham has kept going for a decade with just a breather or two from international cricket. The wonder is that he has been able to approach the game with his customary *élan* for so long. W. G. Grace may have been the game's most creative cricketer in the sense that he formulated the basic principles of modern bats-manship, but although he was noted for kidding out batsmen with his slow-medium offerings, his Test figures cannot compare with Botham's. Also, Botham has won a far greater percentage of Tests than the good doctor ever managed, and that can be the only valid criterion with which to judge an all-rounder from a different century. Let John Emburey have the last word on Botham, a man totally different in temperament and cricket outlook to the Middlesex off-spinner. Emburey has often seethed at Botham's self-indulgences but through it all he has retained a great affection for him: 'He's someone you admire and want to watch, because he has such extraordinary ability. One of the great things about him is that he's done things in life that we others just dream about. He lives out his fantasies, he wants to be Roy Rogers as well as the bandit. He is an amazing bloke and, as all-rounders go, we'll be lucky to see one like Ian Botham in the next fifty years.'

STATISTICAL APPENDIX

by Robert W. Brooke

1. IAN BOTHAM; FIRST-CLASS RECORD, SEASON-BY-SEASON

	M	In	No	Runs	H.S.	Av'ge	100s	50s	Ct	Overs	Mns	Runs	Wts	Av'ge	5	10	Best Bowling
1974	18	29	3	441	59	16.96	–	1	15	309	76	739	30	24.63	1	–	5/59
1975	22	36	4	584	65	18.25	–	2	18	605.3	132	1704	62	27.48	1	–	5/69
1976	20	35	5	1022	167*	34.06	1	6	16	563.4	104	1880	66	28.48	4	1	6/16
1977	17	27	3	738	114	30.75	1	5	15	665.5	149	1983	88	22.53	6	1	6/50
1977/78	9	12	4	397	126*	49.62	2	1	7	210.4	41	691	35	19.74	3	1	7/58
1978	17	20	0	538	108	26.90	2	1	11	605.2	143	1640	100	16.40	10	1	8/34
1978/79	9	14	0	361	74	25.78	–	3	14	239.3	44	848	44	19.27	2	–	5/51
1979	15	20	1	731	137	38.47	2	1	21	436.4	111	1318	46	28.65	3	–	6/81
1979/80	6	10	1	331	119*	36.77	2	–	5	242	81	532	34	15.64	4	2	7/48
1980	18	27	0	1149	228	42.55	2	6	24	453.3	122	1387	40	34.67	4	–	4/38
1980/81	8	14	0	197	40	14.07	–	–	8	224.2	43	790	23	34.34	–	–	4/77
1981	16	24	2	925	149*	42.04	3	4	19	574.2	156	1712	67	25.55	4	1	6/90
1981/82	11	15	1	760	142	54.28	2	5	7	317.2	64	928	25	37.12	1	–	5/61
1982	17	29	1	1241	208	44.32	3	7	7	491.4	114	1517	66	22.98	4	–	5/46
1982/83	9	18	0	434	65	24.11	–	2	17	319.4	63	1033	29	35.62	–	–	4/43
1983	14	21	0	852	152	40.57	3	2	10	232.2	55	728	22	33.09	1	–	5/38
1983/84	7	10	0	409	138	40.90	1	2	8	193.5	49	589	16	36.81	1	–	5/59
1984	17	26	1	797	90	31.88	–	7	7	449.4	93	1562	59	26.47	4	–	8/103
1985	19	27	5	1530	152	69.54	5	9	17	406.2	67	1376	44	31.27	1	–	5/109
1985/86	8	16	0	379	70	23.68	–	1	6	180.5	26	671	15	44.73	1	–	5/71
1986	13	20	2	863	139	47.94	2	5	8	311.1	65	1043	25	41.72	1	–	6/125
1986/87	8	14	2	481	138	40.08	1	2	11	182.1	41	496	18	27.55	1	–	5/41
1987	16	22	2	598	126*	29.90	1	2	10	260	47	883	21	42.04	–	–	3/51
1987/88	11	19	0	646	70	34.00	–	7	18	311.5	82	805	29	27.75	–	–	3/12
										449.7	85						
Career	325	505	37	16404	228	35.05	33	81	299	8337	1883	26855	1004	26.74	53	7	8/34

NB In the English seasons 1974 to 1986 inclusive Botham's first-class cricket was played for Somerset & England; in 1987 his teams were Worcestershire and England; in 1987/88 he played for Queensland. In 1977/78 Botham toured Pakistan & New Zealand; in 1978/79 he toured Australia; in 1979/80 he toured Australia & India; in 1980/81 he toured West Indies; in 1981/82 he toured India & Sri Lanka; in 1982/83 he toured Australia; in 1983/84 he toured New Zealand & Pakistan; in 1985/86 he toured West Indies; in 1986/87 he toured Australia. Where overs and maidens are underlined – 8-ball overs.

2. TEST CRICKET RECORD; SERIES-BY-SERIES

		M	In	No	Runs	H.S.	Av'ge	100s	50s	Ct	Overs	Mns	Runs	Wkts	Av'ge	5s	10s	Best Bowling
1977	A	2	2	0	25	25	12.50	–	–	1	73	16	202	10	20.20	2	–	5/21
1977/78	NZ	3	5	1	212	103	53.00	1	1	5	101	17	311	17	18.29	2	–	5/73
1978	P	3	3	0	212	108	70.66	2	–	4	75.5	19	209	13	16.07	1	–	8/34
1978	NZ	3	3	0	51	22	17.00	–	–	2	142.1	42	337	24	14.04	3	1	6/34
1978/79	A	6	10	0	291	74	29.10	–	2	11	158.4	25	567	23	24.65	–	–	4/42
1979	I	4	5	0	244	137	48.80	1	–	10	179	49	472	20	23.60	2	–	5/35
1979/80	A	3	6	1	187	119*	37.40	1	–	3	173.1	62	371	19	19.52	2	1	6/78
1979/80	I	1	1	0	114	114	–	1	–	–	48.5	14	106	13	8.15	2	1	7/48
1980	WI	5	9	0	169	57	18.77	–	1	2	131	41	385	13	29.61	–	–	3/50
1980	A	1	1	0	0	0	–	–	–	–	31.2	3	132	1	–	–	–	1/43
1980/81	WI	4	7	0	73	26	10.42	–	–	5	145.2	31	492	15	32.80	1	–	4/77
1981	A	6	12	1	399	149*	36.27	2	1	12	272.3	81	700	34	20.58	3	1	6/95
1981/82	I	6	8	0	440	142	55.00	1	4	3	240.3	52	660	17	38.82	1	–	5/61
1981/82	SL	1	1	0	13	13	–	–	–	1	24.5	2	65	3	21.66	–	–	3/28
1982	I	3	3	0	403	208	134.33	2	1	1	93.3	16	320	9	35.55	1	–	5/46
1982	P	3	6	0	163	69	27.16	–	2	9	150.5	33	478	18	26.55	1	–	5/74
1982/83	A	5	10	0	270	58	27.00	–	1	9	213.5	35	729	18	40.50	–	–	4/75
1983	NZ	4	8	0	282	103	35.25	1	1	3	112.5	27	340	10	34.00	–	–	4/50
1983/84	NZ	3	4	0	226	138	56.50	1	1	3	109.4	25	354	7	50.57	1	–	5/59
1983/84	P	1	2	0	32	22	16.00	–	–	4	30	5	90	2	45.00	–	–	2/90
1984	WI	5	10	0	347	81	34.70	–	3	5	163.2	30	667	19	35.10	2	–	8/103
1984	SL	1	1	0	6	6	–	–	–	–	56	12	204	7	29.14	1	–	6/90
1985	A	6	8	0	250	85	31.25	–	2	8	251.4	36	855	31	27.58	1	–	5/109
1985/86	WI	5	10	0	168	38	16.80	–	–	4	134.5	16	535	11	48.63	1	–	5/71
1986	NZ	1	1	1	59	59*	–	–	1	–	26	4	82	3	27.33	–	–	3/75
1986/87	A	4	6	0	189	138	31.50	1	–	10	106.2	24	296	9	32.88	1	–	5/41
1987	P	5	8	1	232	51*	33.14	–	1	3	134.3	30	433	7	61.85	–	–	3/217
Career		94	150	5	5057	208	34.87	14	22	109	259.4 / 3120.5	42 / 705	10392	373	27.86	27	4	8/34

Where overs & maidens are underlined – 8-ball overs.

3. TEST RECORDS STILL HELD BY IAN BOTHAM

FEWEST MATCHES TO ACHIEVE 1000 RUNS/100 WICKETS DOUBLE

Matches	Player	Team & Seasons
21	I. T. Botham	England; 1977 to 1979
23	M. H. Mankad	India; 1946 to 1952/53
25	Kapil Dev	India; 1978/79 to 1979/80
27	M. A. Noble	Australia; 1897/98 to 1903/04
28	R. J. Hadlee	New Zealand; 1972/73 to 1979/80
30	G. Giffen	Australia; 1881/82 to 1896
30	Imran Khan	Pakistan; 1971 to 1980/81

FEWEST MATCHES TO ACHIEVE 2000 RUNS/200 WICKETS DOUBLE

42	I. T. Botham	England; 1977 to 1981/82
50	Kapil Dev	India; 1978/79 to 1982/83
50	Imran Khan	Pakistan; 1971 to 1983/84
54	R. J. Hadlee	New Zealand; 1972/73 to 1984/85
60	R. Benaud	Australia; 1951/52 to 1963/64

FEWEST MATCHES TO ACHIEVE 3000 RUNS/200 WICKETS DOUBLE

72	I. T. Botham	England; 1977 to 1984
83	Kapil Dev	India; 1978/79 to 1986/87

No other all-rounder has yet achieved this double. At the time of writing Imran Khan, with an uncertain future, had 2770 runs and 311 wickets in 70 Tests; R. J. Hadlee's record stood at 2770 runs and 373 wickets in 74 Tests.

4. 100 CATCHES IN TEST CRICKET

Botham became the eighth player to take 100 Test catches during the 1986/87 series against Australia. There follows a list of all those players with 100 Test catches, number of Tests played, and average catches per Test.

Player	Catches	Tests	Average per Test
G. S. Chappell (Australia)	122	87	1.40
M. C. Cowdrey (England)	120	114	1.05
R. B. Simpson (Australia)	110	62	1.77
W. R. Hammond (England)	110	85	1.29

G. S. Sobers (W. Indies)	109	93	1.17
I. T. Botham (England)	109	94	1.15
S. M. Gavaskar (India)	108	125	0.86
I. M. Chappell (Australia)	105	75	1.40

5. At the end of the 1987 Test series with Pakistan, Botham – with 20,801 balls in Test cricket – lay second to Derek Underwood among English bowlers. Of those who have bowled more than 20,000 balls in Test cricket Botham is the only purely pace bowler.

Player	Balls Bowled	Wkts.	Av. Balls/Wkt.
L. R. Gibbs (W. Indies)	27115	309	87.75
D. L. Underwood (England)	21862	297	73.60
G. S. Sobers (W. Indies)	21599	235	91.52
B. S. Bedi (India)	21364	266	80.31
I. T. Botham (England)	20801	373	55.76

6. BOWLING MILESTONES PASSED BY IAN BOTHAM

Matches Needed to reach 100 Test Wickets (20 or fewer)

Matches	Player	Team & Seasons
16	G. A. Lohmann	England; 1886 to 1895/96
17	C. T. B. Turner	Australia; 1886/87 to 1894/95
17	S. F. Barnes	England; 1901/02 to 1911/12
17	C. V. Grimmett	Australia; 1924/25 to 1930/31
19	C. Blythe	England; 1901/02 to 1909/10
19	A. M. E. Roberts	West Indies; 1973/74 to 1976
19	I. T. Botham	England; 1977 to 1979
20	W. J. O'Reilly	Australia; 1931/32 to 1936/37

Matches Needed to reach 200 Test Wickets (45 or fewer)

36	C. V. Grimmett	Australia; 1924/25 to 1935/36
38	D. K. Lillee	Australia; 1970/71 to 1979/80
41	I. T. Botham	England; 1977 to 1981
42	M. D. Marshall	West Indies; 1978/79 to 1985/86
44	A. V. Bedser	England; 1946 to 1953
44	R. J. Hadlee	New Zealand; 1972/73 to 1983
45	Imran Khan	Pakistan; 1971 to 1982/83
44	J. Garner	West Indies; 1976/77 to 1984/85

Matches Needed to reach 300 Test Wickets (72 or fewer)

56	D. K. Lillee	Australia; 1970/71 to 1981/82
61	R. J. Hadlee	New Zealand; 1972/73 to 1985/86
65	F. S. Trueman	England; 1952 to 1964
68	Imran Khan	Pakistan; 1971 to 1987
72	I. T. Botham	England; 1977 to 1984

APPENDIX A

DETAILS OF CAREER RECORD AFTER EACH 50 WICKETS FOR EACH BOWLER WITH 300 TEST WICKETS

(NB. Since it is not always possible to ascertain a bowler's figures immediately after the taking of the relevant wicket, the figures quoted were as they stood at the end of the innings.) The players are listed in the order in which they reached 300 Test wickets.

Player	Tests	Runs Cons	Wkts.	Av'ge	Av Wkts. Per Match
Fred Trueman	10	1152	51	22.58	5.10
	25	2218	100	22.18	4.00
	37	3292	153	21.51	4.13
	47	4431	204	21.72	4.34
	56	5395	250	21.58	4.46
	65	6383	301	21.20	4.63
Total for career	67	6625	307	21.57	4.58
Lance Gibbs	13	1191	52	22.90	4.00
	24	2321	105	22.10	4.37
	34	3545	151	23.47	4.44
	46	5334	200	26.67	4.34
	62	7125	254	28.05	4.09
	75	8536	300	28.45	4.00
Total for career	79	8989	309	29.09	3.91
Dennis Lillee	10	1100	51	21.56	5.10
	22	2372	100	23.72	4.54
	31	3780	154	24.54	4.96
	38	4692	201	23.34	5.28
	48	5866	251	23.37	5.22
	56	6913	301	22.96	5.37
Total for career	70	8493	355	23.92	5.07

Bob Willis	17	1590	50	31.80	2.94
	28	2644	100	26.44	3.57
	41	3653	151	24.19	3.68
	58	5090	201	25.32	3.46
	70	6302	251	25.10	3.58
	81	7359	300	24.53	3.70
Total for career	90	8190	325	25.20	3.61
Ian Botham	10	860	50	17.20	5.00
	19	1897	100	18.97	5.26
	29	2929	151	19.39	5.20
	41	4284	202	21.20	4.92
	55	6050	254	23.81	4.61
	72	7987	305	26.18	4.23
	85	9656	357	27.04	4.20
Total for career	94	10392	373	27.86	3.96
Richard Hadlee	14	1728	50	34.56	3.57
	25	3058	101	30.27	4.04
	34	4125	154	26.78	4.52
	44	5165	200	25.82	4.54
	53	5933	251	23.63	4.73
	61	6860	302	22.71	4.95
	69	7874	351	22.43	5.08
Total for career	74	8334	373	22.34	5.04
Kapil Dev	16	1805	51	35.39	3.18
	25	2624	100	26.24	4.00
	39	4306	152	28.32	3.89
	50	5867	200	29.33	4.00
	65	7014	250	28.05	3.84
	83	8715	300	29.05	3.61
Total for career	92	9454	319	29.63	3.46
Imran Khan	13	1765	50	35.30	3.84
	26	3239	103	31.44	3.96
	37	4139	152	27.23	4.10
	45	4905	206	23.81	4.57
	55	5607	252	22.25	4.58
	68	6615	302	21.90	4.44
Total for career	70	6903	311	22.19	4.44

Ian Botham; Broken down in each lot of 50 wickets

Matches	Runs cons	Wkts	Av'ge	Runs per 100 balls	Wkts per 100 balls	Wkts per match
10	860	50	17.20	41.58	2.41	5.00
10	1037	50	20.74	43.15	2.08	5.00
10	1032	51	20.23	42.57	2.10	5.10
12	1355	51	26.56	48.23	1.81	4.25
15	1766	52	33.96	50.95	1.50	3.46
17	1937	51	37.98	57.47	1.51	3.00
13	1669	52	32.09	59.50	1.85	4.00
10	736	16	46.00	50.93	1.10	1.60

The total of matches is 3 more than Botham's total of Tests due to 3 instances of 'overlapping'.

APPENDIX B

The true all-rounder should be capable of at least one outstanding *all-round match* performance during his Test career, and I feel that 100 runs and 8 wickets in the same match is the sort of standard which should be aimed at. The following table tends to suggest that today is the age of the true all-rounder – that the giants of the past could not usually produce the goods. The bare figures are misleading, however; half the feats came before the 1960s and there have been about the same number of Test matches since then as before, so in fact the frequency of the feat has remained about the same throughout Test cricket history.

INSTANCES OF 100-RUNS & 8 WICKETS BY ONE PLAYER IN A TEST MATCH

G. Giffen	161, 41; 4–75, 4–164; Aust v Eng, Sydney 1894–95
A. E. Trott	38*, 72*; 0–9, 8–43; Aust v Eng, Adelaide 1894–95
J. H. Sinclair	106, 4; 6–26, 3–63; S. Africa v Eng, Cape Town 1898–99
G. A. Faulkner	78, 123; 5–120, 3–40; S. Africa v Eng, Jo'burg 1909–10
J. M. Gregory	100; 7–67, 1–32; Aust v Eng, Melbourne 1920–21
H. Larwood	70, 37; 6–32, 2–30; Eng v Aust, Brisbane 1928–29
G. O. B. Allen	35, 68; 3–71, 5–36; Eng v Aust, Brisbane 1936–37
W. J. Edrich	191, 22*; 4–95, 4–77; Eng v S. Africa, O. Trafford 1947
K. R. Miller	109; 6–107, 2–58; Aust v W. Indies, Kingston 1954–55
R. Benaud	100; 4–70, 5–84; Aust v S. Africa, Jo'burg 1957–58
O. G. Smith	100; 3–94, 5–90; W. Indies v India, Delhi 1958–59
A. K. Davidson	44, 80; 5–135, 6–87; Aust v W. Indies, Brisbane 1960–61
G. S. Sobers	174; 5–41, 3–39; W. Indies v Eng, Leeds 1966
Mushtaq Moh'd	121, 56; 5–28, 3–69; Paki v W. Indies, P. of Spain 1976–77
I. T. Botham	103; 5–73, 3–38; Eng v N. Zealand, Christchurch 1977–78
I. T. Botham	114; 6–58, 7–48; Eng v India, Bombay 1979–80
I. T. Botham	30, 81; 8–103, 0–117; Eng v W. Indies, Lord's 1984
Kapil Dev	41, 89; 5–125, 3–43; India v Eng, Lord's 1982
Imran Khan	67*, 46; 5–49, 3–66; Paki v Eng, Leeds 1982
Imran Khan	117; 6–98, 5–82; Paki v India, Faisalabad 1982–83

APPENDIX C

These figures are worked backwards from their most recent Test matches until a 1000 Run/100 Wicket 'double' is reached; the resultant figures give a more acceptable assessment of recent Test all-round form than are given by figures for their whole Test career. The figures are up to the end of March 1988.

PLAYER	Mtch	Runs	Av'ge	Wkts	Av'ge	Bt/Bl Avs	Seasons covered
Imran Khan	25	1086	45.25	105	19.02	2.37	1982–83–date
R. J. Hadlee	27	1025	33.06	161	18.24	1.81	1983–84–date
Kapil Dev	37	1648	33.63	103	30.93	1.08	1983–84–date
I. T. Botham	33	1708	32.84	102	36.19	0.90	1983–date

The figures show, unsurprisingly, that Botham's form has deserted him of late.

APPENDIX D

PERCENTAGE OF DISMISSALS OF FIRST 5 IN THE ORDER BY LEADING PACE BOWLERS IN TEST CRICKET

Bowlers with 300 wkts	Dismissals of 1–5	% of Total Dismissals
Kapil Dev (India)	185	57.99
R. G. D. Willis (England)	187	57.53
Imran Khan (Pakistan)	171	54.98
D. K. Lillee (Australia)	194	54.64
R. J. Hadlee (N. Zealand)	197	52.81
F. S. Trueman (England)	159	51.79
I. T. Botham (England)	189	50.67

Also note the following pace bowlers

W. W. Hall (W. Indies)	116	60.41
R. R. Lindwall (Aust)	132	57.89
K. R. Miller (Aust)	98	57.64
G. D. McKenzie (Aust)	139	56.50
J. R. Thomson (Aust)	113	56.50
J. A. Snow (England)	114	56.43
A. K. Davidson (Aust)	104	55.91
M. A. Holding (W. Indies)	134	53.81
A. V. Bedser (England)	125	52.96
S. F. Barnes (England)	100	52.90
M. D. Marshall (W. Indies)	126	52.50
J. B. Statham (Lancs)	132	52.38
A. M. E. Roberts (W. Indies)	105	51.98
J. Garner (W. Indies)	124	47.87

Also note the following, not pace or purely pace, bowlers

D. L. Underwood (England)	160	53.87
G. S. Sobers (W. Indies)	125	53.19
L. R. Gibbs (W. Indies)	134	43.36

APPENDIX E

IAN BOTHAM'S FAST SCORING

Where does Ian Botham stand in the hitters' hierarchy? Pretty high must be the answer – but just who in fact are in the opposition? Certainly noted smiters like Arthur Wellard, Alan Watt, Fred Barratt, G. F. Earle, C. I. Thornton and G. J. Bonnor cannot be spoken of in the same breath. All certainly hit hard – Wellard indeed hit over 500 sixes in his career – but none could be thought of as top-class batsmen, whereas Botham's eye and technique suggest that if he isn't, he should be. Possibly Botham may be more easily compared with Learie Constantine; the latter scored his runs, including his five centuries, at a rattling pace but overall his record – going by average runs per innings – 24 – is unimpressive.

Another group sometimes mentioned in the same breath as Botham are the specialist, high-scoring batsmen who generally score quickly and hit a large number of sixes. Certainly among current batsmen Viv Richards and Gordon Greenidge score a lot of runs from hits over the ropes and in the fairly recent past one can name Harold Gimblett, John Jameson and, until health problems hindered his ability to hit, W. J. Stewart. All included a fair number of sixes in their run tally, but again one feels comparison with Botham is invalid.

When all others have been swept away, however, one name remains against whom even Ian Botham tends to pale. Gilbert Jessop played in the 21 seasons prior to the First World War and incredibly made at least 14 of his 53 centuries in one hour or less. Jessop also hit a double century in two hours, and on three other occasions reached 200 in less than $2\frac{1}{2}$ hours.

It is difficult to compare Jessop's feats with Botham's, though on the face of it his 14 fast hundreds outshine Botham's 3 in under the hour. When one considers that until 1910 a ball usually had to be hit out of the ground for six to be awarded, Jessop's feats look even better, but against this is the generally accepted theory that the over-rate in Jessop's time was substantially faster than it is now. Just how much faster is impossible to say, but after a lot of delving into match reports I feel the difference may have been exaggerated somewhat.

I would estimate that for every six-ball over faced by Jessop, Botham faces only five balls. On the other hand, because of the pre-1910 custom that sixes should be hit out of the ground, this would have added perhaps three minutes to each Jessop century.

Where is the artificial tampering with the timings of Jessop's century getting us? Perhaps nowhere – but equally it may enable us to make a slightly less unacceptable comparison between Jessop's and Botham's fastest centuries. The change is in fact quite dramatic; transfer Botham's conditions to Jessop, and Jessop's centuries in an hour or less are reduced in number from 14 to 2. Only the first two survive with revised timings of 45 and 47 minutes respectively, as against timings of 49 and 50 minutes for Botham's top two.

Do the switch the other way, and make Botham play under Jessopian conditions, and Botham gains a couple of centuries 'under the hour' so his figures hardly compare with the genuine total of 14 obtained by Jessop.

What conclusions can we draw from all this playing with statistics? Perhaps none, but we can confirm that Jessop scored more really fast centuries than Botham, but Botham's top few suggest that since maturing as a batsman he has become almost Jessopian in prowess.

APPENDIX F

Figures for obtaining wickets of batsmen 9–11 from members of the '300 Club'

Ian Botham	84 wickets	22.52%
Fred Trueman	72	23.45
Bob Willis	58	17.84
Dennis Lillee	61	17.18
Richard Hadlee	72	19.30
Kapil Dev	62	19.43
Imran Khan	64	20.57
Lance Gibbs	75	24.27

It will be seen that of the '300 club' (excluding Gibbs – the only slow bowler) Trueman's return was obviously improved by the fact that he obtained a larger proportion of 'cheap' (9–10–11) wickets than anyone else; his lead over all bar Botham is in fact considerable.

APPENDIX G

I. T. BOTHAM *v* West Indies
4 Series; 1980–1985/86

Mtchs	Inns	n.o.	Runs	H.S.	Av'ge	100	50	ct
19	36	0	757	81	21.02	–	4	16

Overs	Mdns	Runs	Wkts	Av'ge	5 in mtch	10	B/B
574.3	118	2079	58	35.84	3	–	8/103

R. J. HADLEE *v* West Indies
3 Series; 1979/80–1986/87

Mtchs	Inns	n.o.	Runs	H.S.	Av'ge	100	50	ct
10	15	3	389	103	32.41	1	1	4

Overs	Mdns	Runs	Wkts	Av'ge	5 in mtch	10	B/B
417.4	101	1124	51	22.03	4	1	6/50

IMRAN KHAN *v* West Indies
3 Series; 1976/77–1986/87

Mtchs	Inns	n.o.	Runs	H.S.	Av'ge	100	50	ct
12	23	2	534	123	25.42	1	1	3

Overs	Mdns	Runs	Wkts	Av'ge	5 in mtch	10	B/B
432.3	90	1225	53	23.11	4	–	6/46

KAPIL DEV *v* West Indies
3 Series; 1978/79–1987/88

Mtchs	Inns	n.o.	Runs	H.S.	Av'ge	100	50	ct
17	26	4	988	126*	34.06	3	4	16

Overs	Mdns	Runs	Wkts	Av'ge	5 in mtch	10	B/B
626.3	133	1831	71	25.78	2	1	9/83

APPENDIX H

COMPARISON OF LEADING TEST ALL-ROUNDERS

All cricketing comparisons are fraught with riders and qualifications – none more so than when one seeks to compare the effectiveness of Test all-rounders, since one cannot even take the easy option and fall back on averages.

One method of comparing all-rounders by averages – dividing batting by bowling – has been used in various publications for more than forty years. It may be felt that any all-rounder worthy of his bread should have a higher batting than bowling average, and the method also prevents differing conditions helping one facet or the other. The results are also objective; the figures cannot be 'adjusted' to obtain the 'correct' result.

However, the method does have its weaknesses, with the high scoring batsman who bowls just enough to qualify being definitely favoured. Also it is all about career figures, with no account being taken of all-round performances in matches. Even so, the results, on the whole, seem convincing; one feels that among current all-rounders Imran Khan *is* the leader. Botham however is in a false position, as APPENDIX 'C', covering the most recent performances of the four current leading all-rounders, emphasises.

RANKING TABLE FOR TEST ALL-ROUNDERS BY 'ASSESSMENT FIGURE'

Method; Dividing Batting Average by Bowling Average. The lower the resultant figure, the higher the ranking for the all-rounder. Qualification; all Test cricketers with at least 1000 runs and 80 wickets.

Player	Runs	Av'ge	Wkts	Av'ge	Assessment Figure
G. S. Sobers	8032	57.78	235	34.03	1.69
K. R. Miller	2958	36.97	170	22.97	1.60
W. R. Hammond	7249	58.45	83	37.80	1.54
G. A. Faulkner	1754	40.79	82	26.58	1.53
Imran Khan	2770	32.97	311	22.19	1.48
T. L. Goddard	2516	34.46	123	26.22	1.31
I. T. Botham	5057	34.87	373	27.86	1.25
A. W. Greig	3599	40.43	141	32.20	1.25
R. J. Hadlee	2770	27.42	373	22.34	1.22

M. A. Noble	1997	30.25	121	25.00	1.21
A. K. Davidson	1328	24.59	186	20.53	1.19
J. M. Gregory	1146	36.96	85	31.15	1.18
W. W. Armstrong	2863	38.68	87	33.59	1.15
W. Rhodes	2325	30.19	127	26.96	1.11
Kapil Dev	3889	32.14	319	29.63	1.08
F. E. Woolley	3283	36.07	83	33.91	1.06
T. E. Bailey	2290	29.74	132	29.21	1.01

Index

●